E.J. "SAMADHI" WHITEHOUSE

Circles in the Sand

© Copyright 2005 E.J. "Samadhi" Whitehouse.
All rights reserved. No part of this publication may be reproduced, stored in a retrieval system, or transmitted, in any form or by any means, electronic, mechanical, photocopying, recording, or otherwise, without the written prior permission of the author.

Note for Librarians: a cataloguing record for this book that includes Dewey Decimal Classification and US Library of Congress numbers is available from the Library and Archives of Canada. The complete cataloguing record can be obtained from their online database at:
www.collectionscanada.ca/amicus/index-e.html
ISBN 1-4120-4190-2
Printed in Victoria, BC, Canada

Printed on paper with minimum 30% recycled fibre.
Trafford's print shop runs on "green energy" from solar, wind and other environmentally-friendly power sources.

Publishing. On-demand
for retail sale to the public
ng. On-demand publishing
accounting and collecting

SPECIAL THANKS TO:

Patricia Anderson, Ph.D. and Literary Consultant. You became so much more than an editor—you are a true Goddess and mentor. Your enthusiasm, support, and encouragement fuelled my belief in myself. Thank you for holding my story—my truth—within absolute integrity and trust. You believed in me, and for that, I am forever grateful. [www.helpingyougetpublished.com]

Sarah Van Male [www3.telus.net/sirendesigns]. Thank you for "getting me," for getting inside my head, and knowing how to create my book cover in a way that expressed my journey.

Front cover picture—on top of Pinnacle Point, Najad desert, Saudi Arabia.

DEDICATION

This book is dedicated to all those who are struggling to find their voice, to women who live in oppression, to those who feel they've never belonged, and to the next generation of children. My hope is that every child will know that they are pure love, and that they are never, ever alone.

To Lorraine—you are my sun, my moon, my passion, my love, my first star—thank you for *you*. You are my inspiration. You are the brightest colours on my life's canvas. I adore you into infinity...

To TLK—I wish you the most magical journey through life. May you find joy behind your sorrow, love behind your hurt, and may you know in your soul that you will always have a cocoon to nestle into. Our spirits know our truth—I have loved you forever, my precious...

To my angels and spiritual guides—Dorinda, Dr. Karen Quinn, "Medicine Woman," Tema Dawn [www.temadawn.com], "Terri," and to authors Neale Donald Walsch, Caroline Myss, and Louise Hay, whose books have opened up a new way of seeing life for me.

To my family—this is who I am.

For each book purchase, I will donate a percentage of the proceeds to Women for Women International, a gift from all of us who are finding freedom to express ourselves—thank you.

AUTHOR'S NOTE

This is my truth, my voice, spoken from my heart. There is no malicious intent to hurt anyone, especially my family.

For the sake of clarity and brevity, and to protect privacy, the chronology of events has been slightly altered and some identities disguised. The overall story, however, happened as recounted.

CHAKRA SYMBOLS

FIRST CHAKRA

SECOND CHAKRA

THIRD CHAKRA

FOURTH CHAKRA

FIFTH CHAKRA

SIXTH CHAKRA

SEVENTH CHAKRA

TABLE OF CONTENTS

My Father's Mistress [1974-1978]	13
Fight or Flight…or Both [1979]	27
Running Backward into Time [1980]	37
Saved—at Last! [1981]	55
The Road to Lebanon [1982]	63
Oh, Wretched Soul That I Am	83
Thou Preparest a Table Before Me in the Presence of Mine Enemies	93
Inside Out [1983–1990]	101
My Broken Heart [1991–1993]	111
Out of Body, Out of Consciousness [1993-1994]	127
My Tasmanian Devil	147
The Secret Underground—Known to Everyone	155
A Peek Under the Veil	169
Sinking Relation*ships*	181
The Other Side of the Door	193
Travels Through Time and Spirit	205
Those Who Have Not Sinned—Cast the First Stone	215
An Answer to My Letter [1995]	231
An Angel, a Rose, and Jesus	239
Shalom Israel	259
A Cup of Tea with a Spoonful of Forgiveness [1998]	267
My Vision Quest	279
Ahlen wa Sahlan, My *Habibti*	299
Dying to Forgive [1999]	311
You Can't Run without Your Big Toe	321
Mothers and Daughters and Mothers and Daughters	327
New Endings, New Beginnings, New Millennium	333

1974-1978

My Father's Mistress

"*K*indly ensure your seats are in the upright position with your seat belts fastened securely. The pilot has advised us to expect heavy turbulence throughout the flight."

The roar of the engines temporarily muffled the sound of my heartbeat as we headed into the black night sky. As I sat there, frightened and childlike, nestled into his shoulder, he wrapped his arm around me, giving me a false sense of security. I must have had a break from reality, for my only other memory is of the lights dimming until the cabin was completely cloaked in darkness, except for one light at the front. Within its circle glowed an image of the Mother Mary, arms extended, hands outstretched. Being raised Catholic explained my vision, but at the time I wondered if she was truly reaching out her arms to save me.

As we made our grand entrance through the doors of the Queen Elizabeth Hotel in downtown Montreal, I speculated about where on earth he managed to get the finances to pay for such opulence. He'd always had struggles with money, never owned a home, and moved almost yearly, sometimes on a moment's notice—but you wouldn't know it by the façade he presented to the world.

Carrying himself with a sense of assurance and empowerment, he held my arm as we walked up to the reception.

"Bienvenue to the Queen Elizabeth Hotel, Monsieur et Mademoiselle. May I have your name please?"

"Tell me, what do you think?" he nodded in my direction. "Do you think she's my mistress? Look at her? Would you say she could be my mistress?"

"Sir, I really don't know. Now, your name please? Will you be requiring a double room?"

I stood, frozen in fear, unable to breathe, never mind speak.

"Well, take a guess. Does she look like my mistress to you?" He appeared excited at his game and showed no signs of concern for the awkwardness of the moment.

The reservation clerk, visibly agitated, replied, "I must ask you once again for your name and what type of reservation you have. *Please*, Monsieur—your name?"

"The name is Whitehouse." His voice had taken on an irritated edge.

"Will that be a double room?"

"Of course. One double room."

My quiet voice disguised an inner explosion of panic. "*Dad, please. Can we not have separate rooms?*"

Aware of the clerk's face turning white, I braced myself for an outburst from my father. Things were not going his way, and he was growing increasingly angry. "Don't be ridiculous. What did you expect? Do you think I can afford two rooms for us? Do you have any idea how much I am paying?"

All I could think of was that I had to share a room with my father. All of this behaviour was new to me, and I was not equipped to deal with it. I felt more alone than ever before in my life.

Walking to the elevator, we passed bellboys, maids, and various hotel guests. My father stopped each one, asking over and over, "Say, what do you think when you look at her? Would you say she was my mistress or my daughter? Take a guess." He showed no understanding of how inappropriate his behaviour was.

Two single beds dominated the tiny room as I tried to find breathing space within those four walls. To get out of there as quickly as I could, I suggested we go for lunch.

As the waiter and servers came to our table, Dad became even cruder. "Say, what do you think of this good-looking babe? Does she look like my mistress to you?"

"Dad. Please, please stop."

"What's wrong with you? You're being stupid. Everyone knows I'm joking. Eat your bloody lunch."

Unable to stop the sun from setting, I prayed as darkness arrived. *Please, please let me fall into a deep sleep until morning.* I crawled into my bed and pulled the covers up to my chin. My dad sat on his bed, watching me. Exhaustion took over and, finally, I fell into a sleep.

"Edna? Edna?" I woke up, startled to see my father kneeling beside my bed. His fingertips caressed my cheek as his arm rested down the centre of my chest. As I tried to move, he forcefully shifted his position and kept me pinned down with his hand wrapped around my wrist, which happened to be resting on my breast as I tightly gripped the blankets—his elbow was now pressing heavily on my privates.

"Dad. It's the middle of the night." I was horrified.

"I can't sleep. Can I snuggle with you?"

"Dad. No. That's not right."

"What do you mean *not right*? I miss your mother. It's just like me cuddling your little sister."

"No. Please, Dad. No. It's not right."

"What's so wrong with wanting to cuddle you? Don't be so stupid!"

"It's not right, Dad. Please, go back to your bed."

Enraged, cursing and swearing, he told me how stupid I was as he threw on his clothes and stormed out of the room.

I breathed a sigh of relief. *Please don't come back. I've got to get out of here.* I remembered the image of Mother Mary. *Please help me . . .*

I lay there, my wounds still fresh from having made so many screwed up choices already. I was still brokenhearted at having to say good-bye to my beautiful baby. How I longed to hold her—or maybe it was me I was longing to hold and protect.

I had fallen into a depression and refused even to go out. I began just existing in time and space. Only months earlier, I had been forced to give up my baby for adoption. My parents made threats to institutionalize me and to charge the father, a heroin junkie, with statutory rape. They didn't have to—he was already in prison for trafficking and drug possession. They told me my baby would be a freak because of all the drugs and booze. My drug of choice had been MDA, the "love drug." When I was stoned, everything, and everyone, was absolute love—I was hooked.

Within only a few painful heartbeats—almost immediately after I walked out of the hospital, without my baby—my father began displaying a lust for me. From that time on, he took every opportunity to pounce on his already injured prey.

My mother and I had stood physically side by side in the living room, while my dad insisted that I fly to Montreal with him. Although Mom tried to tell him I didn't want to go, he refused to back down. She didn't know what I needed, he told her.

"Look," he snapped at me, "you're seventeen years old. You haven't been out of the house since you had the baby. How the hell do you expect to travel Europe with your mother? It will be good for you to come to Montreal."

"But Dad, I don't want to go. I'm okay. Mom and I will be fine in Europe. I really just want to stay home."

Frustrated and afraid, my mother tried in vain. "Honest to God. Listen to her. She doesn't want to go."

"How do you know what she wants? How does *she* know? I'm telling you both. This will be good for her."

As if Mom had one last fighting breath, she pleaded, "You heard her. For God's sake, she doesn't want to go."

"I've heard enough. She's coming with me to Montreal, and that's that. End of discussion."

I've spent a lifetime carrying enormous guilt because I was seventeen when all this happened. I was old enough—why couldn't I have handled it better? I never really got it that I became a child, frozen in fear, when I was around my father. It would have taken enormous self-abuse off my shoulders if I had realized that not even my own mother was able to stop him. So how could I?

It took almost as many years to come to another realization: My mother had been my only true witness to that night. She had stood there, beside me, and seen how he overpowered both of us. Her coping skills allowed her only to choose denial and to blame me. We were both trapped. This was bigger and more powerful than me—and Mom.

Morning came and he still wasn't back. I stood, gazing out of the window, picturing the highway home. *I wonder how long it would take me to walk home? Five, six days? Ten days maybe? If I just keep walking...* I whispered to no one, seeing myself alone and walking down an endless highway. The door opened.

His voice cracked with emotion. "You know I would never do anything to hurt you. I love you. I walked the streets of Montreal all night."

The only way I knew how to survive was to pretend nothing happened. "I know Dad. Let's just go for breakfast."

Touring and visiting my aunt took up most of the day. Dad had grown up on the streets of Montreal with four sisters, a mother who I had only heard described as a crazy black Irish gypsy, and a father who was an abusive drunk. Dad was also an alcoholic but had stopped drinking when I was two.

The story told was that Mom had moved on her own from Prince Edward Island to Montreal, where she met and married Dad. Four babies later, she left him because of his alcoholism. I was two months old when she dropped her four kids off at her mother's on the Island, moved alone to Calgary, and then reunited with Dad two years later—once he was sober. Our family settled in Calgary, where my parents went on to have three more babies, as well as adopting a two-month-old baby boy. There were always questions surrounding that adoption—because my parents had no money, but more significantly—because Danny's birth mother appeared in our home on several occasions. This was not how adoptions worked in the 1960s. It was only one of many mysteries within our family.

Being back on his home turf seemed to bring out the street smarts in Dad. He looked and acted like a hoodlum, wearing jeans and a jacket with the collar pulled up. I had only ever seen him in business suits, so this was quite a shock.

Visiting old Mount Royal, I looked up to the hundreds of steps leading to St. Joseph's Oratory, where pilgrims pray their way to the top. If I knelt and prayed on each step, I wondered, would God answer my prayers and rescue me?

The night arrived. Crawling into bed, I wished I felt safer after his apology, but I didn't. Through the blackness of the room, I felt his presence.

"Dad? What are you doing?"

"What does it look like I'm doing? I'm sitting here? Is that a crime?" He sat in the chair, very close to my bed, resting his legs on my bed, and making the sheets so tight that I couldn't turn easily. He glared at me with what looked like disgust in his eyes.

"No, it's not a crime, I guess. But it's very late and—"

"Then go back to sleep!"

"But—"

"I'll sit here as long as I bloody well want to."

I rolled over, forcing the covers to move under the weight of his legs. I didn't move a muscle—just stared at the wall in absolute fear.

Morning arrived, but this time, there were no more apologies. "Dad, I'm going to Toronto to see Wendy," I declared. My sister had just moved there, and somehow, I managed to get a hold of her. My father allowed me to go.

I have no memory of flying there or talking with Wendy about what had happened. My sister has maintained that I told her Dad had sex with me, but I don't remember saying such a thing. It's a bone of contention that added to my eventual break from my family—not that I wasn't heading that way anyway.

Although I don't remember even a mention of Dad, I do remember one conversation. Wendy was pregnant, and out of the blue, as we were driving to the airport, she began asking me about being pregnant, giving birth and pain—as if it were nothing to talk about my pregnancy, when now I had no baby to love and hold. It was insensitive, and I felt violated again—there seemed to be no safe place within the walls of family. My brother-in-law was furious with her, and they began fighting amongst themselves as I sat staring out the window. I worried about the imminent need to tell Mom why I was flying from Toronto while Dad was still in Montreal.

As the boarding call sounded, I was jolted back into a reality I had frantically wanted to escape.

"Hey, baby, wanna sit next to me on the plane?"

My heart sank as I turned to see my father peeking from behind a pillar. How did he get here? How did he know when I was leaving? "Dad! How did you know I was on this flight?" I sputtered as my stomach hit the ground. I felt dirty, as though he had followed me and knew everything I said and did.

"I'll have two rum and cokes please," I said to the friendly stewardess as she smiled at us. "I hear you get drunker faster when flying." I tried to keep things light.

"Edna, may I ask you something? Do you mind if I ask you a question?" my dad said nervously.

"No. What?" Down went the first drink.

"In Montreal, did you happen to notice anything different?"

"Different? What do you mean?"

"Anything different about me? My behaviour? The way I acted?"

A part of me was amazed at his insanity, but that all turned to liquid as my seventeen-year-old mind had a meltdown to a little girl with her daddy. "No. Nothing at all. I don't know what you're talking about. I didn't notice anything."

"Good."

Home soon became a torture chamber for me. As Dad continued in his ways toward me, it separated me more and more from the family. At the dinner table, Dad would tell Mom to keep quiet because I was speaking, or he would direct questions to me, or tell jokes, and watch my reaction. I would try and turn conversations toward Mom, but the tension could have been cut with a knife. Seven other siblings and my mother were unable to support me.

I had the silly notion that I could win my mother's love by taking her to Europe. As the stewardess handed me a magazine, the headline screamed *"INCEST..."* My mother and I just looked at each other, saying nothing. I put down the magazine. When we arrived in England, she asked me what had happened in Montreal, and I told her everything. We never discussed it again—ever.

With the unspoken hanging heavily between us, we travelled on to France. My Catholic confirmation name is Bernadette, because I had long ago fallen in love with the movie *Bernadette of Lourdes* and, in truth, had a crush on the actress Jennifer Jones. When my mom and I walked into the grotto in France, I was very excited to see the actual place where Bernadette had lived. There was a shroud of peace and tranquility over the grounds. I sat very quietly in front of the grotto where the Mother Mary had appeared to Bernadette, and I secretly remembered my own visitation on the plane.

Upon our return to Canada, it was more than clear that I had to run away. Mom had found time to think while she was away from her husband. She chose him.

My mother and older siblings suggested I move out of the family home. Within weeks of my nineteenth birthday, I moved into my own apartment. My Dad occasionally dropped by, as did a couple of my siblings, but my mother never saw my apartment. As time went by, my siblings, speaking on behalf of my mother, told me I was not allowed to sleep over at the family home for Christmas or holidays because Dad was acting weird. Although the other siblings would stay, I always had to leave.

Strangely, I occasionally visited my dad's office, which was located a few blocks from where I worked. I don't know why— maybe it was some sort of Stockholm Syndrome. My family blamed me and wanted nothing to do with me, but my father continued "loving" me.

It was there that I met Denny, who worked with Dad. In noticing our attraction, Dad warned me that he believed Denny was homosexual.

After dating for three months, I remember dancing seductively to let Denny know it was time to have sex. But when he took me home, I changed my mind—I was very good at using my sexuality as a tool for power and control. Denny didn't like that—he picked me up, took off my dress, and flung me on the bed completely naked. With his pants down around his ankles, we "made love" for thirty seconds.

On that foundation, our relationship was built. We quickly began living together and presented another reason for my family to disown me. I stopped visiting my dad.

Denny and I broke up within the year because, he said, I refused to have sex. We soon got back together for another year. I became obsessed with wedding plans, although he had never asked me to marry him. We did have some good times through the craziness, but neither of us knew how to behave. He had been married before, and his wife's reasons for divorce included emotional and physical cruelty, which he denied. I, of course, knew *she* had to be lying.

During my time with Denny, I was very needy—full of fears and doubt, anxious thoughts, and an enormous fear of death. Occasionally, I had phobias of heights, flying, and small spaces. I think these came from my break with reality on that plane ride with Dad.

My fear of being in an elevator by myself sometimes overpowered any logic; once, I waited in the lobby of my apartment late at night, unable to do anything but stare at the elevator door, until finally, someone else appeared and up we went together. On another occasion, I was watching an acrobatic routine at a carnival. A man stood on the outside of a plane, performing stunts, and as I looked at him, I felt faint and had to leave, unable to breathe. I felt the sky was going to crash down on me. At other times, I would have anxiety attacks and feel as though I were falling from the sky.

The worst was sitting on a plane; I kept thinking that the bottom of the plane was going to drop out from under me. My stomach would do a loop-de-loop as the sensation of falling through the air swept over me.

During this time, I worked as a secretary in an all-male sales environment. A man from head office spent the week and, come Friday, invited us all out for a drink at the lounge in his motel. Upon arrival, he met me and said no one was there yet, and suggested we go for a quick drink—I didn't realize he meant in his room, until it was too late. As I sipped my drink, I started to talk to him, letting him know far too much about my past. I can still see myself, as I sat on the end of his bed and talked—I stared down at the floor and felt anxiety wash over me as my thoughts became clouded. I remember how uncomfortable and vulnerable I felt; my mind and body began to shut down in slow motion—I felt myself leaving my body, as I hovered over the girl on the bed.

My memory blanks out from there and picks up as we met the others in the lounge. The next morning, in front of all the guys at work, he strutted around and sang, "When we get behind closed doors, and she lets her hair hang down..." I was devastated, humiliated, and didn't say a word.

I never told anyone; I just kept fighting to survive. And I still don't recall what happened in that room.

Denny often became upset with me, and was always yelling and screaming. One day, when we were together in his car, he worked himself into a fury. He began driving like a madman, reaching for my door handle, threatening to throw me out of the car. I was scared senseless, and yet, I stayed with him for a few months longer. Even knowing that he frequently had sex outside of our relationship didn't give me the impetus to stand up for myself. It finally ended when he slapped me across the face. It would certainly make me feel wonderful to be able to say that I left him, but that didn't happen—he left me, thankfully. Denny was the only man I ever lived with in a long-term relationship.

By this time, I was sneaking into bars and discos—alone.

Although I was "disowned" by my family, I still occasionally saw my siblings and, less often, my parents. Things had been this way for the past few years, so I was surprised to hear that I was welcome at Thanksgiving dinner—my sister Rona passed on the invite. By then, I didn't even know where my parents lived.

Arriving alone, I was very nervous. This home certainly didn't convey a welcoming feeling. I bunkered myself down in the basement, barely greeting my mother and not even seeing my father.

As we sat down at the dinner table, with Dad obviously not present, Rona stood up. "Could everybody listen? I have a letter from Dad. I promised I would read it."

> To my family:
> I know you're all wondering why I'm not at Thanksgiving dinner, but your mother has asked me to leave because of the lies being told about me. Edna's lies and disruption to our family have caused me such pain and are ruining my marriage to your mother. I felt it best not to be present tonight.

I sat amongst my own flesh and blood, feeling like the lamb that had once again been led to the slaughter. My mind was swirling. *My God. What's going on? They deceived me into coming for a family dinner. No one told me Dad had moved out. I have to get out of here.*

I don't remember the rest of the evening or how I coped—maybe having no memory *is* how I coped. The funny thing is, I didn't talk to anyone about him. Nobody asked me. They all witnessed events unfolding at the same time I did, but they kept in a tribal pack, and I kept to myself. Dad moved back in the day after Thanksgiving.

I carried with me a troubling secret. On top of all that was happening in my life, this felt like a cruel joke.

As long as I could remember, I'd always had crushes on girls. I loved looking through the Sears' catalogue, with all the ladies in bras and panties. This went as far back as my elementary school years.

In the middle of all my teenage escapades and sexual promiscuity, women were often the centre of my desire. Somewhere inside, I knew I was at home with them. After Denny left, I flung myself into the gay nightlife, often going to the bars alone. My family caught wind of this, and even more hell broke loose. There was no coming-out party.

"What's it like hanging out with those dykes?" my mother sarcastically asked.

"It's great!" I would say with a defiant look, and that was it. Another war had begun. A rare phone call from my mother would tell me of a support group—Homosexuals Anonymous—where I should go to redeem my soul.

My struggle with homosexuality out of the closet, I felt a heightened need to run. My ventures into the gay world were pure icing for my Catholic family's belief that I would forever rot in hell and damnation. They thought my sins were well past admission to purgatory. I was going straight to hell.

I had a nightmare in which I was sitting on a boat and enjoying the surrounding sea. I saw a tidal wave surge forward, rising hundreds of feet above me. I dove into the bottom of the wave, going down until I hit the seabed—underneath the force of the wave. Bouncing my feet off the bottom, I began my ascent toward the surface. I felt my lungs about to explode from lack of air. I could see the sun's rays piercing through the water, but couldn't quite get to the top. I focussed on the sky with an ever-increasing sense of death. Only seconds away from the surface, I felt my lungs exploding as I woke up.

My nightmare defined how I felt about my life—it was crashing over me like a tsunami as I tried not to drown. I didn't know then that water represents life force.

Escaping, on the other hand, was becoming very familiar to me.

1979

✻

Fight or Flight...or Both

"*I* am Ferzat al-Assali, from Damascus, in the Syrian Arab Republic."

Turning to connect a face with the voice that had just whispered in my ear, I thought *Wow! The Middle East!* I suddenly felt very far from home. This was my first big travel adventure alone through Europe. Now in Greece, I was already feeling intrigued that I was right next door to countries like Turkey and Iran.

Ferzat was very handsome. He lived in the village of Paleochora, on Crete, and worked as a waiter. With his quiet assuredness, exotic looks and accent, he was also a tourist attraction. Physically, we were opposite: he had black hair, dark eyes, and olive skin, while I was a strawberry blonde with blue eyes and fair skin. Ferzat was not aware of the baggage I was lugging around with me and I was most definitely naïve to his world. We embarked on a relationship that would change my life's direction.

If you are a backpacker, you know life takes on different perspectives. Everything becomes more intense. You fall in love quicker. Friendships develop on a very deep level. What, in the real world, could take six months to create, in a gypsy's world, takes one day. The knowledge that we are all just passing through makes it less of a risk to open up completely or to become anything we want. I could be anyone I wanted to be. Nobody had to know I was running away from my life.

Before my awareness of my father's desires toward me, I had already developed an intense self-destructive behaviour. Traumatic life dramas only seemed to worsen as I went through my teens and entered my twenties. I was in way over my head, always trying to stay a step ahead of my shadow. The last seven years had been anything but good fortune.

My promiscuity began as early as age thirteen. I repeatedly ran away and got into heavy drugs; I shot up a few times, hung out with the junkies and had blackouts after my binges. My friends included alcoholics, drug dealers and addicts, guys in and out of prison, and even a close friend convicted of murder; he had drug-induced schizophrenia, believed the communists ruled the world, and shot a Chinese man to death. Other friends died through overdose or suicide, and eventually, AIDS took several others. This was my circle—my tribe. My nickname was Alice in Wonderland, but inside me, nothing was wonderful.

Although my awareness of my father began at seventeen, I have often wondered why I was so hell-bent on abusing myself from such a younger age. Something must have taught me to loathe myself; somewhere, early on, I had learned that I was not worthy of love or respect.

Sex was a way to be "loved" and held; it was a place where I could pretend I was wanted—even though it led to a number of nasty encounters. My so-called sexual freedom had me in chains. I'd go to a party dressed in a shirt and jeans, only to wake up in someone's bed with a different shirt on—and nothing else; then I'd have to crawl around looking for my clothes and find them shoved in a corner somewhere in the basement. On other occasions, I would get just a little too stoned and find myself lying on yet another bed, with three guys touching me, and a room full of strangers watching. I fooled myself into believing that my sexuality was my power. Dead wrong!

With women, I never felt violated—they weren't predators. The sexual freedom of the '60s and '70s had not yet come to a halt, and it seemed quite acceptable to be bisexual. For a time, I was very much into a girl I had met travelling, who came with me to Paleochora. But I turned my attention to Ferzat, as I saw the village mating to be primarily heterosexual. Being a hippie, with gypsy blood, gave me freedom to be and do anything I wanted. Too bad I didn't take that philosophy and use it in a way that would make me happy, rather than accepted. After all, I was merely passing through. I never shared my life experiences with Ferzat.

Paleochora was a sleepy fishing village, where the hippies, gypsies, and punkers cohabitated. Peace and love were still very much the mantra, and in Paleochora, there was much peace and even more love. The east side of the island was rugged, wild, and windy with daily tempestuous surf. This was my private place to wander off in solitude, mesmerized by the orchestrated chaos of the elements.

The tourists spent their days at the west end of the island with the gentle sea, a beautiful sandy beach, gorgeous sunsets, and a disco where dancing gave way to the dawn. Early evenings were spent sitting at the outdoor cafes dotted along the main street, drinking Retsina and enjoying the delicious Greek foods. It was at Foti's café that Ferzat and I first laid eyes on each other, and later that night in the disco, we joined in a mating ritual.

Our relationship was very popular amongst the tourists and villagers, who all loved him. Within weeks, we were talking marriage. Ferzat wanted me to go to Syria to meet his family. The thrill of going to the Middle East captivated my sense of adventure. I knew that I was not exactly the girl his parents would want him to bring home—and that was as I stood in that moment—never mind my history. The thought of Ferzat discovering I had already had a baby petrified me. I couldn't risk discussing my history with anyone, especially my potential future husband.

A group of us sat drinking morning Nescafe, discussing our different plans for moving on down the road. My wandering gypsy friends were quite animated in their excitement at the thought of Ferzat and I riding off into the Arabian sunset. But sadly, their enthusiasm fell short of inspiring me.

My immediate plans were to meet my best friend in Athens, before making my final decision on Syria. The buzz of everyone charting their destinies was interrupted as we stared in disbelief at the huge writing on the wall: "Death To Americans" and "Americans Go Home." The red paint dripped from each letter as if the words were bleeding. We began hearing about an uprising and violence in Turkey. It was my second experience with hatred on a global scale.

The first time was when I had taken my mother to Europe. As we lay across the hard, wooden bench of second class, well into the darkness of night, the jolt of the train's brakes jarred us awake. The force of gravity threw us forward, with our luggage crashing onto the floor. As the train came to a screeching halt, panicked passengers began rushing toward the exit. We tried to find out what was happening but everyone just kept running and yelling in Spanish. Finally, someone grabbed my arm. "Bomb. Run."

Jumping off the train, over the tracks and through a tunnel, I felt my ears reverberate to the sound of tick, tick, tick. Within the darkness just before dawn, this seemingly quiet village, resting on the border of Spain and France, had mayhem thrust upon it. Out of the darkness, we heard sounds familiar from European movies—police sirens echoing through the streets, becoming louder and louder as they raced toward us. There were police vans with German shepherds clearly at the ready to do their mission. Detectives in black suits jumped out of unmarked cars, along with an onslaught of both French and Spanish police. Everyone made way for the vehicle holding the bomb squad. I wondered how so many detectives had descended upon the scene so quickly. This was clearly not their first dress rehearsal.

At daybreak, we were herded onto a train bound for Paris. It was the headline news the next morning. We read that they had found and dismantled a bomb. It had been placed on the track just ahead of our train.

And now, our sleepy Greek village was awakening to another terrorist threat, with newspapers warning American tourists to lie low. Europeans, Canadians, and Australians began visibly displaying their country's flag. Nothing came of those threats sprawled on the wall, except for the disturbance that their gruesome visual caused.

Ferzat and I took the boat to Athens, where we met up with Dale for his two-week vacation. Dale was my very gay "brother" and best friend who, not surprisingly, fell in love with Ferzat's handsome, rugged looks. He was the only one who knew of my struggles with my sexuality, and that I was on the run from me. What he didn't know was my difficulty in having a sexual relationship with Ferzat. So many times, after *he* was finished,

I would turn over with a desperate desire to be with a woman. Ferzat had many difficulties with the female body and sometimes acted like he hated it. He of course loved to receive oral sex, but when asked to reciprocate, he said it made him vomit, and it was disgusting—not the kind of thing an emerging lesbian, or any other woman, wants to hear.

I shared my feelings about Ferzat with Dale while sitting in a beautiful park in the middle of Athens. Alone with him, I felt free to be myself again, at least partially. Ferzat and being gay were enough to deal with; all my other secrets could just stay buried deep within.

We talked about the woman I had run away from in Canada and how much I missed her. We laughed at all the times we danced and partied to the wee hours of the morning. Dale was honest with me, sharing his fear of how sad I had become. He questioned where the happiness of the all-weekend party-girl had gone, and more intensely, he questioned what the hell I was doing with a man, when it was so clear that it was not meant to be.

In my memory, I see Dale talking compassionately to me, trying to bring me to my senses, but sadly, I see only an empty shell of me responding to, but not hearing him. I was betraying my inner truth. My outward choices were choking and deadening my painful internal struggle so that I was feeling nothing. When I told him about the girl in Paleochora that I had a huge crush on, Dale just shook his head in dismay at my dual life. He thought I was crazy. He came all this way to be together with me, but when Ferzat was around, I became a puppet and allowed him to manipulate my strings. I was a stranger to Dale.

Later, as Ferzat and I sat in Syntagama Square in Athens, his black eyes pierced through me, as he said with controlled anger, "I think you are a lesbian." I nervously laughed it off, even while realizing that I had been flirting with and staring at a gorgeous woman the whole time. Ferzat became very quiet and distant. He told me he was afraid to come to Canada, that the differences between our countries were too vast for him—not to mention the differences between us. I felt quite relieved and, without hesitation, said *okay*. It was just like that—we would not get married. We were supposed to meet Dale in the Plaka, and I said I would go ahead and tell him the news. I suggested that Ferzat stay behind and wait for Mustafa, his Egyptian friend.

I skipped with lightness in my step, relieved that I was now free to reconnect to the gay lifestyle—this time, I wasn't going to hide my desires by sneaking off to bars alone—I wanted a full throttle party. How odd that I could not make this choice on my own. I had been a willing participant in a life decision that held no happiness whatsoever for me. My self-worth was null and void, and this was just the continuation of a pattern of being abused. Jumping from one abuse to the other, having sex with strangers, and mistaking it for love and caring were all coming with a price tag. My soul was dying.

Somewhere between our last conversation and my meeting up with Dale, Ferzat changed his mind. As I was eating a souvlaki sandwich and telling Dale I was free, Ferzat suddenly appeared. Walking in and nonchalantly sitting down, he declared he had just been nervous and proceeded to inform me that we would get married after all. My stomach literally dropped to the floor, and yet I acted happy. How absurd and crazy.

Dale watched this fiasco in horror and couldn't believe the depths to which I would sink, to try and please my parents and God. It affected him so much that our friendship ended right there. He thought I had totally lost the plot and was disgusted with my lack of caring for my own happiness. I knew he was right, but I was unable to stop. My ship was sinking, and I wore no life jacket.

Ferzat's friend Mustafa was a sleaze. He looked at me as a means to make him money. It was through him that I first heard about men marrying foreign girls to get entry visas into western countries. As he spoke, he laughed and said I was childish not to know this. Ferzat muttered something in Arabic to him and then told me he was not like this. I dismissed the possibility that he could be lying. My mind was already preoccupied with a "favour" I was about to do for a man that gave me the creeps.

Ferzat, Mustafa and I stood in line at the Bank of Greece as Mustafa whispered instructions on how I was to act with the teller. I was to request that my Greek drachmas be converted to U.S. dollars. After asking how I was to answer if questioned over the large amount of cash in my possession, I was told not to worry. For once, I listened to my gut. As I flung the money back into Mustafa's filthy hands and walked out of the bank, I realized just how close I had come to participating in laundering money. Could I sink any lower?

Under the guise of apologizing and showing concern for my loss of Dale, Mustafa suggested we go for a nice walk together. His tone was one of exaggerated sympathy. "Forget about your friend. He is nothing to you now."

As he wrapped his arm around me, I began to feel scared of him. He was trying to convince me to stay in Athens and work for him in a nightclub in the Plaka. All I had to do was entice men in by offering to have a drink with them. Oh, yes, the only other minor detail was to sit on their lap and maybe "do some favours for them"! As he spelled out my job description in broken English, Mustafa's arm coiled around my neck like a snake, as he held me in a death grip. Saying I was uncomfortable, I asked politely for him to remove his arm. The moment felt like being with my father. Mustafa hugged me even tighter and said there was no problem; he was just expressing his love for me like he would to his sister. He enjoyed my nervousness and discomfort. He did not let go.

With darkness fast approaching, he took me to the Acropolis. I was afraid that he would hurt me, which is what he wanted, and I was unable to break free. *If I just pretend to be interested in this job proposition*, I said to myself. And it worked. I said I would go home, shower, and meet him at the bar.

I then made the mistake of telling Ferzat, in the hope that he would protect me. Instead, he was furious. Before long, his anger turned into rage. He raped me. As he thrusted his body forcefully into me, he yelled disgusting insults in English and Arabic. He acted as if he were a man I had enticed into Mustafa's bar. "Do you like *this?*" he asked, as he became increasingly violent and aggressive.

In my mind's eye, that encounter is as clear as if it happened this morning. I remember that I again detached and looked down at the girl on the bed, watching her silent horror. I saw the fear in my own eyes as his force bashed me against the headboard and I began coiling up the wall. I shut down. I never discussed it. I never left him. I was not yet able to hear my soul crying out to me that I did not deserve this. At this point in my life, abuse was all I expected from men, and my expectations didn't let me down. I stayed with him. I was in too deep and had no understanding that I could walk away—if only I chose to.

I don't remember the flight to Damascus.

1980

Running Backward into Time

We arrived in Damascus in the middle of the night, and darkness covered her mystery. When he awakened his family, Ferzat was met with cries and kisses, while I was greeted with stares and confusion. I don't think Ferzat had told his family about me. There was quite a buzz amongst his many siblings about the western redhead he had brought with him.

"*Marhaba, ishmeh Edna*—Hello, my name is Edna." I proudly said. "*Arabi, Fatima*—in Arabic, Fatima." They laughed and seemed impressed that I had chosen an Arabic name for myself.

A large wall hid the family house from the street. Opening the large gate, you walked down the open-air entrance, then stopped to rinse your hands and face in a water basin with a spout mounted on the wall; a trough below caught the water. The entrance hallway led to the centre of the house, into an outdoor courtyard, complete with a cold floor of black and white mosaic stone, a small water fountain, and various trees, some with lemons hanging from their branches. Four doors opened from the courtyard, and each led into an interior room of the house.

The back room was apparently where special guests were welcomed. I was never invited into that room, except in secret.

Another door opened to a slightly modern living room with a small black and white television, four mismatched chairs squared off against opposing cement walls, and a plastic-covered love seat. Scattered about the room were assortments of tacky, plastic flowers. This room screamed for Martha Stewart. This is where Ferzat and I slept, on the hard floor with a blanket over us. To my surprise, Ferzat's father allowed us to sleep together. I am ashamed now because I know that western women are considered whores to many in the Middle East. I don't know why his father allowed it. When the other siblings headed off to bed, there were always mutterings and laughter. I felt very dirty but wanted to believe that the family, in particular the father, were modern in their thinking.

The third door opened to the main family room, used for daily visiting, relaxing, eating meals, and sleeping. There was no furniture, and the room's multipurpose use was reminiscent of Bedouin living. Each house I visited had both a sitting and an "on-the-floor" room, with the preferred choice always being the latter. I enjoyed this because it retained the ancestral heritage of the Arab people.

In Ferzat's family room, the walls, in dire need of repair, had chipped plaster, and the green paint was splattered with lightning-bolt cracks. There were several Arabian throw rugs scattered across the floor, with the only seating being a piece of cloth-covered foam running along the base of the walls. Big, soft pillows were scattered along the floor for added comfort. The eight siblings still at home slept crammed together in this same room. At night, everyone would leave their plastic sandals outside the door, find a spot on the hard, cold, thinly carpeted floor, and form a line of bodies curled up with a few blankets between them.

The last door was more like a barroom swing-door, opening to a kitchen full of hanging antique-like brass pots and utensils; there was minimal counter space, which was okay, because the mother always cooked on the floor of the family room. Connected almost like a pantry, off to the side of the kitchen, was the oldest part of the house—the toilet.

Not one room had a window in it, but with each opening into the courtyard, there was never a sense of being closed in—at least not physically. A set of steep steps, sans a hand railing, led to an open-air rooftop.

It was still dark when I first heard the wailing. Ferzat joked that it was wild animals in the hills. I envisioned wild dogs and coyotes yelping away. Those yelps however, were the sound of the various imams' calls for prayer. From each mosque on every corner, the prayer call rang out to the men of Damascus to awaken and come pray. It was sunrise. Neither Ferzat nor any of the men in the family ever went to prayer—more reason to believe Papa al-Assali was a modern guy.

Arising that first morning, I went up to the rooftop terrace with curious anticipation of what the light of day would reveal. I stood in silence, wide-eyed and open-mouthed, as culture shock paralyzed me. Time seemed to have ticked backward while I slept, and I had awoken to the world of two thousand years ago. I was transported back into Biblical times. The twentieth century seemed a distant memory.

Most of the men wore floor-length robes, called *thobes*, which had started out white but were very stained and dirty from their environment. On each of their heads was what looked like a black-and-white checked teacloth, known as a *goutrah*. Women wore head scarves to cover their hair and long dresses under ankle-length coats. Young girls wore school uniforms that looked like lab jackets and long pants underneath long skirts. Ferzat's father always wore a long grey *thobe*, his mother always wore a head scarf, even in her home, but all the siblings, including the sisters, wore jeans.

Boys as young as six ran up and down the street, carrying silver trays full of tiny gold-trimmed crystal glasses brimming with *chai*—tea. They took orders and served all who called out—all *men* that is. The *chai*-runners would serve men working in their souqs, older gents sitting out front playing backgammon, and even passengers hanging out the windows of passing buses. At a brief stop, they would yell for their glass of *chai*, drink it down, then throw the money and glass back toward the boy, as the bus cut off anyone in its way.

Most of the shops had one or two old chairs propped out front, with the older men sitting watching the world go by, enjoying their *chai* and smoking their hubbly-bubbly pipes. All the men dangled and manipulated their prayer beads, which were more like appendages than possessions. Prayer beads are similar to a Catholic rosary, minus the crucifix of course. Seemingly unaware of their actions, men obsessively caressed each bead and twirled the strands about their fingers. The beads I saw were made of plastic, wood or, like Ferzat's, a heavy Bedouin silver. Donkey carts trotted by, stopping momentarily while men of all ages flung one-hundred-pound sacks of beans, lentils or rice over their shoulders, and others unloaded various bins of beautifully coloured spices or coffee beans to sell. Money changed hands quickly, and off the carts would go—the donkeys trotting to the next souq.

Everything and everyone seemed impoverished. The sandstone souqs, or market stalls, were very, very old, and had probably been family businesses dating back generations. Very old men would sit either on the ground, or on a tiny stool or rickety chair, with a small row of gum, cigarettes or tiny bins of beans lined up on the sidewalk to sell to passersby. It appeared only a step away from begging. Shoe shiners would yell out their services, chasing the occasional businessman in his long white *thobe, goutrah,* and black business shoes. This could not have been a lucrative business, because 99.5 percent of the feet I saw were all wearing sandals.

As I stood on that roof, mesmerized by life in Damascus, someone from below noticed and pointed up toward me. The entire street began to take notice and turned their eyes upward. Curious men, women, and children stared and argued amongst themselves about who this foreigner was.

My future brother-in-law happened to be on the street, buying the daily pita from the bakery. He ran into the courtyard calling for Ferzat, who immediately came upstairs and pushed me back, saying, "Get away. Don't let the people see you like this. Look at these men staring at you!"

I was offended by his push but kept it to myself. I was equally staring back at their world and, in truth, I was enjoying the sense of celebrity, even if it wasn't exactly my full fifteen minutes of fame.

Damascus is known to be the oldest inhabited city in the world, dating back eight thousand years. The hole-in-the-ground, otherwise referred to as the al-Assali toilet, was not much younger. After my learning curve regarding waist-long hair, squatting, and peeing, I tried not to panic at the coordination required for the task at hand. The added necessity of holding one hand over my nose, or wrapping my hair over my nostrils so as not to smell or gag, required even more of a balancing act. Allah forbid if you became constipated or took longer than anticipated. Not only did I need strong quads to hold myself securely over the hole, I also needed fairly good balance to reach for a tiny hose attached to a rusty old faucet. There was no two-ply in sight.

I sheepishly asked Ferzat about wiping and he stuck his hands out saying, "Use these." Although it was mine, I was unable to get that familiar with my own waste. Soon, a small bucket appeared next to that tiny hose—I knew it was just for me.

Hanging on to the thousand-year-old brick with one fingernail, I could lean toward the hose, fill the bucket with water, and cleanse myself. Dripping dry depended on how much my quads were trembling. Once in a while, probably for humour, there would be a box of Kleenex outside the loo. Using this did not turn out to be fun because the water pressure was so minuscule that it just wouldn't go down that hole.

My first shower was an interesting experience. I was given a towel and told to have a shower in the kitchen. I looked around and only saw a small bucket of water. As I stood naked, staring at that itty-bitty bucket for the longest time, I knew my body was way too big for it. I put my foot into the cold water. I squatted over and tried to wash my long hair inside the bucket without spilling the water. Being in the kitchen seemed nonsensical and I couldn't figure it out. It was futile.

I called Ferzat repeatedly, but he never came. Wrapped in a towel, I tiptoed through the courtyard and knocked on the door, asking for him to come out. Seeing me standing there in a towel, he was furious and, as he brought me back to the kitchen, yelled at me never to do that again. He bent over and started grabbing handfuls of water and throwing it all over me.

"Like this," he said. "The water goes down," he added, pointing to a hole in the floor. This was yet another collision of two worlds. If any of them had snuck a peak at me dipping my toes into the bucket, trying not to spill water—*oy vey!*

For meals, everyone would sit on the floor or on the cushions along the walls, while the mother cooked in the middle of the room. Rather than utensils, pita bread was used to pick up the food. They laughed amongst themselves as I struggled to get more in my mouth than an empty piece of pita. Discreetly, they found me a fork. I still kept trying and became quite refined, with minimal droppings. Forget about the rule "no double-dipping." It was fun to watch the family drink out of a communal water jug, a very old Arab urn with a long, skinny spout, as it passed from person to person. The spout never even got close to lips, with each person holding it further and further away from their mouths. As I reacted to the ever-increasing distance, those inches became competitively more and more but never a drop was spilled. I tried and dribbled down my face, neck and shirt while, in a disappointed tone, Mamma told them to get me a glass.

Seeing the freshly dead carcasses hanging in various souqs, I couldn't handle eating the meat, mostly lamb. Mamma al-Assali noticed that I liked her stuffed eggplant dripping in oil, along with tomatoes and eggs. In the beginning, she would motion toward me, expecting me to help her cook. I panicked. I felt lost in any kitchen, never mind cooking Arabic-style on the floor. That's one link in the chain of mothers and daughters that was broken—my mother and I had never, ever stood cooking side by side in her kitchen. I was never shown anything about how to prepare a meal. With eight kids underfoot, all she wanted was to get them out of her way while she prepared meals.

I was embarrassed at my lack of skill, even in peeling fruit and veggies. When handed a clove of garlic, with her motioning me to chop it, I just stared at it, not having a clue how to peel, separate, and then chop—I felt humiliated at my lack of ability and basic knowledge of food preparation. Mamma al-Assali would get impatient and take them out of my trembling hands. I'm pretty sure she thought I was an oddball. If I couldn't share cooking with her, what good was I to a man?

She saw how much I enjoyed her delicious tabbouleh, hummus, tahini, and creamy yoghurt, with all sorts of olives and salads, and there was soon a plate just for me. It was a bit embarrassing because everyone else shared from a common plate. I tried to explain that I would nibble along with them, but they just shooed me away and motioned for me to eat my own little meal. There were always dishes of dates and figs to chew on. Another fun treat was the daily supply of pomegranates. With all these delicious nibbles, it was easy to do without meat.

Of the ten children, only the two eldest were married and lived outside the parental home. Mohammed was in his forties and Karam, in her thirties. The youngest son was around eight years old. I imagine his birth must have been a shock, because so many years had gone by between the first and tenth child. His sisters were more like mothers and took care of his every wish and demand. I never developed a relationship with the brothers. They pretty much ignored me, put up with me, or were amused by me, but showed no interest in who I was or where I came from, as they carried on with their daily lives.

The grandmother, who was nearly one hundred but looked closer to three hundred, used to constantly mutter under her breath at me. It was clear she was angry and cursing at me, as she would point her finger toward me and shake her head in dismay. She seemed annoyed with everything I did. The women used to yell at her to be quiet. The day I took her picture, she became very upset. I was told, after the flashes, that the older Bedouin women felt their spirits were being taken out of their bodies if someone captured their image on film. I wish I had understood and respected that; I thought she was just muttering her usual hostilities and had no idea how deeply upset she was as I clicked away.

Ferzat's younger sister, Maha, and I became fast allies. She spoke no English but her body language spoke volumes. Maha was a dyke through and through. She was so obviously a lesbian that I wondered how she would ever escape Damascus and her fate of being married off. Maha and I would sneak off into the special guest room and smoke. No one ever seemed to come into this room, nor did she seem to care about the consequences if they did.

Occasionally, there would be two or three other young girlfriends, secretly waiting in the room for us. It appeared like she smuggled them in to see me. Discussing me amongst themselves, they would stare at me and try to sum up what I was about. Maha would stand on guard, almost as if she were my security, and answer their questions. I watched as they lifted their chins toward me, asking something. Maha, looking at me to find the answer, would respond. I felt like a dress in the window, or a piece of art she was trying to interpret. Sometimes our eyes would lock for a moment as I felt Maha's yearning to be free. I wish I could have kidnapped her.

Little did I know that I was a hostage myself.

No one, not even the eldest son in his forties, was allowed to smoke in front of the father—but I was. Again, I don't understand why I was allowed such freedoms. Rules were so strict and women did not get the luxuries that I was given. If a grown man could not smoke, then why could I? The father would leave the room and all the brothers would light up their cigarettes. One evening, he returned unexpectedly.

To warn the children to be respectful, it was customary for the father to knock on the door before entering. Simultaneously, as the door creaked open, three cigarettes came flying toward me, one of them landing in the father's drink, to stand upright in the thickness of his Arabian coffee.

Staring at me, now with two cigarettes in my hand, and then looking down questioningly at his coffee, he muttered, "Fatima, why? Your cigarette in my coffee—why this?"

Holding in my laughter while the brothers looked sheepishly at me, I had no answer. I cannot imagine what this man thought of me.

The women led separate lives from the men and were very different when the men were away. I spent many days at Karam's house. Karam, Maha, and Anna—Ferzat's beautiful, exotic cousin with her ultra-blue piercing eyes and olive skin—along with a multitude of aunts, cousins, and nieces would all gather in the family room. The music, with its sensual and exotic beat would start, and each woman would cup one hand over her upper lip as she sounded the *zilagheet* shriek of rejoicing. This was a "lalalalala" with their tongues, as they began to clap their hands and prod the first girl on as she wrapped a scarf around her hips. The belly dancing began and the women loved it. They were very sexy and flirtatious with each other. It was as if all their sexuality and spirits became free with the beat and they held nothing back. The dancer would seductively take off the scarf and wrap it around the next girl chosen to dance and she would continue—all around the circle, each one dancing and flirting and being sexy.

As Anna seductively took off the scarf from around her hips and proceeded to wrap it around mine, I shyly said, "No, no. *La shucrun*—no thank you," as they twirled their tongues in joyous chanting. "*Yella, Fatima! Yella, habibti*—come on, darling, go!" they urged me. I began swirling my hips and imitating them, going up to them, shaking my shoulders and flipping my hair. The crowd went wild. We all fell to the floor laughing and giggling. Soon, I heard the beat of disco.

"Fatima! American dance. Disco. *Yella, omi*—come on, get up!" they shouted. I stood in the middle of the room and, for fun, started dancing completely out of rhythm. Nobody laughed. Realizing my humour got lost in translation, I began to rock on to the disco beat as they all jumped up and started dancing around me with scarves intertwining us.

Every time I said something, one of the ladies would ask, "*Shoo bak*—what did she say?" This eventually became lots of fun. When they talked and I didn't understand—which was always—I would quickly respond, "*Shoo bak?*" and was always met with lots of laughter. Though I was a young woman trying to leave behind her gay lifestyle, I must admit I was in heaven dancing, flirting, and being the centre of attention among these beautiful Arabian princesses who oozed sexuality.

They, too, left the reality of their lives outside the room. And then, there was a knock on the door.

The music died as everyone scurried for their head scarves and quickly changed into demure, passive women. Ferzat and his brother walked in, demanding *chai*. Karam jumped up to make it before they finished their sentence.

Only moments earlier, there had been a sense that we were caught up in the eye of a storm. Everything was loud, boisterous, and jubilant, as excitement, laughter, and movement aroused the essence of our womanhood. But, with that one knock at the door, the frenzy collapsed, crushing us under its weight, burying us alive. There was an instant calm as the women hid behind their scarves and dress, vanishing into quiet death.

Life did not imitate art. There were only two television channels in the home, one being nothing but infamous Arab soap operas or musicals. These were over-the-top in drama, makeup, clothing, and the love relationships they portrayed between men and women. Watching these shows, you would think that men adored women and enormously enjoyed female sexuality. Songs were always stories of love or broken hearts, full of drama and intense love between a man and woman. It was as if the only way they were allowed to express a male/female relationship was through music and soaps, because nowhere that I saw was this kind of love a reality for anyone.

The other channel was an all-day propaganda machine, showing Israel bombing Syria and Palestine. There were imams preaching and showing a steady stream of graphic pictures of how Israel has attacked the Arab nations. There was no hesitation in showing dead women and children or close-ups of dead Israeli soldiers—repeatedly. I only knew a little about the Middle East because, before, it was always "over there," but now, it was "here."

I asked Ferzat what he felt about the troubles in his part of the world and he angrily said, "Israel is this big." He held his thumb and index finger an inch apart. "And we want it *this big*." He pinched his fingers tightly together to symbolize the crushing of Israel. I looked at him and realized I had never before seen the hatred that I had heard about. I had never looked into black eyes so full of rage toward another race. I was also brainwashed by my western indoctrination that Israel was God's chosen people. Ferzat took me to a part of Damascus and showed me where the Israelis had bombed the city and killed hundreds of people.

"This is where your apostle Paul was blinded by your God," Ferzat said with a laugh as we continued on to the only city tour I was given, which included the famous market—the oldest in the world! This market was astounding, like nothing I had ever seen. A domed iron-trestle roof gave way to minimum light as we wandered through a labyrinth of souqs. The market seemed to stretch for miles, with offshoots to the left and right, and back again. The fragrances of spice tantalized the nostrils until the stench of butchered animals, suspended right next to rows of hanging gold jewellery, had me using my hair as a nose-covering again.

The quantity of gold was epic in proportion, dazzling and blinding in the same instance. Ferzat would say, "Smell. That's oil! Smell the money! These are Saudis."

Ferzat bought my mother a huge wall tapestry of *The Last Supper*, beaming proudly that he picked out something Christian. It was a nice gesture that my mother would laugh at and think tacky.

Back at Karam's house for a late afternoon visit, Ferzat had not mentioned we were having company. Or, should I say, *he* was having company. As his guest entered the home, I was not introduced, nor were any of the women acknowledged. The sisters and cousins scurried around, preparing food and coffee for the gentleman caller. The men sat in the fancy drawing room with the door closed. There was an air of pomp in the house. Karam put a tray of coffee and sweets on the floor and was about to knock on the door, when I asked what she was doing.

"We cannot go inside." I asked why, and she nervously said, "They are the mens. We are woman. It is not allowed."

I huffed toward the door as Karam begged me not to. I knocked and opened the door, picked up the tray and brought it in, introducing myself to the male guest. Ferzat turned pale and I felt his disgust. "Get *out*," he furiously muttered. Frightened and angry in the same moment, I backed out of the room while Karam just shook her head. I was later told, "You are forbidden to do this again. Women do not sit with the mens." Man, Ferzat sure wasn't like this in Paleochora.

That evening, Mohammed and Karam came over to the house with their spouses. Mo's mother-in-law was a regular visitor at the al-Assali house, appearing friendly to everyone except her son-in-law. This visit had the feeling of "odd." There was a lot of angry shouting, and cries of hysteria mounted as the discussion became quite heated. Finally, Ferzat told me that the mother-in-law just said she had helped breast-feed Mohammed as a baby, and, he was therefore her son. Apparently it is a Bedouin belief that any woman who helps breast-feed is considered a mother. It was not uncommon for women to share the breast-feeding amongst themselves. Because Mo married her daughter, he was being accused of marrying his sister.

Wow! This was better than those juicy soaps I had started watching. Ferzat told me that, according to ancient belief, this violation of marital rules could lead to death. I never got to hear the outcome because everyone stormed off, disowning as many family members as possible. Karam and Mohammed never returned for a visit for the remainder of the time I was there. The mother-in-law seemed pleased at the chaos she had created, and I felt a brief moment of being home.

Damascus was not a tourist attraction in 1980. I saw no foreigners and definitely no backpackers. I was over the moon to finally meet an Irish girl married to a Syrian whom she had also met while backpacking. It was fantastic. To have a friend who spoke English and who understood this culture and these families. We loved each other's company.

When we were sitting alone, Shivon would tell me of her fears. Her Irish Catholic parents never knew that she was married, because it would break her father's heart that she married outside of her faith. She had asked to go home to Ireland for a vacation but her husband had refused. She felt trapped in Damascus and was trying to get out without raising suspicion. Shivon spoke Arabic and understood it even better. Having been in Syria for the past ten months and hearing no English, she was forced to understand or remain isolated.

Shivon quietly shared with me that her husband and Ferzat often talked of ways for Ferzat to marry me in Syria. She also warned me that he spoke in very controlling ways and that I must be careful. I told her of some of the places we had been, and she fearfully said it was the same route her husband took to get their marriage licence. As we were talking, I sensed he was giving Ferzat further suggestions on where to go and whom to talk with. They would often look toward us, apparently suspicious of what we were saying to each other. My naivety about the situation I was in became increasingly clear. I never thought my freedom was in jeopardy. I thought I could leave at any moment I chose to.

Ferzat wasted no time. The next day, we made a visit to the recommended government agency. Ferzat told me that once I signed the document, I did not have to be present to marry him.

Walking up the steps, I remained silent. Where was *my* voice, and what the hell was I doing? My thoughts were interrupted by Ferzat's continuing conversation. He had already progressed to our imminent divorce, stating that, in the Muslim world, a man needs only to repeat three small words three times, and *hallas*—it is finished: "I divorce you. I divorce you. I divorce you."

The interviewer was kind enough to speak minimally to me in broken English. For some reason, his questioning Ferzat about his military background was in English—at least, enough for me to know that Ferzat had lied to me. Ferzat had a scar on his knee, and he had previously told me a lengthy story of how he took a bullet from an Israeli during his military service. As the interviewer requested his military papers, they began to have a heated discussion, now in Arabic. I chimed in, much to Ferzat's anger, and learned that he had just admitted he did not have to do military time. His father apparently had managed to arrange for him to skip the army. Maybe that's why he had been living illegally in Greece for the past several years.

I have a clear memory of my internal dialogue and my emotions of anger, even rage. I felt empowered, knowing that I was going to end this charade. I have an equally clear memory of the exact following moment when my fury and anger turned against me, into denial. The topic of military service was never mentioned again. I asked no questions and, somehow, stuffed my emotions inside.

Walking out, he sheepishly put his arm around me, surely wondering what I would say after discovering his lie. My recent internal moment echoed a previous episode in my life—with my father. Here I was, on those steps in Damascus, with the exact same emotional reaction. I froze. I denied. I remained silent. It is disproportionately illogical how or why I chose to choke my impending empowerment. Although I was tough and, according to my parents, had a mouth from the gutter, I wasn't able to speak my anger toward Ferzat. It defies explanation. As we continued on down the street, I turned off a switch inside and pretended that nothing was wrong.

Although I couldn't save myself, it would turn out to be a gift that no papers were signed that day. My fate was not yet sealed.

I had been misled that we were going to visit Shivon. Instead, we went to Ferzat's uncle's home. I sat there while they spoke Arabic and shared their lives together—without me. I was just a person sitting in the corner. It was calculated and cruel, giving me a message of who was the boss.

After only a few short visits with my Irish friend, I was abruptly forbidden to see her or to call her. *Hallas.* There was no discussion. That meant I had no chance to get her address or a letter to give to her parents—the opportunity had passed.

On the drive home, Maha hopped in the open back of her brother's truck, and I said I wanted to sit with her. Ferzat yelled his disapproval; I ignored him and jumped in the back. Police sirens began to wail, as we were motioned to pull over. Ferzat and his brothers had to show their military papers, and I had to show my passport. With Ferzat not having done military time, I have no idea what papers he showed. Maybe he had a dishonourable discharge—I don't know. They questioned the men about me for quite some time and then, yelling at me in Arabic, motioned for the truck to drive on. I think they thought Maha was a younger brother.

Arriving home, the brothers were furious with me. They yelled and screamed, and the whole house became hysterical. Ferzat would not speak to me. The next day on television was a news report that the police suspected an increase in western prostitution, particularly from Russia, and they would be clamping down! I watched the news while Ferzat interpreted what was being said; the brothers and father were discussing it in angry tones.

Ferzat yelled at me in front of everyone, "See what you have caused my family." I never saw any other westerners and found it remarkably dramatic for such a reaction to a western woman sitting in the back of a truck at night. Needing to be alone, I stormed out of the house. I got one block and had to turn around in fear. Men were touching me, grabbing me, pulling my hair, and saying unquestionably filthy things to me. I shouldn't have been surprised, because even when walking with Ferzat, men would whisper things as I walked by. At one point, Ferzat slapped some guy across the head, yelling at him to keep quiet.

Ferzat just laughed at me as I came running back into the courtyard. "I tell you. This is not safe for you. You must listen." He informed me I must now wear a scarf to cover my hair. He warned me that men kidnap western women and put them in their harems as prostitutes.

I covered my hair and began to panic about the mess I was in. The family was beginning to grow tired of me. I was very unhappy. No one seemed to care that I was more and more a prisoner in their world. The rules were slowly becoming stricter. No going outside alone. No uncovered hair. No more western friends. I was now expected to sit quietly at the family gatherings and my participation would depend on my learning their language. Even my smoking buddy, Maha, seemed always to be called away when she tried to spend time with me.

Thank Allah, we were unable to get a marriage licence in Damascus, though not for lack of trying on Ferzat's part. I would have to fly back to Canada and apply on my home turf.

The airport was full of travellers. All the men were screaming and yelling. The women and children sat in circles around the airport floor.

I asked Ferzat if I could kiss his father good-bye. The male customary farewell to the father was to kiss his hand, then lift it to your forehead, kiss again, tap your forehead again and then kiss five times on one cheek and then the other. I didn't wait for permission. I picked up his father's hand, lowered my lips to the back of his hand, immediately raising it to touch my forehead. With a rhythmic beat, I moved closer and kissed his left cheek—smack, smack, smack, smack, smack—and quickly progressed to his right cheek. Nobody had time to react. Upon the last kiss, I looked into his father's bewildered eyes. Taken aback, he stared at me and seemed unable to decide whether to be angry or to laugh.

I thought he was going to blow, and I stared back into his eyes, as I continued my farewell. "*Shucrun. Ma'arsalama. Ana bahabick.* Thank you. Good-bye. I love you." In the last instant, his anger turned to laughter.

I don't remember sadness about leaving Ferzat. I was just going through the motions, knowing that I had to get on that plane. I felt like I was following a script and reciting my lines according to how the world told me I must be. No one knew what world I was going back into. I was in no hurry. Inside, I was already keeping a secret from Ferzat.

I was supposed to fly to Athens and connect with an ongoing flight to Canada. I didn't think Ferzat needed to know that I was planning a longer stopover in Greece to head back down to Paleochora and see if my girlfriend, Dawn, was still on the island. I was so excited at the thought of being with her again, although three months had passed, and the chances of her being there were slim. As my heart and soul were already with a woman, my body stood alone in Damascus, void of personality. I cannot remember saying good-bye to Ferzat.

As I sat on the Russian plane back to Athens, I couldn't help but wonder what would happen to my Irish friend.

1981

✽

Saved—at Last!

Dawn was still in Paleochora. We were so excited to see each other and went off to the beach to share our experiences—but not before I was asked to give her a message. Much had changed in both our lives. Dawn had become involved with a gorgeous green-eyed Greek man, Leksi, who had been a friend of Ferzat. In his broken English, Leksi asked me to tell Dawn that he had gonorrhoea, and she must see a doctor. He conveniently had to leave town.

As Dawn and I cozied up on the beach, we shared the past few months. She showed me some very sexy nude photos of herself on a deserted beach and seemed to be teasing me. The game would have been so much fun, but I had to tell her what Leksi had been afraid to confess. Any sexual momentum went out the window when she heard the news. She was more shocked than furious, and quietly, we packed up and went to the city of Chania, where she saw a doctor. I went on to Athens. Time and choices had changed both of us, leaving us to individually find our way "home."

Upon returning to Canada, I continued in my insanity, fully anticipating bringing Ferzat over, marrying him, and naming our firstborn Mohammed. I had been out of the country for a year, and I went to my parent's house, in the hope that time and the news of my upcoming marriage had changed things on the home front.

Several of my siblings, a neighbour, and his two daughters were all going to the swimming pool. Though I had just gotten off the plane, I agreed to go—mostly because I was scared to be alone with just my mom and dad. Dad never ever went to public pools, as he hated the germs and people peeing in the pool. I thought I was safe.

Lying in the sun with a towel over my eyes, I felt someone lie down very, very close to me. I heard the hollers from the pool: "Hi Dad. We can't believe you came to a public pool. Come in the water. Hey, guys—Dad's here!"

I froze. I could feel him almost touching me. His head was only inches away from my hips. I felt something so horrible oozing from him—his thoughts, his desires. In that moment, I didn't have an understanding or awareness of energy. To me, it was his *vibe* and it was disgusting.

Don't move, I cautioned myself and prayed for this to go away. If I didn't move or acknowledge him, I hoped, it wouldn't really be happening. When the other kids came out of the pool and distracted him, I jumped up and ran into the water, so thankful that the silence was broken.

As my siblings and I stood in the parking lot of the movie theatre the following evening, they huddled in a circle and secretly discussed something. I stood off by myself, beginning to feel uncomfortable. I guess they had been deciding who would speak to me.

Jimmy started. "Look. Mom asked me to get you out of the house. I know you just came back from Europe, but Dad's acting weird since you've been here. You have to leave."

Wendy continued, "You know, Mom cried the other night. Did you know that she tells me everything? Mom said all this is your fault. I don't like hearing all about her pain, but she obviously needs someone to talk to about this stuff."

I didn't have time to absorb the bombardment as my sister continued, "Did you know that Mom told me Dad raped her in a drunken rage? Then she got pregnant with you. Mom said she had wanted to kill him and had even tried. I think you were right—she has always turned her hatred on you. Yeah, she pretty much said that she has never loved you."

All this in less than twenty-four hours—and in a parking lot. I guessed my upcoming marriage wasn't going to guarantee me a place at the dinner table. My father's behaviour and my subsequent disownment by family members had felt so far away while I was travelling, but here it was again—still very much alive, with a choke hold on all of us.

Rona and her husband Ray, both born-again Christians, allowed me to stay with them until I got reestablished. I wanted to jump back into the gay scene. I wanted to make love to women but I needed to do the right thing. Dale, who had abruptly ended our friendship in Athens, now called me to patch things up. He and other gay buddies wanted me to go out dancing and couldn't understand why I was saying no.

My appointment with immigration was at 9:00 a.m. The officer told me I had only one more paper to sign and Ferzat would be able to enter Canada immediately. Talk about time management—I found Jesus only days before that final signature.

I had reluctantly gone to a church service with Rona and Ray, and behold, I met the Lord—and collapsed into my seat in a ball of tears and sorrow. I had been running out of ideas on how to crash through the gates of heaven. And acceptance by my family was costing me dearly. Maybe this would make them love me. Being a fiery passionate Libra, I went full-tilt into being born-again. Evangelist extraordinaire! I was a Jesus-freak. I was saved.

Sitting across the desk from me, the immigration officer said, "Now, let me get this right. You have one more paper to sign and you have decided not to? You're leaving this poor bastard in Syria? He's expecting to hear from us this week. Now, what am I going to tell the Syrian Embassy? Have you told him what you're doing to him?"

I held firm to my decision, although internally I felt like a piece of crap. Did the officer have to make me sound so cruel? Did he not realize how this marriage would be a scam?

"I'll let him know tonight," I said quietly, though I knew that the papers would arrive before my phone call. I kept thinking, *He'll kill me when he finds out. What will his family think? I've brought shame to him.* The fact that he emotionally, physically, and sexually abused me did not enter into my self-battering thoughts. I did eventually make contact with Ferzat and told him he must accept Jesus before I would marry him. I went as far as to mail him an Arabic New Testament. After a few phone calls, including some from Leksi back in Paleochora, I began to distance myself from trying to save Ferzat and to focus on my own salvation.

Because I loved to travel and escape to foreign lands, I found an evangelical school in Switzerland. I saved up for the year in order to take off and learn how to be an evangelist. Ferzat was now behind me.

I threw myself into being born-again. As I prepared for my trip, with a newfound zeal I threw out all my pictures and possessions from Damascus. They were of the devil, I now thought. I had wonderful photos of an Arab family behind closed doors; I had prayer beads from Ferzat made of gorgeous Bedouin silver and a few cool clothes—all thrown out. To this day, I feel annoyed, because how many chances does one western person get to live inside a Syrian family? But Rona stood over me as she explained why they were of the devil, and convincingly encouraged me to rid myself of my demonic possessions.

At least, I finally had some hope of God accepting me. But, within a few short weeks, the leaders of the school believed it wasn't just my possessions that were possessed—it was me. They believed dark spirits consumed me. After all, in their eyes, I had danced with the devil.

I felt pretty worthless throughout the first three months in my new evangelical world. So much criticism, all in the name of love. When I first fell to my knees in acceptance of Jesus, the song being sung cried out, "I come as I am. As I am, I come to Thee." The leaders of the evangelical school seemed to feel differently. They were trying to change everything about me; even the way I worshipped the Lord seemed too needy.

They encouraged me to break up my friendship with Joe, one of their staff, because they felt we were a bad influence on each other. Joe had come from a rock band; he was very good looking and had all the girls fawning over him. Our friendship brought out the "fun" in our personalities, but to the school, we were too "secular."

In the end, our friendship ended for a different reason. While we were having lunch together, Joe shared a secret. He showed me a list he had written years earlier of all the qualities he wanted in his wife. At the top of his list was *she must be a virgin!* I went crazy with internal anger. There was no doubt that Joe had enjoyed his share of one-nighters and now, as a born-againer, he felt his wife needed to be a virgin. It made me sick and, because of my already well-established hatred of myself, I took it personally; I felt like a filthy slut. I allowed his chauvinism to affect me. I sobbed at what a wretch I was. It also made me think of the "Virgin Mary," and how I had been taught that she *was* a virgin—pure in the eyes of God. Not having dealt with my anger toward men in general, this just added to my confusion and questions about how the scriptures seemed structured and defined by man—for man. Could it just *possibly* be that the word "virgin" was symbolic?

On a sad, rainy, lonely day, I tape-recorded a "letter" to Rona. In it, I finally shared everything about Dad and what happened and how I felt about it. It was the first time I purged; my heart ached. My words were private and intimate—from my soul—and I never imagined they would come to the ears of my parents.

After three months of living in a Swiss chalet, my evangelical education was complete. I had studied in class day and night, and along with my classmates, had made weekend excursions to evangelize and preach on the streets of Lucerne, Geneva, and even at the International Montreux Jazz Festival. Many times I had stood, microphone in hand, giving my "testimony," sharing how even a wretch like me could be saved. Now it was time for us students to disperse on a three-month outreach mission. Team leaders were announced and several destinations were revealed. Each student had to pray on where they felt the Lord wanted them to go.

It was 1982. Israel had just invaded Lebanon. My heart was telling me this was my calling. The mission was to send a Christian group to lead the Lebanese to Christ. I was first to volunteer.

1982

The Road to Lebanon

The senses are never prepared. Maybe that's why shock is such a wonderful gift. It does not allow the full extent of the truth to penetrate all at once.

Driving by building after building, I tried to absorb the array of devastation—all around, facades were blasted away, leaving wires and steal beams suspended in midair. It was the overwhelming number of bullet holes that captured my gaze. "Now they know how many holes it takes to fill the Albert Hall"—words from a song by the Beatles played in my mind. I wondered how many soldiers raised their machine guns in unison, shooting row after row of perfectly aligned bullets. It would be impossible for anyone behind those walls to have hidden from the onslaught.

Salu was the leader of our group, which consisted of myself and four Swiss mates: Suzanne, Gabriella, Malais, and Oscar. Suzanne was my closest friend, as the others spoke better German and French than English.

Being a Canadian able to speak little tidbits of Arabic was an advantage for me. I was looked to as the co-leader of the group and gave interviews to the worldwide press and got my picture in the papers. The Swiss team members were somewhat meek and quiet, while Salu and I were more animated and involved.

Salu was from Africa and, as a teenager, had been saved from the ravages of his country's war. Missionaries had taken him out of the jungle and given him his first pair of shoes. He had no idea when his birthday was or how old he was. His skin was charcoal black, and he had a thick accent and an infectious laugh.

Salu and I had become great friends and were very comfortable with each other. Although he was the leader, our relationship grew into a deeper sharing of each other's lives, concerns, and loves. He knew more than anybody about my personal struggles, and I knew about his. I took on the role of helping him understand women, including our sexuality, because Salu was sensing the Lord telling him to marry a young woman he had met while in Sweden. He was afraid, because he had never been with a woman. We discussed female sexuality, and he became a quiet listener as I talked and drew pictures.

"Is this okay? Are you sure?" I felt uncomfortable drawing the female anatomy for my spiritual leader.

Sweet Salu seemed desperate and pleaded, "Please ma'am—help me. Married people do *that*?" he kept asking. "I thought only gay people do these things."

I assured him that he *must* believe me—even straight women would like what I tried to show him. I think my pictures scared him. I wasn't a great artist and had arrows pointing here and there—he had no idea and watched with a frightened look on his face. It was very innocent and sweet. They eventually had three babies.

Salu loved the Lord.

Our first few days were spent in the coastal city of Sidon, on the floor of a hospital that had been destroyed in the bombing. We were greeted by an American, whom I nicknamed DT-II (Deep Throat Two), because he was so secretive and mysterious. Settling in, we spent the evening with a team of missionaries who were leaving after their two-month stay. We listened to their stories of how each time a bomb fell, they realized lives were being taken. They never mentioned anyone coming to Jesus but seemed satisfied with their efforts to spread the Gospel.

In the morning, Salu met with their group leader while the Swiss team went off for supplies and I stayed back to talk with DT-II. He took me aside and said he wanted to show me something. We walked across the street and met up with an Arab man who greeted us both with a handshake.

"I want you to walk very slowly and do not stop or speak to anyone. Do not look up, but know this: Tanks and machine guns are being pointed directly at you. They are following your every move. It is not safe but I have been given permission to show only you."

Through the corner of my eye, I saw the Israeli soldiers; their weapons and tanks pointed directly down on us from their perch above everyone. The arm of the tank was ever so slowly moving in harmony with our every step. I saw the guns and felt fear, both my own and the Palestinians'. My heart was pounding in my ears. I was being escorted through a Palestinian refugee camp. Up to that moment, I didn't know that a refugee camp was simply a bombed-out neighbourhood where people were forced to live in squalor and filth.

We walked in silence. Dark, saddened, hostile eyes stared into my blue eyes. I longed to hug the children, who were closely following me, but I could not. I did, however, say hello and smile at them. I could not pretend they did not exist. All buildings and homes were reduced to broken shards of glass, and brick to dust. This had once been a beautiful 'hood, with tall swaying palm trees, right on the sea in the city of Sidon. Now, it was all death and decay. Israel had done what was called "saturation bombing," relentlessly bombing over and over, completely destroying whatever was deemed enemy territory belonging to the Palestinians. As we turned a corner, I asked about the rubble I was looking at. It was clearly a multi-floored structure that was now pancaked into the ground. It had been a school. Our guide quietly said that there were many dead children and teachers underneath, some buried alive. I felt acid form in my stomach.

As we left the camp, DT-II said he had wanted me to see how they were living. The Arab stranger disappeared and we walked back to join the rest of our team. I don't fully understand why I got to go. Maybe it was because I was Canadian and DT-II felt comfortable with me. Salu, being a black man, could possibly have been harmed in the camp because many Palestinians are of very dark skin. I kept the walkabout to myself.

After only a few days in Sidon, our team relocated to the south of Lebanon under the protection of Major Sa'ad Haddad, head of the Lebanese Christian Militia. I naively thought if he were Christian, he was doing God's work and helping the people of Lebanon.

We moved to Arnoun, under the Beaufort Castle. Arnoun, a Shi'ite Muslim village, was the stronghold of the PLO, who regularly bombed northern Israel, blasting Russian-made *katyusha* rockets into *kibbutzim*. The PLO had taken over southern Lebanon, making it their Palestinian stronghold, and as a result, Arnoun was now completely destroyed. Every family we met had lost someone. By the time we got there, only a handful of families remained. Others had come from Beirut, feeling it was safer now that the PLO had been removed from the village.

The villagers began gathering around, inspecting the strangers in their midst. Filthy, dusty, dirty, they all had worn faces—small children, mothers, brothers, grandfathers. Young girls had their baby siblings hanging off of one hip, carrying far too much responsibility for their ages. The men predominantly wore western-style pants and shirts along with their *goutrah*s. Women and girls wore long dresses, with pants underneath, and head scarves to cover their hair.

"*Salem malenko,*" I greeted them.

"*Malenko salem,*" they returned with surprised giggles. What a strange greeting in a strange land—peace be with you.

"*Ishmeh Edna. Arabi, Fatima!*" I continued, enjoying their chuckling. "*Shoo bak?*" Now I was just showing off.

They started speaking to me, assuming I understood more than my basic greetings. I got as far as to say, "*Schwai, schwai. Ana taki schwai Arabi.*" They laughed as I begged them to slow down, because I spoke only a little of their language.

"*Hum'da'allah*—praise be to God!" everyone chimed together.

In Arnoun, our digs were the remains of yet another bombed-out school. The children followed us up the collapsed staircase, as we crawled over mounds of cement slabs, broken away and lying along stairs piled with rubble and debris from the bombing. I looked down to the schoolyard to see two gigantic craters from bombs that had missed the building but hit the school yard. Other bombs had been successful in destroying their only school. I wondered if the children had been in class that day.

It was quite evident that there was no concern about collateral damage; if your enemies were in that hospital or school—*ma'arsalama*. In fact, it seemed that hospitals and schools were the actual targets. Two bomb craters, plus direct hits to the school would lead one to believe that none of this was accidental.

Within only a few days of our moving to Arnoun, the newspapers reported that the Sidon refugee camp had been savagely attacked. We were told that the Israelis simply opened fire. My mind moved in slow motion, as I remembered the faces of the men, women, and little kids sitting around the rubble and filth. It was like watching caged animals at a zoo; their conditions were already barbaric and inhumane, and now they had undergone more brutality. Pictures of blown-up bodies—some of them women and babies lying in pools of blood—covered the pages of the newspaper.

In my current world, the reality of people in the West waking up, showering, having breakfast, and driving off to work or playing in the park seemed very, very distant. All of life as I previously knew it was going on in a parallel galaxy. I couldn't see outside of the world I was in.

Having only just walked through the camp, this news of its destruction was hard to comprehend. Thank Allah for shock absorbers.

We wanted to make as nice a home as possible out of the ruins. We cleaned out one of the bullet-ridden rooms, laid our sleeping bags on the floor, and set up an area to cook. Scorpions would creep toward us throughout the night, and remarkably, one of us would wake up in time to stare them in the face, jump up, grab a broom, and bash them to death. Better them than us. To this day, I shake my shoes before putting them on—in case anything has crawled into them overnight!

The floor was incredibly painful to sleep on, and so, when the ladies eventually saw mattresses on one of their shopping excursions, they dickered out a great price. It was heaven after months of sleeping on the floor. Chores were divided up, with Gabriella being in charge of the shopping, which she did down the road in the larger village of Nabetia—home to the infamous Hezbollah.

We took turns cooking, doing dishes, and cleaning up. I negotiated to get out of cooking dinners, telling them *they* would be very grateful. Fortunately, they all loved cooking, and I loved doing the dishes.

The only source of water came from a well in the ground, which of course was contaminated water. It had to be boiled, tablets dissolved into it, and boiled again. Within a very short time, Oscar and I became very sick with bowel problems. Our hole-in-the-ground toilet was down the treacherous broken stairwell, past the bomb craters, around to the back of the school, and inside a small, enclosed cement enclave built by the guys. Suzanne would help me race to the toilet. It got very scary as I started throwing up simultaneously with diarrhea, all the while squatting over a hole.

Someone decided we should go to a doctor, and off we went to Nabetia, to a Red Crescent makeshift hospital. I was nervous because of the lack of hygiene, the dirt, and the frenzy of the place. It had been used for the war-wounded and now helped people with various illnesses or injuries, many from land mines.

A few years previously, I had been diagnosed with aortic valve disease, a congenital heart disorder. Now, upon hearing the gurgle of my heart, the doctors became concerned. Try begging for Arabic-speaking doctors not to worry whilst you are vomiting, pooping, and generally fearing for your welfare. It was not easy. Fortunately, many Lebanese speak French, and so did Suzanne who, being a nurse, tried to explain. But it all got very confusing.

Just as I settled in to my IV drip and they were about to connect Oscar, DT-II arrived saying we must leave immediately because he had found a private hospital that had offered to help us. He added that the hygiene was much better, but more important, he felt we were unsafe in Nabetia. Staring at the IV drip in my arm, I tried not to be afraid. Wrapped in blankets, IV and all, we left as the doctors were yelling, confused as to why we were being smuggled away. I felt bad because they had been so kind, but I was too sick to think straight.

We walked into what used to be a hospital but now had only one small wing open—the rest had been bombed and destroyed. Being slightly brainwashed as a born-againer, I had believed Israel could do no wrong, but I soon found myself conflicted over the spiritual versus secular state of Israel. Its soldiers were not biblical characters.

Oscar and I had just settled into our eerily quiet hospital rooms, with new IVs hooked up, when I got an unwelcome visitor—my period. Thank Krishna, Suzanne was with me and offered to go out and find supplies. In the meantime, all the nurse gave me was Kleenex.

Shortly after Suzanne left, we began hearing loud, frantic Arabic announcements coming from various loudspeakers. There was a heaviness in the air. I worried about Suzanne. Oscar came into my room, saying he felt nervous. When I told him Suzanne was in town, our fearful thoughts speculated on what was happening. *Shoot first, ask questions later* was a phrase we were becoming familiar with.

A scared-looking Suzanne finally wandered into the room. "Trucks were driving up and down with people standing in the back, yelling on loudspeakers. Everyone is running around. Someone grabbed my arm and told me to get inside, but I couldn't understand what was happening."

Visibly upset, the doctor and his wife came in and began conversing in French. President-elect Bashir Gemayel, a Maronite Catholic, had just been assassinated. By the end of that same day, his brother had been elected president of Lebanon.

A curfew was instantly imposed on all of Lebanon. Anyone found on the streets would be immediately shot. Everyone was under house arrest. I kept imagining a bomb hitting the hospital. God, I was afraid.

The doctor's wife came and sat with us. Speaking English, she told us stories of how the hospital was taken over by the PLO and then subsequently bombed. She and her husband had been thrown out of their own hospital by the PLO and were now attempting to start over. There was only one nurse, but they had high hopes for rebuilding their hospital and staff.

With curfew lifted, and Suzanne now back in Arnoun, I lay alone, trying to communicate with my doctor. It was clear that he was worried about my heart, and I believed he was bringing a cardiologist in to see me. I had not been able to convey to him not to worry. I'm sure with the added fright over possible bombs dropping, my ticker probably sounded even more stressed. He said, "*Bukra, bukra*—tomorrow, tomorrow," as he pointed to his heart. I knew a specialist was coming to see me. Oscar tried interpreting but he barely spoke French. Things were getting complicated. I needed Suzanne back.

DT-II appeared the next morning. It was too dangerous here, he said, and he wanted us back in Arnoun. I told him I was positive someone was coming to see me, but he laughed it off with a casual "don't worry." He would not listen to my concerns about offending this wonderful, kind doctor. I told him we were going to insult him, as he had gone out of his way to help me and was bringing a cardiologist from somewhere to see me. DT-II didn't believe my intuition, but as we were packing up, in walked my doctor with a very well-dressed cardiologist. I think he came all the way from Beirut. The doctor looked surprised and embarrassed that I was up and dressed, as he stood with a specialist beside him. I was so uncomfortable and felt so bad. DT-II finally understood that I knew what I was talking about but it was too late. Why was it so dangerous to be there anyway?

Our illness brought us closer to the people of our village. As we arrived home, feeling much better after IV fluids, we still needed bed rest. The women gathered around; they'd brought a dish made from a Bedouin recipe passed down from the nomads. They tried to feed me the mixture of goat's yoghurt, garlic and other herbs and spices, but it was not what I felt like swallowing. As they pleaded, I saw a chain reaction within all the women. As one became upset with my being sick, she started the *zilagheet* shriek used to express either sorrow, grief or happiness—"lalalalala." This caused a domino effect, and soon, all the women were wailing and upset. I, of course, ate the potion, which turned out to be miraculous. This was the first of many times I would be offered this Bedouin dish known to cure a myriad of illnesses. The Swiss ladies brought some to Oscar, and in no time, our strength returned.

I felt wonderful and insisted that we go back to Nabetia to apologize to the doctor who had taken care of me. We returned bearing gifts of cakes and cookies. Suzanne explained the situation to him and all was forgiven. The doctor told me my bowels would never be the same and I would have intestinal problems for the rest of my life; he was right. To this day, my guts dismiss foreign food within hours of eating. We enjoyed *chai* and treats and then headed back to our village, fresh with a desire to bring Jesus to the people.

Meanwhile, bad news was spreading like a disease. Two Beirut refugee camps, Sabra and Shatila, had been deliberately raided and destroyed. A murderous rampage had been inflicted on people who had already lost everything. Women were brutally raped and murdered. People were lined up and then gunned down like flies. The pictures in the paper were beyond comprehension. Children, women, men, grandparents—blown to bits by bullets repeatedly ripping through their already lifeless bodies. Oh, my God, this was war.

I didn't find out who was responsible until much later. I don't know how we were sheltered from that information, but I would soon understand why DT-II knew we weren't safe.

In my rare time alone, I would go up to the rooftop of our school to pray and meditate. From my perch, I looked out at the beautiful hills and cedars of Lebanon, with the snow-capped Mount Hermon off in the horizon. Behind me would usually be a handful of kids, who followed me everywhere. Israeli jets would fly by on reconnaissance missions, breaking the speed of sound and creating a supersonic *boom*, which sounded like a bomb exploding as it broke the tranquility. Within the confines of a war zone, I had a unique opportunity to learn meditation.

Every week, our group would perform mini-plays, in which we danced, sang, and acted out the death and resurrection of Christ. We had Arabic New Testaments and worked hard to convert the sinners. The village would watch, chuckling and whispering amongst themselves but being polite out of kindness. I only ever saw one young girl read the New Testament we had given her.

I kept my focus mainly with the ladies. I had a hidden mission to give love and honour to the women who had been so abused and destroyed—at least in my heart, that's what I wanted to do. Having experienced a small sampling of how women are generally treated in the Muslim world, I wanted to reach out to them. Sadly, I wasn't in a position to give love unconditionally—I hadn't learned how. I passed along everything that had been done to me in judgement.

Hostility would creep over me. As I watched a teenage girl on her rooftop, circling in prayer as she read her Koran, I looked up at her with a harsh stare. She returned the same glare. If only I had understood that she was a mirror image of me. My whole life, I had never been allowed to be who I was, without judgement and condemnation crushing me down at every turn. And here I stood, passing on the same to her. *Do unto others as you would have them do unto you* was obviously twisted in my head to be *as others have done unto you.* It didn't stop with her.

Sumaiya spoke French and had a great time acting as translator for the village. It became humorous at times as the team would ask her questions in French, speak with each other in German, and translate into English to me. Often, they would be speaking to me in German and I would be listening for several minutes until one of us realized I couldn't understand. It was so funny because I would listen intently, and maybe on some level, I did understand their language.

Sumaiya and I became friends. Although neither of us spoke the same language, we were always together and somehow managed to communicate. Her brother had shown us Polaroids of Israeli soldiers lying dead along the trails to Beaufort Castle. They were very grim and horrifying, and as I looked away, everyone laughed. They had witnessed far more death than a picture and thought it was funny how disturbed I was.

We decided to walk up the pathway to Beaufort Castle and asked Salu to come with us. I wanted Sumaiya to see that it was safe now. It was spooky to walk where so much death had occurred, and I could sense her nervousness as we climbed to the top.

Israeli soldiers patrolled it and, for the most part, were friendly. Not this day. At the top, I was pointing to Israel, showing Sumaiya how close it was, when soldiers started yelling at us and asking what we wanted. As Salu tried to calm the soldiers, he told us to start walking back down the mountain. Machine guns flailing in our faces, Sumaiya and I quickly turned around and left. My heart pounded as she held my hand tight and started crying.

All the way down the mountain, I got her to say over and over again, "Jesus. Jesus. Jesus." I somehow felt that the more she said it, the more accountable she would be for knowing about

Jesus and not accepting him. This is what I had been taught. She was so afraid and just kept saying *Jesus* over and over, all the way down that mountain. I wasn't protecting or giving comfort to her, not on any level, except maybe way down in my heart of hearts—in that place I had not yet discovered.

Outside of showing the way to salvation through Jesus, our primary goal was to fix homes. One house stands out in my memory.

Our team would break into pairs, each working on a different home. More often than not, Salu and I worked together. We were busy mixing the cement to fill the bullet holes, prior to painting, when the family became very upset, pointing downwards. We looked and, sure enough, there was a bomb tucked right beside the house. It had not detonated, but if anything were to touch it—*kaboom*. Knowing the family had no choice but to live in their dwelling and risk the bomb, we chose to continue. My heart pounded through my chest as we worked quietly and methodically over and around the bomb. Eventually, the house was repaired and we painted it a beautiful white and blue. The family had tears of joy. I had tears of relief.

Our village, being Shi'ite, celebrated Ashura, a ten-day mourning commemorating the martyrdom of the Prophet Mohammed's grandson. According to custom, the mosques were draped in black and no music or singing was allowed. Mind you, for the three months we lived in Lebanon, there really wasn't any music or dancing.

The males in our village went to Nabetia to join the festivities. The men and boys beat themselves with chains for nine days. These chains were not just symbolic—they were the real deal: heavy strips of metal, hanging down to form a whip. The men flung them over one shoulder and let the chains crash on their back and then over the other shoulder—over and over, as their backs became redder and redder from the lashings. On the last day of mourning, they donned white sheets and cut their heads with a sword as they rhythmically beat their heads, while chanting and working themselves into a trance, allowing the white sheets to become soaked in their blood.

Even mothers held their young boys and babes, cut open their heads, and hit the wounds over and over—those poor little babies. Many boys and men passed out and ambulances were everywhere. Although the head cuts are typically not huge, they bleed profusely. There was blood everywhere, which further escalated the crowd into a frenzy. Our team was allowed to watch this procession take place in Nabetia but it felt dangerous. There was something very primitive and tribal in the chanting that invoked an emotional excitation and increased the mood to a very intense level. I've seen it reach near hysteria, but within Ashura, it was a more intense frenzy—with everyone almost out of body.

The next year's celebration in Nabetia would turn deadly. Soldiers opened fire into the crowds and killed many bystanders.

Living down the road in Arnoun and being allowed to witness the very private and sacred rituals of Ashura, as well as doing other business in Nabetia, made us acutely aware of a particular daily reality. We lived surrounded by Hezbollah.

Salu and I were on a lunch break and were soon joined by a group of guys from our village; they had just returned from Ashura celebrations. We all sat around in a circle, talking in French and English—those who spoke only Arabic made sure their words were translated—each wanting to be heard. I asked about one of the elders, who sat in the same chair everyday, twirling his prayer beads and boldly wearing a Palestinian head scarf. His two houses had been taken over by the PLO, whom he fully supported, and he had therefore had two Israeli bombs dropped on them. His son was killed, and his son's wife subsequently ran away. The guys just laughed it off.

They began bragging that they were part of Hezbollah. They knew how much they were disturbing us, and laughing and chanting, they declared their pride in being part of a Jihad against Israel. Although Hezbollah carries with it terror and fear, behind its name stood these young boys and men who had simply been taught to hate. They were very fiery about Hezbollah, and we tried matching their passion with talk of Jesus.

As we headed back to work, I sensed they were up to something and felt a tangible nervousness. As Salu and I resumed our job of repairing bomb holes and painting a house a beautiful cobalt blue, a bullet seared past Salu's head. He ducked at the swishing sound, and the air was thick with danger as we took a moment to pray for our safety. We never found out which one of our village brothers drew his gun. Salu was a wreck, as he put my hand over his pounding heart, and told me that he felt the bullet pass by his head.

With death and danger biting at our heels, I felt that every step was a possible land mine. Living and being in the moment took on a much deeper meaning—this was no joke. Lebanon is where I started a lifelong habit of watching the sunset and wishing on the first evening star. I was thankful for every sunset I saw and even more thankful for every sunrise.

There was a constant stream of Israeli soldiers coming in and out of southern Lebanon, from Kiryat Shimona in northern Israel. Watching their tanks roll by, I would often flash them the peace sign and they would reciprocate. They were all so young.

Occasionally, they came into our village for *chai* with us. This made the villagers a bit uncomfortable, but it was good public relations. I doubt that the Hezbollah guys thought so, however.

The Israelis spoke both Hebrew and Arabic and would chitchat with the kids. Time ran in slow motion while I watched an Israeli soldier look down at a small Arab boy, cup the boy's face with his big hands, and speak lovingly to the child, as if no one else mattered. His spirit consumed the young boy's eyes, and they shared a brief moment of peace, compassion, and love. I watched and wished it could all go away. *You're both descendants of Abraham—you are brothers. All this fighting and dying. It's crazy.*

During our tour of duty for Jesus, we had asked to go to Beirut but were told it was too dangerous because we were "connected" to Major Haddad. None of us understood this, and sadly, none of us questioned it. We just innocently trusted our leaders. Major Haddad was an enigma, but we were under his protection. The politics and religious connections were not made known to us—until I started snooping around and finally figured it out.

I don't know how they managed to hide the truth from us; I felt so naïve and passive. It was *his* militia who raided, raped and murdered all those Palestinians in the Sabra and Shatila refugee camps. I wept. Christian Militia is quite an oxymoron. DT-II was closely connected to Major Haddad; that's why he was so bloody secretive. He seemed to know intimate details and was very protective of his secrets. DT-II appeared to be the eyes and ears for Major Haddad—at least, on some level. My imagination ran wild and I thought DT-II might be a drug lord, selling opium from the Bekkhae Valley. He seemed to have friendships everywhere, including with the Syrian soldiers.

I also thought that we as missionaries could do no wrong, and that "we" included Major Haddad and his *Christian* militia. What was I thinking!

Our three months were up. It was time to head back to evangelism school in Switzerland. One by one, we had dinner or *chai* with almost every family to say our good-byes. A family who lived away from the village, high up on a hill, offered us the use of their shower, proudly saying it was just like an American shower. All we had been using was a small bowl of water. It was quite a feat for four women, all with long hair, to sponge bathe and keep clean. Packing up our supplies, we excitedly climbed to the home with the shower. The family must have been rich in Beirut because they did not mingle with the village people much.

Entering their bathroom was like winning a million dollars and then having someone take it away from you. The shower was a rusty pipe with a drip. Drip, drip, drip. Cold-water droplets hit the rusted out tub. It was the offer that was appreciated. There was not to be a glorious cleansing but they didn't have to know that. He was so proud, saying, "Edna. Like Canada? Yes?"

I was tired and wanted to scream, *Are you freakin' kidding me?* But instead, I replied, "Yes. Yes. Like Canada."

As we finished packing, the women, girls and children of Arnoun started congregating around us. We had been through a lot together. Almost all the worst homes were repaired. We had laughed, loved, and judged.

We began making our rounds through Arnoun to say goodbye. We promised to try and come back in a few months, during our next field trip after the School of Evangelism II.

Walking through the village, with all the kids around me, I felt a tiny hand softly slip into mine. I looked and there she was: a precious, beautiful green-eyed angel who, up to that point, had not smiled or laughed and would not let anyone touch her or get close to her. She had been so full of fear and totally shut down. For three months, I had tried and just kept on loving her—*schwai, schwai*—slowly, slowly. I felt something terrible had happened to her—physically and emotionally—and I knew her scars were very deep. I would always see her, standing off in the distance, alone and watching. And now, here she was, with her head held high, proud as could be, holding my hand, walking through the village.

As one woman began the infamous Arabic women's wail, another and another and another joined in, until there was the beginning of hysteria. They closed in around us, touched us as if we were more than human, and then pulled at our arms, pleading for us to stay. I felt a bit scared. Salu told us to pile into the Mercedes (Did I mention that *everybody* drives a Mercedes?) and get out of Dodge.

Before we left, one of the men asked if we would mail a package to his brother in Paris. I looked at Gabriella and she said, "Why not? We trust him." We took the package.

I have never been successful at getting through airport security. There is just that something about me that tends to send out alarms with custom officers. I don't know if it's my rebellious nature, my long hair, or my tie-dyed clothes. Ben Gurion airport was abuzz with people. We entered security clearance number fifteen, and the guard asked, "Where are you coming from?"

"Lebanon," we replied. Why lie?

"*Lebanon?* What were you doing in Lebanon?" he asked between Hebrew calls for more security to surround us. Our group was broken up; Salu talked to one group of guards, Oscar to another, and we ladies spoke with yet another. We began explaining that we were missionaries, thinking that should make things easy, but they weren't buying it.

"Did anyone give you any packages to mail for them?" Seeing Gabriella and I look nervously at each other, he asked it a second time, only harsher.

"Well, yes. It's here. But we lived with these people. We trust them." Suddenly, all those news flashes started filling my mind.

"*Don't touch it,*" he shouted. Within a heartbeat, the bomb squad surrounded us. This brought a bit of attention to our group. We could have started preaching to the masses and saved a few lives if we hadn't been so concerned about our own. As the futuristic-looking, head-to-toe covered bomb squad gently removed the package into another room, I stood staring at Oscar. I knew by his face what he had done.

In Arnoun, there were large fragments of blown-up bombs lying everywhere, as well as smaller bombs that appeared to have not detonated on impact.

Oscar had said he wanted to take a warhead home for a souvenir. I told him he was crazy, and now, looking at his face, I knew. Oscar had a *katyusha* in his luggage!

I said, grinding my teeth, "*Oscar!* You must tell them."

Oscar, being slightly odd to begin with, started talking condescendingly to the security, informing them that he saw nothing wrong with having—and he pulled out the warhead. All hell broke lose. Security went ballistic—never mind the bomb. Their English was very good, and they proceeded to scream into our faces about the dangers of having weapons on a plane and the stupidity of taking a bomb, not to mention breaking the law. They screamed that we could have blown up the plane. Oscar was furious at me, but I was on the side of the Israelis on this one.

The bomb squad brought back a now imploded package of film, shredded to bits, and handed it back to us. Were we really to send this package to Paris?

Thank Yaweh that Security clearly saw our ignorance and our naivety. Miraculously, they let us through, albeit with an escort onto the plane. It would not be my last escort onto an El Al Airline.

Oh, Wretched Soul That I Am

*B*ack safely in Switzerland, I endured three more months of evangelism school, again with students from all over the world. I had endless troubles and was rebuked many times, as I questioned things and continued to show a rebellious spirit—at least to the leaders.

I spent hundreds of hours crying and pleading with God to change me. In my scrapbook, under almost every picture, is a comment about how sad I was, or that I was going through a hard time. Even while in Lebanon, I shed many tears and had enormous internal conflict. I hated myself and felt worthless and still not worthy of being loved. Being saved didn't help me with loving myself and didn't release me from the bonds of homosexuality's gripping desires within me. Nobody touched my relationship with my dad. There was little discussion about it. I was just to forgive him and move forward. They were much more concerned about my *choice* and desires to be gay.

The leaders became convinced I was demonically possessed and eventually took me to "the room." Stories abounded that Satan was cast out of student's souls inside that room. Exorcisms were not unusual in our quaint chalet.

Leslie and I shared a room right next door and often heard strange noises through the wall. One particularly disturbing exorcism was done on Theodore, a British aristrocrat, who was enormously wealthy and yet, dressed like a pauper. Only his accent and mention of friends during "forgiveness prayers" gave it away—he would make reference to Sirs, Knights, Earls, Dukes and Duchesses, whilst he prayed for their forgiveness, or forgave them.

Leslie and I just happened to see the staff taking him into "the room," and we immediately put our ears to the wall. We heard the staff shouting at the devil, demanding he not only leave Theodore, but also that he leave the building. There was so much noise, it sounded like a struggle was going on. I later told Salu that we "inadvertently" heard the "horrors" and were petrified that Satan's spirit saw us and could harm us. Salu, being my friend, shared what happened, beginning by saying we had nothing to fear because they commanded Satan's spirit to not harm anyone within the chalet. He told me that Theodore and his brother used to practice levitation, and through this exorcism, Theodore's body levitated almost to the ceiling. All of the staff's strength combined could not pull his body back down. When I asked why levitating was sinful, Salu said that it was because the power to do so was not from God.

In prayer time, I remember feeling the gaze of one of the leaders and I looked over at him with a hostile glare. He felt it was the devil's glare, and a part of me did as well. After hearing about Theodore, I was quite numb with fear as they sat me in the designated chair, surrounded by my leaders all praying feverishly, demanding that Satan show himself—but nothing happened.

Later that evening, I talked with my group leader, Janet, and she was furious with me. She said she knew I wasn't telling them everything, and made me feel like I was hanging on to Satan. It was hard for them to swallow that just maybe, Satan did *not* dwell within me.

They weren't the only ones upset. How could I change my spots? It was like asking a white person to become black—it couldn't happen. Maybe it's a few too many XY chromosomes. We are what we are, aren't we? God knows I tried to shed not only my skin but also my core.

Mentioning some of my episodes of being stoned on drugs didn't help me. I tried to explain that when I was doing drugs, I often tripped out and imagined that we were all just souls in one room. We had no eyes or bodies, and nobody could see our "images." We were all androgynous—there was no male or female, just our spirits. I always felt that we would end up loving a soul that we probably would have hated if we'd seen it. Was that so far from what God's plan is? Doesn't God just want us to love the soul of a person and not the physical? Maybe our souls are our "auras"—just hovering around our bodies. After all, the body dies but the soul lives. Why did the leaders think I was possessed? Dating all the way back into my days of getting stoned, my "visions" seemed to make sense to me. I had been spiritually searching a lot longer than I realized.

The leaders wanted me out of the school because I wasn't an easy convert, and they felt my soul was doomed. My questions were met with disdain, particularly if the leaders didn't have an answer. Was it so wrong to question the logic of Adam and Eve being the only humans to procreate? That meant, to me, that their children would have had incestuous relations in order to keep the human race growing. Again, I questioned the possibility of biblical events being symbolic? This was making more and more sense to me. I don't believe I did anything outrageously wrong, other than cutting a few classes, questioning things, and not wanting to change my outer appearance. The leaders wanted me to be quiet, to wear more dresses, and to cut my hair because I looked like a hippie. And would it hurt me to put on a bit of makeup? Just crazy things—how would makeup and a dress heal my wounded soul?

The timing for a letter from my father seemed perfect. Just what I needed—a confirmation that I was full of crap.

The first five pages were about an apparent confrontation my siblings had with my parents. I'd heard that my parents were being evicted and had asked for financial assistance from their kids. But rather than money, they got an "intervention."

My parents always had money troubles and yet managed to live in the most beautiful homes in the richest 'hoods. Granted, we moved almost yearly. I never knew what my dad did for a living, but I knew he had troubles. Police in uniform and plain-clothes detectives had even raided one of our homes while the folks were away. We were teens and sat watching detectives fling out drawers, empty them on the floor, and ransack the home. None of us ever learned why.

And now, my parents were again in dire straits, only this time, I was far away and wasn't involved. Because I wasn't there, Dad's letter should just have been about my siblings, but never one to miss an opportunity, he managed to throw in a curve ball. The portion pertaining to me said:

> As to the situation with Edna, she was not sexually abused; in fact, I never put a hand on her. This was the result of a change of life, over which I had absolutely no control, even though I prayed day and night for this situation to be removed from my life. And I might add that during all of this time, Edna never did very much to discourage this situation, and one could even say she might have encouraged it a little.

On the heels of this letter, my mother for the first time sent her own letter. It was short and to the point:

> As for dealing with the situation that existed during the male menopause of your father, that was dealt with, and Edna knows she was not sexually abused.

I encouraged him? And yet I lied?. *Menopause?* My parents had figured it out together. But it still made no real sense. Why wouldn't he have apologized for his menopause, instead of casting stones at me? I was now a child of God. Why were they being so cruel? I slid out of my skin, repulsed by everything around me—including myself.

Though I was held in low esteem by almost everyone, I must have had angels and fairies around me. To be so worthless in my world was crushing, and without some sort of love holding me up, I surely would have been buried alive.

Somehow surviving the classroom, I, along with about fifty other born-againers, embarked on another outreach. From Europe, into Greece, Turkey and on to Israel, we were about to spread the Gospel again. I don't know how I believed I could spread the love of God when I stood in my own skin, full of hatred and self-loathing, unsure that I deserved to be any part of God's plan. As for being part of the body of Christ, I didn't even feel worthy enough to be an infected baby toenail. But off we went again—to save the wretched sinners of the world.

We entered villages where religion was a no-no, where gypsies stole our belongings, and where Satan clearly had taken up residence.

While we were in Czechoslovakia, our leaders quickly piled us on the bus, a bit panicked to get out of town. As we evangelized on the streets, the locals began getting annoyed, rumblings erupted and police began to appear. At that time, communist countries did not allow open discussion of religion in public, and they wanted nothing to do with us.

I don't remember anybody ever getting saved through our efforts—in any country. Today, I am so happy that I never managed to pull down the foundations of someone else's beliefs. Not that I didn't try.

It felt good to be back in the Middle East yet again. Maybe I was most comfortable in a barren desert.

When we arrived back in Kiryat Shimona, a man greeted us and asked, "Is there an Edna in this group?" My fellow students were surprised, as was I. Who could be asking for the problem child?

"I'm here," I said, wondering what was happening.

He proceeded to bring out newspaper clippings of me at work in Lebanon. Apparently I had made a bit of a stir—in a good way—and was known within the Christian community. Wow, I wonder how much they would have loved me if they knew all the demons I was battling with. It was uncomfortable standing in the middle of my classmates and leaders, knowing some of them felt I was more of an abomination to God.

We had heard that Major Haddad was ill, but this was incredibly top secret. It turned out he was dying of cancer, but it had to be kept hush-hush because of the ongoing war. Interestingly, it was DT-II who gave us the initial information, saying only that Haddad had a flu—if word had gotten out that he was dying, it would have had grave consequences. DT-II was obviously still working alongside Major Haddad, but other than that, he remained as mysterious as ever. *Who* was he?

I pleaded to go back to Arnoun to visit. After all, here we were standing at the barbed-wire freedom fence created by Israel. I could look down and see our village, but our leaders wouldn't give us permission. It was too dangerous, they said. There had been much fighting there recently and a lot more bloodshed.

I walked over to the fence and stood looking down to our tiny village, wondering if they were all right. I felt guilty that I had been able to freely leave, while they had to stay behind. Now, we were only moments from them—Sumaiya and my precious green-eyed angel, and all the families there. The answer remained *no*. It was not safe to go.

We camped throughout the country, evangelizing in the land of Jesus and seeing every religious site possible to see. I will never forget an encounter with a young Palestinian man as I walked along the Via Doloroso, where Christ carried the cross to his crucifixion. When I stopped at the man's souq to talk with him, the subject of Lebanon came up and, of course, I felt in my heart that Jesus had given me this opportunity to save his soul. I preached the Gospel, essentially telling him his belief system was dead wrong. He became very upset and started yelling at me but was soon overtaken with grief. His voice cracked with emotion as he tried to get me to understand the Palestinian plight and what Islam meant to him. We both became still and, for one quiet heartbeat, looked eye-to-eye, soul-to-soul, and I knew that I was no better than he. I was not saved, and he was not condemned.

Israel certainly is an enchanted world, especially if you are there to spread the Gospel of Jesus. Seeing where Christ was born and raised, and where he died—visiting the Garden of Gethsemane, Golgotha, the Wailing Wall, Jericho, Bethlehem, Nazareth, the Dead Sea, Masada, the Sea of Galilee, and a myriad of holy sites—brought the Bible vividly to life.

Projecting my own anger, I was always reacting to the role of women. Women were not allowed to go to the main area of the Wailing Wall to pray, but the men were kind enough to section off a tiny piece of the wall in the corner for the weaker sex. Did God really create women to be so much less than men? Why weren't my fellow female born-againers angry? They believed in being submissive—the Bible told them so. This was not working for me.

As we wound our way back up into Europe, I was hating the rules and hating how the others were always annoyed at my character flaws. By the end of the trip, feeling not quite sane, I kept mostly to myself.

Originally planning to stay away from Canada for only three months, I had been gone for a full year. Having no money, I was only able to remain abroad and travel because *secret angels* supported me. Funds and gifts found their way into my mail slot or they were given anonymously to the leaders. One way or another, my various brothers and sisters in Jesus paid for the entire year. Even when my passport was stolen in Israel, and I had to get a temporary replacement, hands would be outstretched, slipping money into my palm. Although I felt very isolated and a bitter failure, their kindness was startling to me. Looking back, I wonder if I had been somehow trying to shove them all away, just to see if they would love me, no matter what? With my emotional and spiritual maturity being quite murky at the time, this would have been a completely unknown and unconscious behaviour, but in hindsight, I can see how often I pushed everybody away—before they left me.

As we sat in the classroom, funds were divvied up in secrecy—I wasn't the only one who didn't have money. When it was announced that all my costs had been taken care of, I stood up and thanked everyone who had supported me. I apologized for not being successful at finding peace and promised I would continue my quest. The amount of financial support and kindness was astonishing, considering I spent so many hours being miserable and confused.

With absolute sincerity, I spoke with as much gratitude as I could, feeling very humbled. My classmates and I cried. They must have seen something good in me.

After my year abroad, I came back to Canada, compliments of my mother—which should have aroused my suspicions. She bought me a plane ticket and sounded like she was welcoming me back. I had the crazy notion that I would save up again and head off to yet another evangelical school. I had to keep trying to be born-again, because it was so drilled into my head that any other choice meant eternal damnation. I didn't know what else to do. Talk about the fear of God. I never had a settled feeling. Although I didn't realize it, I was constantly planning where to run next. I was running myself into the ground—burying myself alive.

※

Thou Preparest a Table Before Me in the Presence of Mine Enemies

My mother and brother met me at the airport. My mother seemed standoffish and quiet, while Jimmy hugged me so tight, I thought he could crack my back. That hug was the kiss of Judas.

As we were supposedly driving to a family barbeque and welcome-home party, Jimmy said we needed to stop off at his apartment before we continued on to Mom and Dad's. I walked in and saw a man sitting in a chair with his legs on the bed.

As my mother stood silent, my brother's voice cracked. "We believe you have been in a cult and are brainwashed. Our whole family agrees that you have to be deprogrammed." My mother had gotten it into her head that I was in a cult. Although she phoned the Swiss Embassy and they gave their highest praise to the school I was attending, she had not been convinced.

I stood in shock and horror at what I was hearing. The stranger stayed silhouetted in the bedroom, with his legs still resting on the bed. He never moved. I felt fear enter from the tips of my toes and consume me.

Mom remained silent as Jimmy continued, "We have been working with an ex-Moonie and he believes you are brainwashed. He has undergone deprogramming himself. Look, he knows what it's like to be in a cult and has no doubt that you have to be deprogrammed."

My eyes flashed to the windows, which were all boarded up. Unable to say one word, I bolted for the front door. But my brother locked me into a death grip and threw me into the room with this creep. I finally cried out, pleading with him not to do this to me. Thrust into the chair, two feet away from this stranger, I asked for a cigarette and immediately started chain smoking, after quitting for a year.

The Moonie proceeded to play good-cop/bad-cop for the next thirteen hours. I tried to go to the bathroom and was told I had to remove my belt for fear of my wanting to hang myself. I was not allowed to go pee alone. My brother stood next to the toilet while I urinated.

I tried running for the door again and this time his force was stronger. In another headlock, he screamed at me, "He said you would do this. He said if you were in a cult, then you would act like this!"

I tried appealing to my brother's common sense. "Who wouldn't bloody try and get out?" To my brother, all my behaviour, including putting my sunglasses on at the airport, apparently resembled that of a cult member. To him, I was hiding my deadened eyes, *not* shading them from the sun. To me, it felt quite normal for a flight/fight survival mode to kick in, considering that I was a hostage in a prison with boarded-up windows and a crazy ex-Moonie. And he, by the way, had a chip on his shoulder and raged against God and the church.

This complete stranger to my circumstance called me a liar and told me how I had hurt my father. He flung my tape recordings from Switzerland across the bed. I was stunned that my mother had managed to manipulate my sister into surrendering those tapes. Now, my most private, intimate thoughts were exposed to my mother and this maniac. I felt so betrayed.

He forced me to agree with him that my parents were right in calling me a slut and a whore. After all, I was involved in sex and drugs, which led to various tragic events that were all my own doing. What else did I expect?

"Do you love your parents? Why then would you accuse your dad of such atrocities? Have you not read your Bible? Have you not heard of honouring your father and your mother? Do you know what pain you have caused your family? Were you going to try and get money from your family to give to this cult? Don't you think God will condemn you for your homosexuality?"

"Why would a cult allow me to leave?" I retorted, trying to control my rage at what he was spitting out at me.

"I'm asking the questions, you bitch. Now shut up."

In the next moment, he would turn from angry to calm, telling me he understood me. As I was lulled into believing in his compassion, he would again charge forward into a barrage of hostilities. He told me that when he was done with me, I would be so broken in spirit that I wouldn't know what I believed and didn't believe. A halfway house for deprogrammed cult members was arranged for me in Texas, and I would regain myself through them. Inside my head, over and over, I kept repeating: *The truth will set me free. The truth will set me free.* This war zone felt more dangerous than Lebanon.

Well into the thirteenth hour, Mr. Moonie confessed that he had stopped believing I was in a cult within the first hour—triggered by my asking him why a cult would allow me to leave—but he decided to continue with his brainwashing for safety purposes. After all—and I quote—"I'm getting paid to break you."

As dawn was fast approaching, he broke the news to my mother and brother that I was just messed up and a religious fanatic. In my memories of the event, my mother never said a word through the entire kidnapping and deprogramming attempt. There were no apologies.

My brother proceeded to inform me that I should get a few hours rest because we were going to talk to Dad in the morning. Dad had apparently admitted everything and wanted to apologize. Sleeping was out of the question.

We drove to see Dad in silence. Sitting in the living room, my mother told me to tell Dad what I had told her during our trip to Europe, which had never been discussed or mentioned since. I had felt so exposed because upon speaking the truth, I had been met with a stone-cold silence that lasted to this day.

Here I was again, having to repeat everything, only now, it was in front of my father. I told my story, and upon its completion, my mother started crying. "That's the exact same story she told me in Europe." She looked toward Dad pleadingly.

It was Dad's turn. Staring me down for what felt like an eternity, he began. Somehow, I had a suspicion that this was not going to be an apology. "Well, you have your bloody nerve. How dare you! Do you have any idea how many tears and prayers I have made to God Almighty? Do you have any idea what I have been through, and how I've prayed for this to go away? The pain this has caused me! And you sit there with these lies. Yes, it's true. I fell in love with my daughter but I most certainly did not act on this or hurt you. I refuse to sit and look at your face for one more minute!" He stormed out.

My mind was racing with overloaded emotions and exhaustion. *Did he say he fell in love with his daughter? That's worse than the excuse of menopause! Oh, my God! I've got to get out of here.*

I sat, shell-shocked and silent.

My mother looked me square in the eyes. "Alright. That's enough now. You have hurt your father enough. I don't ever want to hear you mention this again. Ever. This is the last conversation about this. Your father has been hurt enough."

They told me Dad had confessed to everything, I mumbled to myself. *I've been set up again!* I sobbed internally, completely overwhelmed by my experiences of the last twenty-four hours. *My father's been hurt enough? How the hell do I get out of here—I need to get on a plane. Maybe I can prostitute myself this afternoon—how many men would it take to get enough money?* My thoughts were stumbling over each other.

Apart from my parents and the one brother, none of my family had even known I was back in Canada. The kidnapping and confrontation with my father had been kept a secret. Call it what you may, my family continually responded like a textbook case of a family dealing with incest. I was to blame and I was the outcast.

Unbelievably, immediately following this confrontation, we all drove to my sister's house for that family barbeque. Astoundingly, I rode with my parents—alone! My brother was coming later. Before Jimmy left, I went out to meet him at his car. "Do you believe me? It is important for me to know that you believe me?" He hesitated, and I knew his answer.

As Dad filled the car with gas, my mother sat in the front seat, her eyes fixed straight ahead and said, "You owe your grandmother $3,000 for the plane ticket." I was speechless. When Mom called me, telling me it was a gift, I had asked her to let me book my ticket because I knew how to fly cheap. I'd found a flight for only a few hundred dollars, but because Mom thought I would steal her money, she paid for a business-class fare on a very expensive airline. And now, I had to pay it back.

Everyone was surprised to see me, and I sat through the afternoon and evening, saying nothing of the day's events to anyone. I would have done anything to get on a plane back to Switzerland, or anywhere, but I was flat broke.

I had a sense that born-againers looked to God as they looked to their fathers—or maybe it was just me that did so. From the moment I was saved, I looked at God as an authority figure and a father figure. No wonder I had a scared and rocky relationship with him and always felt unworthy of his forgiveness. No surprise that I doubted God's love for me. I doubted my salvation. I hated myself. The leaders in school were right. Nobody, including me, accepted me as I was. I had run out of places to escape to. If I couldn't find peace with God, where was I to go? I would get myself to another school of evangelism. Maybe it would work the next time. It would have to. What a wretched soul.

While in Europe, I had sublet my flat to a friend. He decided to move out before my return and called my mother to ask permission to store my belongings at my parents' house. My mother told him not to bother and to just throw everything out! And that's what Tom did. From my king-size water bed to my knives and forks, what little I had was gone. My mother laughed when she told me.

Rona and Ray had a new baby, and there was no room for me to stay with them. Jimmy took down the boards from the windows and let me stay with him while I found a job. We never discussed the kidnapping or my dad. Rona's explanation for handing over my private tapes was that she had felt overpowered by Mom's aggression and succumbed. My plans were to get out of the city as quickly as I could and continue on with my higher education. I would attend another evangelical school, this time in Hawaii. I settled into a job and found my own apartment.

I had another nightmare that again portrayed my inner truth. God, how I wished I'd understood that my soul used my dreams to beseech me to set myself free.

I was a bride, dressed in a beautiful white wedding gown, standing at the front door of the church I'd been attending in real life. My brother—not my dad—stood next to me, about to walk me down the aisle. I stood frozen, staring at the long walk to the altar, and seeing my faceless husband waiting for his bride. I whispered to Jimmy that I just couldn't do it; he said, "Run." I turned and ran as fast as I could down the street.

I awoke in a panic, desperately confused about why I had to try so hard to be something I wasn't. Nothing made sense anymore, and I felt like a puppet controlled by the strings of religious dogma.

1983–1990

Inside Out

I soon backslid into my dance with the devil. Frances, an ex-boss who happened to be gay, had earlier tried to lure me from the grips of salvation, right up to the night before I flew to Switzerland. When she heard I was back, she began pursuing me relentlessly, which I, of course, encouraged. I was already 90 percent out of my family tribe anyway.

The news of my latest fall from grace soon reached the ears of my family. And what happened next was no surprise to me. Once again, the family door slammed in my face.

I now openly espoused a gay lifestyle, and became intimately involved with Frances, who was several years older than myself. Our relationship lasted almost five years with a breakup and a whole lot of chaos in the middle of our time together. Because of her age, I thought she represented safety and security. If I were with someone more mature, I reasoned, I wouldn't want to get wild and party too much. I was wrong. Her maturity was no safeguard against my learned disdain for order and stability. I treated myself and others with nothing but disrespect. I was dysfunctional on many levels and carried even more fear than ever before. After all, I'd chosen homosexuality over Jesus—that couldn't be good.

After cheating and hurting Frances senselessly over and over, I desperately tried getting out. I didn't want to be with her, but I also didn't want to be alone—I was too scared. I was obsessed with my own damnation and finally succumbed to my enormous guilt. I needed to run back to Jesus—if he would have me.

I managed to get myself to Hawaii and tried to become reacquainted with God. Just prior to flying away, my parents ran into me at Rona's. They weren't overly kind but managed to say they were relieved that I was turning from the devil.

They weren't the only ones judging. During the short time I was a Jesus-freak, I took the opportunity to judge my parents and condemn them, rather than being condemned. Being *saved* made me feel as though I were in the driver's seat. It was *they* who were now going to hell.

I'll never forget a night where, again, we were in a combative mode because of my father. I tried to talk with my parents about Jesus and how we all needed to be saved from this incestuous relationship. But my father stormed out of the room—as per usual.

My mother looked into my eyes. "What about Lourdes? How can you say there wasn't something there? What about the Virgin Mary? How can you say that wasn't of God?"

Because we born-againers were so busy condemning everything outside of Jesus, I had trashed the notion that Mary, Mother of God, was allowed to show herself in spirit. I went so far as to say that worshipping the *Virgin* Mary was of the devil! But my mother had a point. I, too, had felt something very mystical at Lourdes. I also knew that Mother Mary had appeared to me previously, though I couldn't tell my mom that. Anything outside of Jesus was of Satan, who would use these techniques to turn us away from Jesus.

My heart said one thing, but my words said another. In that limited window of vulnerability that my mother showed to me, I could only look back into her equally lost eyes. "I don't know," was all I could muster.

I didn't allow myself to honour the Mother Mary in my life—even while sitting in the darkness of that airplane with my father. It was hard enough for me to try and honour a Father God without feeling stressed—I had such a warped image of "father-anything." Never mind putting a mother into the equation.

If only we could have seen how much energy we spent telling each other we were no good. If only...

The Hawaii school was an affiliate of the one in Switzerland, and one of my ex-leaders, Janet, was now a counsellor there. She invited me to stay with her while I settled in. The Hawaii School of Evangelism was full of lesbians trying not to be lesbians, including a counsellor Janet had arranged for me to see. This just wasn't going to work.

I had another vivid nightmare, in which I was simultaneously dead and alive. I stood looking down at me, dead and lying in a coffin. The dead-me opened her eyes and started talking. I felt her hard, cold body and told her I wasn't coming to her funeral. As she spoke of the violence against her, which caused her death, my dad suddenly appeared beside us. This shut her down, and she again lay there dead.

Seeing that she was dead and silenced, my dad then disappeared. As I looked back into the coffin, she again opened her eyes and started talking, but this time, I couldn't understand what she was saying. I could only see her desperate face trying to explain something to me, but I just couldn't hear. Her face began morphing—going back in time, until she looked like a six-year-old girl, silent and dead.

Disembodied hands closed her coffin and took her away, and I stood there, alone.

I have forever had a fear of being buried alive. I tell everyone that I must be cremated; I imagine myself waking up, buried...

I felt dead.

Had I been dead from the age of six, when I vividly remember believing that Mom didn't love me? I remember making a card for my mother and writing, "From the daughter you love—I hope." I was a little girl and she laughed at me. All through elementary school, I told my classmates that I was adopted.

I also started to believe that native Indians lived in the wheat fields of the surrounding farm country. My family used to tease me and say that the rolled-up bushels of hay sitting in the farmers' fields were Indian homes, and I believed them.

The Calgary Stampede is a famous rodeo held yearly, where Indian tribes from all over North America showcase their culture. I loved to watch their powwows—the drumbeat, spiritual dances, and chanting were all mystical to me. I had always wanted an Indian princess doll, but never did get one. I also became fascinated with graveyards, and whenever we drove by one, I would stare and wonder about death.

Did the young woman-turned-little-girl lying in the casket try to tell me a truth that I needed to hear? Why couldn't I hear her? What was I doing in another evangelism school? With a bunch of lesbians trying not to be lesbians. It was crazy. Could it be killing me? Within two months, I quit.

I met up again with Frances in Honolulu and flew back with her for another year. My fear of God, death, and damnation flew back with us, and religion and Jesus were off-limits for discussion.

The one and only correspondence from Janet in Hawaii was to tell me she was praying for me and that she was moving to Washington. In a postscript, she wrote, "Salu died in Camaroon, after having an allergic reaction. Love in Christ, Janet."

Nina kupenda, Salu—I love you. Salu taught me Swahili. I kept thinking that now, he knew all the secrets of the universe.

Throughout my relationship with Frances, I had very infrequent visiting rights to my parents' home. They had made very clear their disgust that I had again left God for homosexuality.

I knew my dad's aunt from England was visiting. Because I had met her while travelling with Mom, Frances persuaded me that it might be a gesture toward healing if I were to go and visit. It was also my dad's birthday.

Frances dropped me off, and I instructed her to pick me up in one hour. She, my "gay lover," was most certainly not welcome in the family home. I walked into the backyard and, to my surprise, was coldly greeted by my great-aunt. My parents did not even acknowledge my arrival and proceeded to ignore me completely. None of my siblings were there yet.

Getting up as soon as I arrived, my father said, "Enjoy the sun while I make us a snack." He directed his remarks exclusively to his aunt. I sat down, feeling completely alone. I was also deeply embarrassed by the clear message that I was not welcome. My great-aunt must have been told what was going on, because her disdain toward me was flagrant.

After about fifteen minutes of sitting in this tension, without a word being spoken to me, I slowly got up and walked out of the yard into the street. Fifty-five minutes later, Frances drove by to see me sitting on the curb. I must have looked like I felt inside—a broken, sad little girl.

I was very close to my youngest sister, Lorita. We shared our experiences and talked about family often. Lorita had a bad relationship with our parents but still saw them and tried to work through the dysfunction. Her life had also taken some sharp turns, and she, like myself, was using her sexuality as a means of feeling empowered.

Not having great impulse control, Lorita often let her emotions get the better of her. After hearing of my attempt to visit our parents and great-aunt, she made an angry phone call to Dad. She yelled at him to tell the truth—not surprisingly, another letter soon appeared from my father. This one was addressed to Lorita, with copies sent to all his kids.

Dear Lorita:
I remember you calling me in tears about Edna. I was furious and said I would not even discuss it with you, because I suspected Edna told you entirely out of context so that she would have you on her side against her evil father.

Edna has been able to create the "poor me" syndrome ever since she was five or six and she's a master at it.

I will not continue letting my children think, and keep on thinking, I have done to Edna what she says I have done—on the tape she made in Switzerland. My letters are perfectly truthful, sincere, and very considerate in view of the circumstances, and Edna has not denied any of my statements to date!

I only just found out about the incest business from your mother. How could Edna ever have made a statement like that about me? I suppose if she's confronted, she'll say that she wasn't sure what incest meant. Edna went to Europe with your mother after she came home from her trip to Montreal with me. Why didn't she tell your mother about this incest business on that trip? She is a strange person, and quite frankly, I worry about her mental state, because I have observed her for many years, and I honestly believe that there are psychopathic tendencies—in my other children as well—but more pronounced in Edna.

On my birthday, Edna willingly came over and was extremely friendly with me but would hardly talk with your mother...

So much for a gesture toward healing. And then there was that mention of me as a five- or six-year-old. What was the significance? It was as if he chose to forget the confrontation after my kidnapping, when my mother insisted I repeat what I *had* told her about the events in Montreal—how could he pretend that didn't happen? Even my father had listened to my private tapes. I had unwittingly exposed my soul.

Shortly after coming off the streets, Lorita "shacked up" with a guy, and had a baby who died at ten days of age. Hours before life support was removed, our mother snuck a priest in to perform the Catholic Last Rites, against my sister's wishes. Upon Lorita's arrival at the hospital, Mom looked at her and said, "God sure has a way of bringing you to your knees." Her intent was to blame Lorita for her baby's death. I wasn't the only one who was at the receiving end of our parents' wrath.

The section of the graveyard had a sign, "Babyland," where only infants and small children were buried. I stood off, by myself, and watched the sorrow of burying a baby. Rona spoke to me later that day to say she had watched me and, for the first time, had some sense of what it must have been like to surrender my baby—that it must have felt like a death. I was shocked and sadly happy to hear someone finally say words of comfort and understanding. I thanked Rona for her love. I never shared how I *had* buried my baby—deep within my soul. I felt Rona was an angel, honouring myself and my baby girl.

Lorita spent the next few months seeking out my company and support. I stood by her and watched her take one tiny step at a time toward healing. I listened and loved her through her grief. I felt I understood her pain.

Lorita went on to have two more precious babies.

With family life and emotions all but shattered, it was small wonder that I continued to be unsuccessful in love. It was impossible for me to know how to love anyone, and I brilliantly sabotaged the love Frances had for me—even if it was dysfunctional love. I only knew how to betray her and myself, and to ensure that things did not work out. Finally, in our fourth year, and after two unsuccessful attempts on my part to end the relationship, it was over. Her jealousy over my spending time with Lorita was the last straw. Nor had she met my expectations that she could tame me. Being with her did not curtail my enthusiasm for living wild. She put up with way too much crap from me, and I put up with her need to have me all to herself. My heart was out of the relationship long before I physically left.

After finally breaking free, I just wanted to be alone and to be a wild child. I didn't know that my family was hiding the love of my life in the palm of their hands.

With two sisters expecting babies two months apart, it had been an exciting time for them. Naomi didn't do well when Lorita's baby died. Lorita extended an incredible gesture of love and offered to host a baby shower for Naomi after she gave birth to a son. I think it was a passage of healing for Lorita.

It was there at the shower that I first met her. Lorraine was great friends with both Lorita and my sister-in-law, Verna, *and* she lived with my cousin. My own mother also knew her and had even invited her for Christmas dinner. Why no one had shared Lorraine with me before is a mystery. But upon meeting her, I knew I liked her.

We got together within a week of my breaking up with Frances, and although I didn't intend anything more than a fling, Lorraine ended up being an angel in the guise of a lesbian. She was my soul mate.

I had a turning point and still remember the exact moment, even though I was drunk and stoned. We were having a midnight snack after a night on the town. I felt Lorraine's sadness as she sat beside me—she was disappointed that I was so high. It was in that moment that I felt my heart want to promise never to hurt her. She was so gentle, kind, and sweet, and I was scared that I wasn't good enough for her. I didn't want to be a drunk or an abuser—she deserved my respect and to be honoured. In sharing that moment years later, I wasn't surprised that Lorraine remembered it, too. She *had* sat there, afraid that I was going to be too much into partying, and she didn't want to get hurt. Amazing how the soul can appear, even through a drunken state of "unconsciousness."

Lorraine quite quickly experienced the fury of my parents. They caught wind of my possible involvement with her and, on Christmas morning, called Lorita to tell her that neither my "lesbian lover," nor I were welcome in their home. It was clear by Lorraine's expression that she had never experienced such a slap in the face. I felt so sad—more for her than for myself. I was used to them.

She had spent Christmas Eve preparing an English trifle to bring to dinner. In all of her sweetness, she gave the dessert to my sister to bring anyway. Because Lorraine's family was in England, she and I drove to the mountains and had Christmas dinner alone in a restaurant. Although I was overly familiar with missing family celebrations, this was a first for both of us, and was bittersweet. We were both sad to be distanced from family gatherings, but happy and grateful to be together.

1991–1993

My Broken Heart

By Lorraine's and my second year together, my heart had finally begun to burst at the seams with all the toxins I had been carrying. I had a broken heart that was leaking badly and needed repair—physically and spiritually. I was put on a waiting list for a human donor valve and told not to get pregnant—my heart would not withstand it. Having already carried a baby, I realized that amongst all the sorrow, there had been a miracle of birth and life. I wished to the stars, asking for my baby girl to somehow know in her own heart that she was a miracle.

The specialized procedure I needed was done only in Toronto, over two thousand miles from our home in Calgary. Fortunately, health care covered the cost of the flight for both Lorraine and myself. Rona and Ray were now living just outside Toronto and graciously drove up to visit before, during, and after surgery. I was so happy Lorraine would have someone to wait with.

One would think open-heart surgery would be grounds for family healing but not with mine. My siblings were unable to respect my wish not to tell my parents.

My mother, in hearing about my upcoming surgery, wrote to me and pretended not to have heard. She had a "mother's intuition," she claimed, which told her I would soon need heart surgery. She was forewarning me and advising me to go for a checkup. It was outrageous:

> All my life I have been blessed or cursed (I'm not sure which) with an inner knowledge when things aren't right with my kids, and for some time now, these feelings about you have been very strong. So I am thinking it is probably time for you to have the heart operation—where and when I do not know, but for sure, it won't be too far in the future. A mother never forgets her child.

Just before finding out that I needed heart surgery, I happened to be in the "wrong" place at the "wrong" time. Lorraine and I dropped by to see my sister's baby, and Mom and Dad showed up, unannounced. It happened to be Mother's Day. As my mother passed by me, she bent over and whispered in my ear, "Happy

Mother's Day, dear," at which I almost fainted. Lorita, who was sitting beside me, also heard her, and we both just looked at each other, unable to speak. Up to that moment, it was the most painful thing my mother had ever done to me.

When I read her letter, the words *a mother never forgets her child* felt like a knife cutting into my heart.

I wrote a hostile and sad letter to my mother. I reminded her that I had been kicked out of their lives for years, and now, since they were still unwilling to accept me, there seemed no reason to communicate. I was furious that she was pretending to be an angel sent from God with a message for me. Part of my letter said:

> My thoughts and my heart are overwhelmed with what I want to get through to you. I want to react and respond to every last pain you've dealt to me. Do you want to know something funny? All that your children have ever wanted was to be loved unconditionally—but that has never been the case, has it? Do you have any idea how hard, how extremely painful, it is for me to continually be stabbed in the heart by you...over and over and over?
>
> I just can't bear the pain anymore—do you have any concept what you have done to me? Do you know that I have wondered if you loved me since I was six? I finally realized that you really don't—that's okay—but stop hurting me. I can't take it anymore.
>
> You and Dad both said that I was to blame for everything with Dad, that I seduced him—my own father. He even went as far as to say that I didn't seem to mind—how dare he say that!! Do you have any concept of what that did to me? I buckled over in pain. I wept for days. I felt like I was mourning a death, and in a way, I was: a final blow to my heart—you both broke me with your words...
>
> All I wanted was to have a mom and dad who loved me. I've tried everything. When I was pregnant, you told me not to come home. You told me "it"

would be a freak and retarded. You told me that if I thought of keeping "it," you would press charges—and yet, you sadistically said "Happy Mother's Day" to my face. How dare you? How evil... how cruel.

Do you have any concept of what it is like to be sixteen and screwed up—and then to go through nine months carrying a baby, and then to deliver this baby totally alone in a back room of the hospital ward? And then to hold a beautiful baby girl in your arms and say to her, *I'm sorry. I will always love you in my heart. Please have a wonderful life. Please come and find me when you can. Please forgive me.* Do you know what that's like, Mom? Maybe not, since you nonchalantly asked me what my daughter would think if she knew I were a lesbian! And then you said "Happy Mother's Day"—as if I have no pain, no ache within my heart.

If only you cared. I refuse to allow my heart for one second to be fooled into thinking you care. I've tried making you love me—you've chosen not to. All my heart wants is to have a mother. You've never even been in one of my apartments before.

I have never stopped loving you. I've tried to be what you've wanted me to be—Christian, heterosexual. What I am is not my problem—it's yours.

I can't take this stress anymore. I just can't handle it. It's breaking my heart...

Phew! No wonder my heart was physically broken. Although I buried my baby girl in an internal grave, it was painfully obvious that the decay was seeping out.

I was absolutely petrified of death. I had given up on religious organizations; each claimed to be the only true way, which meant I was on my own with God. Lorraine loved me through the fear of surgery and death.

At this point in my life, I was minimally aware of how illness was playing a role in my life. My heart was the most serious and caught my attention—I knew my body was trying to tell me something.

What my heart needed was a cleansing. I realized that not forgiving was killing me. Thus began my slow journey to begin finding peace with myself, my family, and with God—preferably just as I was. I didn't want to turn to God out of fear again, and somewhere in the confusion, I knew that it was okay to start talking. Slowly, for the first time since I had run from God, I began thinking about forgiveness.

I had been on a waiting list for almost a full year, during which time I opened up to a friend who was also a natural counsellor. Terri, who was into astrology, energy, and spirituality, had a tremendous gift of helping people and seeing past the physical. She did my birth chart, and noted that it was no surprise I was on a search for peace—Libra being the sign of the peacekeeper.

There are four planets in my sign—the Sun (centre of consciousness), Venus (approach to love and relationships), Mercury (way of thinking) and Neptune (desire for oneness). All of these energies within me are governed by the *soul* purpose of Libra, which is to seek harmony, maintain peace and reconcile conflict. These energies are the biggest influence on my personality, and they are also brought into play in any close relationships or partnerships. I have a lot of energies all in one place, including—not surprisingly—Neptune that can lead to self-deception and illusion in my way of thinking and relating, especially with those I am closely connected to.

Terri and I contemplated how many influential people in my life were born in Gemini—my mother, my baby girl, Denny, Frances, bosses, co-workers, key friends and lovers, and my precious Lorraine. Terri suggested that because Gemini falls in the area of my chart that deals with psychological transformation, those born under that sign have the potential to trigger in me a kind of psychological death and rebirth, which in many of these relationships has been very painful for me. Although Lorraine's planets in relation to my chart also allow for an intensely life-changing relationship, it is one that is compatible, characterized by open communication and the pursuit of inner growth. We are able to bring out the best in each other, challenge each other's fears, and help each other to constructively follow our dreams.

If I choose to consciously work on my "life lessons," particularly through these intimate relationships, my journey will bring me to a place of increased happiness and fulfillment.

This was my first glimmer of consciousness that I was moving forward from a less evolved self into a new place of peace, love and internal happiness. There was hope for me!

As I look back on my life's relationships, particularly with the Gemini-tribe, my natal chart certainly confirmed what I already knew—I had a way to go before discovering peace. The timing to *open my heart* was perfect.

When I finally shared my many fears with Terri, she was shocked at how I viewed God and pointed out that I treated God like a cruel ogre, full of wrath and vengeance toward me. But after I told her about my parents, she understood why.

Her take on God was very different. He/she was *spirit*, as were we. That was just a bit too much for me at the time—to tell me I was actually a part of God, of Oneness—come on now. It certainly was food for thought, however. Her understanding of God felt so wonderful, so free, but I was wrapped up in my fears and didn't dare believe—yet.

Talking with Terri allowed me the courage to speak to God. Although I was still looking at God as an authority and patriarchal figure, I began praying to him, albeit, as a small, scared girl, cowering in his presence, but at least I was trying to communicate.

In prayer, I forgave my parents and asked for help in releasing my anger and hurt. I asked for guidance to come from a higher place of love, rather than from my wounds. Maybe a new heart would be a first step toward a new hope.

I was also introduced to energy and chakras, which explained the flow or blockage of *chi*—life force.

I learned how chakras were energy units, situated in the low back, hips, stomach, heart, throat, forehead, and crown of the head. It seemed so logical that each of my injuries/illnesses correlated with an emotional/spiritual wound. With each illness, my family had never believed me and always accused me of being dramatic for attention, faking it, and lying.

I remember one particularly insane example. On a family outing in the mountains, the front of my bike collapsed, crashing my knee and face into the ground, causing me to momentarily lose consciousness. Though my niece, who witnessed the accident, was frightened by the mess I was in, the rest of my family insisted on having dinner in a restaurant with me sitting there, scaring the patrons and going in and out of consciousness. Several days later, I heard Mom tell my sister that I was faking it, pretending I couldn't walk properly and being a baby for attention. I'm not sure what attention I got, except that I was laughed at and ridiculed every time I had a physical problem. No wonder the energy in each section of my body was blocked and twisted into knots.

A few chakras stood out. I had two back injuries and chronic low back pain; now I learned the spiritual and energetic connection. The first chakra is the root chakra, located at the base of the spine. It is our foundation and represents security, survival, and an ability to be grounded. My back was weak and sore, unable to support me through life, and I certainly wasn't grounded.

The third chakra—located in the solar plexus/stomach, I learned—acts as a clearinghouse for emotional sensitivities and issues of personal power. I had an umbilical hernia removed. There was a possibility they would have to cut out my entire belly button—talk about cutting the umbilical cord to my mother! I was getting it. What a journey...

The fourth chakra is the heart. Mine was in dire need of help. I didn't need much of a lesson in how my broken heart correlated with a broken spirit. Love was missing.

In the early hours of the morning, I was awoken and told to have a bath in a disinfectant dye. I stood, staring at myself in the mirror. *This is it, Edna. Just breathe.* A quiet calm came over me. I was just going through the motions, one heartbeat at a time.

Ray, Rona, and Lorraine arrived. As I was being prepared for surgery, the room was very still. Everything was methodical, as each of us stayed quiet in our own thoughts. I was wrapped up in a cocoonlike foam-padded pouch and mechanically lifted onto a gurney. It was eerie to hear only the sound of the machine.

I suppose the pouch was so that after surgery, my body would not have to be touched. As the orderly began wheeling me to the operating theatre, my brother-in-law asked if he could pray for me—something I was dreading he would do.

"No," I said quickly and directly enough to make him remove his hand from my arm and step back. I couldn't bear to hear him asking for my soul to be spared from eternal hell and praying that I rediscover Christ's love and forgiveness.

How could I explain that I *did* believe in Jesus? Understanding him in symbolic terms spoke to my soul, and it left no one out. Buddhists, Hindus, Muslims—none of us were dismissed. Jesus was symbolic and told us of our greatness: *Ye all are gods. These things and more shall you do. The kingdom of God is within you.* I had already tried to ask Ray and Rona to see beyond their church doors—to see the world's diversity—but to no avail. Our planet, the expanse of the universe, and beyond—it all seemed too big to box God into one religious doctrine. Ray had once told me he was "tired of casting pearls before swine," a biblical quote meaning he was wasting his time showing his Christian values to me, because I didn't understand or appreciate them. To Ray, I was like a pig—unworthy. It would be impossible for me to share my soul with them.

It was difficult for both Rona and me. I knew that she loved me and stepped up to the plate on many occasions. But I was also acutely aware that she was "afraid for my soul," and this often strained our relationship. Neither Ray nor my sister could ever understand that I was on an intense journey within my soul, one that resonated with my spirit. But any talk of spirit, astrology, energy, chakras, or symbolism would have been attacked as being of the devil.

Not now. Not as I'm being wheeled into open-heart surgery.

Going through those doors, I looked back as best I could at Lorraine and saw tears in her eyes. On entering the operating theatre, I took a quick glance around at all the equipment and asked what the huge machine next to me was.

"That's the heart/lung machine, for when we stop your heartbeat during the surgery," the anaesthetist said as she put the needle into my arm. I closed my eyes and went off into the arms of angels.

Having a piece of damaged heart removed seemed to me to be an example of God's expansiveness. Surprisingly, I did not feel as though I were being punished but rather, that I was being cleansed.

While meeting my surgeon the night prior to surgery, I asked for his assurance that Lorraine would be treated as my "spouse," and she would be noted as the immediate family member—he said yes, and left. Sadly, Lorraine later informed me that, during my surgery, she watched other surgical staff periodically come out of the operating theatre to update spouses, but no one ever came to her. When it was time to visit in the ICU, the nurse looked at her dismissively, "Only immediate family are allowed." Fortunately, Rona stood up for Lorraine, and told the nurse she was my partner—which must have been hard for her to say. The nurse begrudgingly took my life partner in to see me, followed by Rona and Ray. We had no energy to deal with this common occurrence of prejudice—we just felt the sadness of not being accepted as a couple, deeply in love with each other.

My valve was replaced with a human donor's valve—a young man killed in an accident. *All of us are one* whispered in my thoughts. Being connected to someone else physically emphasized our spiritual connection to one another. But I couldn't dwell on that reality—it was much too intense to cope with. Upon my discharge, the doctor warned, "Now, remember, you're starting out with a faulty heart, so don't expect to be perfectly healed. This will be the first of several surgeries."

My thoughts raced as quickly as the blood flowed, and I felt light-headed at the doctor's words. *Wow! That was so not positive. What a way to start!* The understanding that I was starting out of the gate "faulty" reminded me that my "new" heart also needed healing and cleansing. Just because I had surgery didn't mean I didn't have work to do.

I arrived home to another letter, this time from my father:

Did you really think we wouldn't find out about your surgery? Are you that stupid? We know everything that transpired from day one. But when I think of it, and what terrible parents we've been, it's understandable.

I suppose this alienation started when your mother began showing her disapproval of your relationships with other women. Do you believe (and obviously you do) that she should have welcomed you and your friends with happiness for you? I have been praying for you—more than once during the day— and for your partners, that you will break away from this sinful lesbian way of life. Also, maybe one day you will find it in your heart to tell your siblings that there was no incest between you and me.

Old Satan really did his job on you, didn't he? If you have no fear of coming face to face with God one day, I say, God help you. I suggest you get your Bible out and read and read and read, and pray and pray, until you come to the conclusion that there's no use praying anymore because the Lord doesn't even seem to know you exist. What if you have a heart attack and die? Facing God is pretty terrifying if you examine your personal status in the eyes of God.

All my love,
Dad.

New heart, I would like you to meet my dad. Dad, my new heart. Was he trying to kill me? Did he not know of my extreme fear of death, and here, only weeks after surgery, he brought up having a heart attack, dying, and meeting Satan. And even worse, to tell me God doesn't even know that I exist. I felt like a punching bag; I'd get a good bashing with a right hook and slowly come up from the floor, only to be kicked in the chest. I had just had my valve repaired and was terrified that these blows would rupture it again.

I vacillated between clarity and fury, trying to stay connected to what I was learning about energy and spirit, but often being overtaken by emotions. I began to feel I was once again like Alice in Wonderland, only this acid trip was an overdose. Lorraine didn't even want me to read the letters and suggested I return them to sender. But how could I? What if it had been a letter of love or compassion, or one asking for forgiveness?

When Lorraine brought out the meditation tapes Terri had previously given me, I actually felt sadness. I had hoped that once surgery was over, I wouldn't need those relaxation tapes. But as I put the headphones on and heard the familiar music, I realized that looking for a temporary fix wasn't going to cut it. I had to be in this race for the distance. One tape was particularly peaceful—it was native Indian drumming—the drum's rhythm was of a powerful, beautiful heartbeat.

Terri, Lorraine, and I spent many evenings discussing energy and spirit. It was so wonderful to be able to talk about these things. Energy was a fairly new concept, but it all made so much sense to me. I could feel when my own energy was sucked out of me by circumstance. I didn't quite know yet that I had control over my own energy through my choices.

A strange thing began happening in my family. My siblings suddenly began having memories of their own sexual abuse—and not only from Dad! I was stunned, surprised, and angry. All these years, and no one had truly supported or honoured me, and now, half my siblings laid claims to abuse. No one called to say they now understood because they, too, were abused. It was as if the "Dad-thing" had never happened with me, because now, it was all about them. I didn't want sympathy—I just wanted to be part of my family—I just wanted to be heard. I couldn't stand it.

Naomi and Lorita were part of this rising tidal wave but, with me, shared only bits and pieces of what they were remembering. I tried to listen and support them, because I cared and wanted their friendship. They seemed to deliberately keep me out of the situation and their confrontations with Mom and Dad. I felt I was a spectator, sitting up in the nosebleed section, barely able to see the game. It was better that way, because each sibling was going through their own intense time with parents I scarcely knew anyway.

Watching the family drama unfold, I pondered what eruption all our different memories would invoke. Eight kids and two parents, all under the same roof, but living in such individual isolation—such circumstances could provoke an array of reactions.

At about the same time, after a few years of "backsliding," Naomi turned back to Jesus, and Lorita turned to native Indian spirituality, something she and I both shared a fascination with; we loved the native customs and the mysticism behind the ceremonies. Lorita went full-tilt, even going into the forest alone for a weekend of cleansing and being one with nature. She would come back with extraordinary insight about her life and share her beautiful moments of clarity. Although I felt a connection to their spiritual culture, I never immersed myself as deeply as my sister. I would have been scared senseless sleeping in a forest by myself, although it sounded like something I would have loved to do—if I could have gotten past the fear factor. I was also afraid to delve too deeply because, somewhere in the recesses of my mind, I heard a warning, *It's not Jesus.*

I told Lorita about my talks with Terri and how it was now making sense that we have lived many lives. I was relieved to find that Lorita also believed in reincarnation, and the evolution of the soul. The born-againers believed reincarnation was of the devil. Native beliefs include the idea that we return many times over. They believe that their ancestors were great wolves or whales, and that all mankind came from the sea—it all felt so natural and lovely.

Lorita was soon the only family member I had regular contact with. It was through her phone message that I heard that Naomi's husband was killed in an accident. The thought of our family coming together for this crisis seemed impossible, but somehow, we needed to support Naomi.

Naomi's Christian friend was screening calls. "Naomi does not want any of her family here. She does *not* want to talk to any of you." I wrestled with that for a bit and then thought, screw it. I had to get to my little sister.

I saw my parents' car parked out front and knew this was going to be awkward.

After walking through the empty house, I saw Dad sitting in the backyard—alone. I cautiously approached him and said hello. He stood up, walked toward me, and hugged me, as he said how sad this whole thing was. Mom had taken Naomi for a walk and, upon their return, said nothing to me—no greeting, no nothing.

And so, from there, we tried to bury my brother-in-law and help my sister cope. Naomi kept saying over and over, "Where is he now?" She feared that he was in hell. As her congregation surrounded her, they convinced her that Wyatt in his last moment on earth had called out and accepted Jesus Christ as his Saviour. God, this was all so sad.

Within a week of the funeral, everyone got another letter from Dad:

> To my children:
> I see Edna once again has you all deceived. And now, I hear accusations from my other children of the evil abuses I have done to you as well. Edna has always lied. I firmly believe she is the one who has inappropriate love toward me. She has proven it by her actions.
>
> When her brother-in-law died, I distinctly remember her walking through the house and into the backyard. She saw me and yelled, "Hi Dad," and raced into my arms. She threw her arms around me. But when her siblings are around, she acts angry, as if I'm not in the room. She has you all fooled.
>
> Edna is well rehearsed in heterosexual sex, lesbian sex, the gay bar scene, and many, many, many other experiences, including being a woman at the age of sixteen with her pregnancy and giving birth to a child. As for my behaviour in Montreal, I now understand— and have said before—that I was going through the male menopause. Although I never laid a hand on her, she made every attempt to encourage me and prod me on. Stupid. Idiotic. How many daughters would tell this Montreal story to Oprah and be believed—not one in a thousand!

Oh, my God! His words reminded me of Shakespeare—*Thou doth protest too much.*

He wanted me dead. Why, at the saddest times, did he throw all this at me, and at my siblings? Naomi's husband had just died, and he wrote this kind of crap.

Since I had not participated in the recent family discussions, I wasn't fully aware of just how explosive the sex scandal was. Reading this letter was my first clue that I was partially being blamed for my siblings' accusations of abuse. I had nothing to do with it, but my father thought I had instigated things. I was so tired of being called a liar. Yes, I had walked into the arms of many a stranger looking for some sort of love or affection—but never into the arms of my own father.

I found myself staring at another long, empty highway again. How long would it take *this* time to walk to safety? Again, the only response I was able to give was to allow his words to crash over me. Under their weight, my body collapsed into the fetal position; small and frightened, I wept uncontrollably. *Dad, please stop hurting me. Please.*

I jumped in to help Naomi get through the next few months without her husband. Naomi had dark emotional problems and had lost her ability to parent. I practically moved in, taking care of her now three-year-old son, Nicholas. I would spend most of the week at their house and return home to Lorraine on weekends. Nicholas also had many sleepovers with Lorraine and me.

I kept trying to get Naomi back into life, and finally convinced her to come out and play. An awe-inspiring moment happened when we went swimming. Naomi and I were playing in the pool when a girl asked if we were sisters. We laughingly said yes, and she said she'd been watching us play and laugh together—we reminded her of how much she missed her own sister. We listened to her story of how she had just escaped from Iran, where her sister had been murdered. She told us we should never take each other for granted. She touched our hearts; I'd always longed for closeness with my sisters, and having this time to bond with Naomi was wonderful. Naomi was wide-eyed at her first encounter with life outside of her borders. I prayed that this would help her see the world, and its people, as more than just a church doctrine.

After six months of supporting and loving Naomi, I was devastated when I heard she'd told Lorita that she only allowed me into her home because I "left my homosexuality at the front door." She then proceeded to tell me that Nicholas was no longer allowed to spend any time at our flat because we had pornography on the walls. The pornography consisted of a set of collector plates, titled The Four Ancient Elements—earth, wind, air, and fire. The image for each element was of a woman, with bare breasts showing. Flashes of all the nudity within Michaelangelo's masterpieces—including the completely naked King David and the glorious—dare I say "erotic"—nudes painted on the ceiling of the Vatican's Sistine Chapel—almost made me want to laugh, if it hadn't been so sad.

I had been wrong—Naomi's heart hadn't expanded to accept everyone. In my heart of hearts, I had always longed for my sisters to see how blessed we were to have each other, but that to was just me dreaming. It was the beginning of a slow process of distancing myself from what was left of any family bonds. The pulse of the tribal vibe was intensifying.

All of this—homosexuality and now, pornography—along with the last letter from my father, made me stumble. I kept my rage, and my utter hurt and disappointment, to myself.

From the time of my heart surgery, I knew I was on the cusp of having some kind of understanding about my life and God but couldn't quite cross over and move away from fear. Everything seemed too big to handle—there was just so much darkness at every turn that I couldn't see the Light. Could my new, yet already-damaged heart take much more of this? The pain was becoming increasingly insurmountable. Why was it so hard and seemingly impossible for *love* to conquer all?

1993-1994

*Out of Body,
Out of Consciousness*

Four years into my relationship with Lorraine, one and a half years past surgery, and nine months since my brother-in-law's death, I responded to a newspaper ad to work in Saudi Arabia. With gypsy blood still coursing through my veins and, more truthfully, still needing to run as fast as I could, I applied.

My plan was to go alone, stake it out, and then bring Lorraine over. With me earning tax-free dollars, our dream of travelling would soon be a reality. We did not yet know that only blood relatives and spouses of expats (expatriates) were allowed to visit—there was no such thing as a tourist visa for Saudi Arabia.

Lorraine freely allowed me this experience. Neither of us grasped that we would be apart for the next year. She never took my leaving personally, but saw it as an incredible opportunity for me. I, on the other hand, would have taken it totally personally if Lorraine were the one wanting to go. I would have felt she was leaving *me*.

It was a strangely familiar feeling that my heart was again calling me to the Middle East. I wondered if I had unfinished business in the desert.

I was about to enter a world of mirrors, all reflecting my internal struggles. And my whole family was coming along for the trip. Their roles would be played by bosses, peers, friends—and men.

Unable to look inside and see my own soul, I would soon *see* from the outside looking in. As I stood watching the chaos around me, would I be able to see me?

I had been building momentum in learning to love outside of fear, but that last letter from Dad, along with allegations from my sisters, seemed to shut me down. I was just coming into consciousness and didn't realize that I was about to make a choice to go back, even further, into unconscious living.

My running would cause me to bump right into my past. My soul's journey was about to become a living movie with all the characters representing members of my family and myself: I would soon crash the Mad Hatter's tea party and be ruled by the Queen of Hearts—*off with her head, off with her head*. Only this time, Alice didn't need any little pill: What a trip this was going to be!

Matching coloured "Jeannie" pillbox hats with chiffon scarves draped across the neck almost fooled me. In reality, they were a striking contrast to the fashion statement imposed on the Saudi female population. Fuchsia pink, cobalt blue, and deep purple were for the British and Lebanese Saudi Airline stewardesses, while black on black polyester was for Saudi women.

I had my first altercation with a man before I even stepped out of the airport.

An Arabian knight charged toward me. He was dressed indigenously in a spotless white *thobe*, a floor-length cotton shirt-dress. A white skullcap on his head supported a red and white checked *goutrah*, a cloth that sits on the head. This was folded into a triangle that cascaded over both shoulders and down the back, like long hair. Topping it off was a black braided cord that was wrapped around the forehead and tied at the back of the head, the two ends draping down the length of the cloth. All in all, the man looked immaculately clean.

He proceeded to demand my papers. No *marhaba*, no *ahlen wa sahlen*—no welcome of any kind. It was clear this stranger was already put out by me.

"You? KEG?"

In my tired state, KEG did not register as an acronym for the hospital in which I was to work at.

I was sent to sit in a corner of the airport with a group of women from Sudan and Ethiopia. Forty-five minutes passed and I didn't know what to do. Finally, my knight decided to compare my name to the list he had been carrying in his hand. Seeing my name, he started yelling in mixed English and Arabic, the gist being that I *was* the person for KEG, and why did I *lie* to him? He pointed for me to grab my bags.

"Why didn't you just *ask* my name? I can't lift them; could you help me get a porter?"

He snapped his fingers, telling me to hurry and pick up my own bags. I started getting ticked.

He stopped, turned, and looked directly at me. "Pick these up. *Now!*"

"I can't lift them!" I really meant *sod off*.

Finally, he barked orders at a porter, as we jumped the long queue for customs. I was furious that he did not help, and he was furious that I did not obey.

At last, I arrived at the compound, the security gates opened, and I entered my new world.

Fortunately, our hospital bus driver, a very nice East Indian man, carried my bags to my room. I glanced around; it did not look like the "brochure," and I asked if there had been a mistake. He said that everyone stayed in the efficiency flats on arrival. The "Efficiencies" were drab, like rooms in a cheap motel; they were small bachelor suites, with a bed, chair and television in one room, a small kitchenette with a hotplate, and a tiny bathroom with a shower stall. Since it was 3:00 a.m., I was surprised at the note on my single bed; it directed me to appear at Personnel at 8:00 a.m.!

I had not slept in a single bed since the age of five and almost fell out of this one. I proceeded to have a temper tantrum throughout my shower, because it, too, was so tiny that the shower curtain kept sticking to my two thousand body parts every time I moved. I felt like I had just ingested the pill that makes you very, very large…

Seeing the compound in the light of day helped my mood. There were fountains everywhere, an array of trees, including my favourites—weeping willows and palms—deep green, well-watered lawns, flower gardens scattered all around, and a row of tennis courts. A tall metal fence surrounded it all so that no one could enter the property, or leave it, without going through Security.

My boss was the medical director, but I would report directly to his office manager, Ginete, a tall, lanky woman of East Indian descent. She immediately emphasized that she was Portuguese, and had the passport to prove it. I wondered why she felt the need to tell me that.

When asked about my arrival, I mentioned my minor altercation. Ginete became furious, picked up the phone, and was soon yelling at someone on the other end. I was a bit surprised at the intensity of her reaction, concerned that I was causing trouble before I even started work. After hanging up, Ginete assured me he would not treat anybody else with such disrespect.

As if she had done me a favour, she said, "I give to you. You give to me. That's how we do things here."

I was taken on a small tour of the hospital and told the Do's and Don'ts—mostly Don'ts! Dresses must be eight inches below the knee. Blouses must cover the elbow. Staff members are *not* to laugh in the hallways. Saudis use the main entrance; staff must enter through the back so as not to "disturb them."

The top floor, off limits to the general staff, was reserved for the Custodian of the Two Holy Mosques, King Fahad bin Abdul Aziz al Sa'ud. His private ward, I was told, was lavishly decorated and included gold faucets and marble tiled floors but sat empty, only to be used by the Royal family. Considering he had his own doctors with him at all times, it was doubtful he would ever walk the corridors of the KEG.

My title was Supervisor of the Medical Staff Secretaries, and there they were—five ladies, each quietly checking me out from top to bottom. My department was a mini-United Nations of three Filipinos, a Sri Lankan, and an East Indian. I hoped they didn't see my nervousness as I wondered how our worlds would blend together.

I then met the Mad Hatter Medical Director, who began with, "I want you to be my eyes and ears and to report anything said by the medical staff to me." He waited to see if I flinched, and I did.

It didn't take long to discover that Ms. Ginete wreaked havoc on everyone and unmistakably controlled Dr. M. H. She was a force to be reckoned with. She informed me I would stay in the Efficiencies until *she* found me a flat, saying she only needed to know if I wanted to live alone or with someone. I said either would be fine but I didn't believe her.

I tried to one-up her and headed to Housing myself where I was met with an "*Insha'allah.*" Although this translates as "God Be Willing," what it really means is "when I feel like it"—a lesson I learned very early on in Arabia. Housing then said they had already spoken with Ginete, at which point I understood I needed to return a favour if I were ever going to get out of the Efficiencies.

After twenty-four hours of travel, no sleep, and a bizarre indoctrination, I was allowed to stagger home. I slept from noon to the next morning, and then began my first full day of work. Jet lag would have to take a backseat.

Personnel asked me to hand over my passport in exchange for an *iqama*, a document stating who my sponsor was, that I was a Christian and on a single contract. Your *iqama* must be on you at all times. It felt strange to let go of my passport, but this was a rule of life in Saudi.

Two documents were then put in front of me along with a pen and a command to sign them. My first signature was confirmation and acknowledgement that I was Christian and a non-Muslim. The second was a statement saying that I acknowledged the fact that import and/or involvement in drugs, alcohol, or pornography was a serious offence and that trafficking in any of these items was punishable by death. I had not yet heard of Chop-Chop Square.

At mid-morning of my first day, I was informed that I would be doing minutes for the medical staff meeting. I couldn't quite believe it—this meeting was attended by every doctor in the hospital, 98 percent men, of course.

It was strange to walk into a room full of doctors from all over the world, dressed in a variety of indigenous dress, including white cloth turbans that wound around and around on top of the head, looking quite heavy and balanced like a tiara. Saudi doctors wore their *thobes* and *goutrahs*; sandals were replaced with shiny business shoes. The Lebanese, Syrian, Egyptian, and Jordanian doctors wore western suits and ties.

Dr. M. H. expected me to do attendance for the meeting and asked me if there was a quorum; a certain percentage of the entire medical staff that needed to be present. This was another hint of what was to come. I was a bit dumbfounded that he expected so much of me so quickly. It was an outrageous request.

And the names—well, Ginete helped me but told me I must learn very quickly and she could not always help me. I had just arrived for God's sake. *You do know I just got off the plane, don't you?* I muttered, barely under my breath.

As Ginete did the head count, checking off names like Wafai, Nasr, Abdulla, Fahed, Faisal, Ghassan, Hussain, Mahmood, Youssouf, Smith, and Jones, I wondered how I would ever remember. Hearing all these different names only exacerbated my anger that they expected me to know everyone before I had even completed my first day on the job.

Put off by having to help me, Ginete reminded me of the system in place. "I scratch your back and you scratch mine," she hissed in my ear.

As the meeting progressed, Dr. M. H. compounded my problem as he began using their first names, making it impossible for me to know who was saying what. And every other name was the same—there must have been fifty Mohammeds!

In the past twenty-four hours, I felt like I had tripped out in an insane asylum. I felt like I did with my kidnapper: If I could just play into their hands and let them believe I was with them, I would get by.

Ginete instructed me to meet her immediately after work to go shopping for my very own *abaya*. Wrapping a borrowed one around me, I wondered about the heat. Asking if they came in cotton or colour met with a grunt of disapproval. All expat women must wear one, as well as a scarf to cover their hair.

We entered a shop and Ginete grabbed the first *abaya* she saw and flung it at me. There is not much room to make a fashion statement from black polyester, but there were design choices: zipped, snapped, or wrapped. It dragged three feet on the floor and when I objected, Ginete replied I could hold it up; besides, it was good to have one too big so as not to attract attention. I wondered if tripping all over Riyadh would be an attention-getter. After we grabbed a matching black scarf, the shopping trip was finished.

It reminded me of when I got my first period—my mother simply threw a pad and a belt at me and said, "Use these." No explanation, no choice, and no discussion. Oh Lord, didn't I leave my mother at home?

Not only did Saudi women wear *abayas*, they also had to wear the *niqab*, a face veil, either fully covering the face or having a small slit for the eyes to occasionally see the light of day when shopping. There was always another layer to cover that slit when you must hide your eyes.

Women had two choices to help them see beyond their veil. Some lifted their veil a few inches from their face, looking down past their nose and chins, trying to catch a glimpse at something they wanted to buy. Others would put their hands on their forehead, press hard into the veils, push their hands down to their mouths, forcing the veil to be taut against their faces so they could see through. Our code name for the women was BMO, meaning Black Moving Objects.

Some ladies also had to wear black gloves if their husbands deemed their hands sexy and provocative. The strictness of fathers was evident from how many little girls had to don their cover, some being as young as six. The rule was that a girl covered upon reaching puberty, but if Daddy was strict, then his little girl began looking through her veil as an innocent babe.

Covering occasionally created somewhat of a sexual mystery, depending on how the woman underneath carried herself. When all you see are chocolate brown eyes, dark eyeliner, and long lashes, the appearance can sometimes be alluring.

Those gorgeous dark eyes were not always sitting on a pretty face which led me to wonder what would happen, should the highest bidder also believe her to be beautiful when, upon his purchase or, should I say, on the wedding night, he lifts her veil...

It was nice to see some of the young women with beautiful henna artwork on their hands; they were fortunate to be able to display some sort of adornment. Hennaing is an ancient custom, made more charming by the fact that it has been passed down through the ages.

The contrast of women having to wear black polyester while the men wore white cotton only showed that no stone went unturned in the mistreatment of women. Having to wear a partial covering myself, I became well acquainted with the unbearable heat under all that black. It was suffocating. Whoever said that black is better in the heat lied.

With my long heavy hair having to be tucked in as well, my back dripped with sweat. I felt choked; the heat seemed to burst my lungs from the inside out; each breath hurt; each heartbeat ached; even my ribs felt expanded. My blood felt like it was boiling inside my chest.

I put on the veil to see how much more enclosed it would be. Seeing life through a thread count of minuscule squares of a cloth was agonizing, like looking through a darkened window screen. I had such anger at the suffering caused by the rules of men, and nothing could convince me that Allah demanded this of women.

I teased my friends that my choice of rebellion was to not wear underwear under my *abaya*. That was enough to stir up some anxieties, but I maintained that it was something I *must* do. I was the only one who had to know that I had on soft cotton breathable undies.

And so, life in Saudi began.

It is forbidden for women to ride in cars with anyone other than a male blood relative or husband. Many cars had dark, tinted windows enabling women to uncover inside, but a law was passed saying that tinted windows were now also *forbidden*. Saudi women must remain completely covered, even in the privacy of their cars, and western women would not be able to hide behind the tinted glass.

It is forbidden for women to be with a man in public, other than a male blood relative or husband. This not only applied to Saudis but to all women. You could not even say hello for fear of being arrested for prostitution, which happened quite frequently.

It is forbidden to have alcohol but you wouldn't know it by the amount of homemade booze and alcoholics.

It is forbidden to even consider that a woman's word is worth any more than half that of a man's.

This cocktail of forbidden fruit was consumed by many, willing to take the risk of getting caught. I drank from the cup more in Saudi than ever in my life, a reaction to being in such an oppressed society. All of us rebelled to the full extent of the broken law. No one would survive Saudi's rules if they didn't break them. But getting caught wasn't so pretty.

And then the western leaders had to add to the mix their own set of insane, controlling laws—three of which stood out:

If your supervisors didn't like you, you were gone.

If your supervisors didn't like you, they could corrupt your records to fire you.

If your supervisors didn't like you, they could harass the be'jesus out of you.

Stir in the *it is forbidden*'s with the *ifs*, add a dash of all the hidden laws that pop up and change according to mood, shake, and voilá—one crazy Molotov cocktail.

There is a hierarchy in Saudi according to your country of origin, beginning with westerners and working down through what was referred to as the TWNs—third world nationals. TWNs included Filipinos, Sri Lankans, Indians, Pakistanis, Bangladeshis, and Afghanis. These groups were treated the worst. Afghanis worked outdoors maintaining the grounds and buildings, regardless of the sweltering heat—they seemed to be the lowest on the food chain, not even allowed to enter the hospital.

Westerners also weren't exempt from prejudice. We were all infidels, and many Saudis viewed us as tools to meet their needs. But the underlying theme was *Go home. We can run the place without you.* There was constant chatter about Saudization, meaning cleansing their world of outside influences and being able to sustain a workforce of predominantly Saudi nationals.

Filipinos made up a large percentage of workers in Saudi, all supporting parents, grandparents, aunts, uncles, and children back home. It's normal for them to leave their children to the care of a relative in the Philippines and to work in Saudi for years and years, in order to have enough money to buy homes and education. They see their children once a year for thirty days. It was sad to hear that this was their only way of giving a reasonable life to their families.

All TWNs received free food vouchers, excluding dessert, which was reserved for westerners. Ginete was considered western because she had a Portuguese passport. Now I understood why it was so important to her to let everyone know that she was not Indian—not for the dessert but because of the status and prejudice. I was embarrassed and offended and would bring up goodies to my secretaries. Seeing the abundance made it even more absurd that it wasn't for everyone—cheesecakes, cream-filled tarts, cream puffs, chocolate-layered cakes, custard puffs. My dedication to working out was intensified as I licked my caramel mousse!

There was also a lot of animosity over salary. My secretaries made $500 per month; kitchen and cleaning staff made $200 per month; and Filipino nurses made half of what western nurses made, which caused for enormous division and tension on the wards. All salaries were paid in U.S. dollars.

As I adjusted to Saudi life, I must have put Lorraine through hell. Because people travelled to North America almost daily, I was able to send a lot of mail, not realizing the impact my letters would have. If it was crazy to me and I was living it, I can't imagine how it sounded to her. She admitted to being very stressed out, hearing about all the madness while she was on the other side of the globe. She hated how I was being treated and wanted me to do a "runner." If she didn't hear from me regularly, she would envision me in prison, another reality of Saudi.

I wasn't alone. Staff, including doctors, packed up their lives and came to Saudi, only to be fired on a *hallalah*—on a dime, that is. It was not unusual to come to work and hear of somebody getting fired and leaving the country within twenty-four hours. I knew that I was walking on shifting sand.

Even more common than firing was what was known as "doing a runner." This was when a staff member left the kingdom and failed to return to complete his or her contract. You would need to plan a vacation prior to doing a runner, because you never had possession of your passport and spontaneity was therefore out of the question. Staff who just couldn't deal with the situation, or who knew they were on the chopping block, or who had personal integrity, and decided not to be treated like dirt, did a runner. I wished I had been that type.

No wonder we all partied like dogs in heat. By the way, there are no dogs in Saudi because they are seen as "unclean," similar to how westerners were sometimes looked at. You do, however, hear the wild dogs in the hills as they howl at the moon. I longed to join them but those hills would have to wait; I had a few parties to attend.

My spiritual quest had temporarily been buried in the sand as I gave in to a semi-hedonistic lifestyle within a kingdom where everything we did was wrong.

Partying with Donna wasn't difficult. Under her *abaya* strode a pair of legs that never ended, accented by the shortest skirts possible. Her dark, curly hair resting on her hips capped off her cuteness. Inviting the same number of women to match her Saudi boyfriend's male friends, I sometimes felt like an escort service.

Donna worked with Judy, whose roommate had just done a runner. I was introduced, pleaded to move in, and Judy said yes—*Hum'da'allah*.

I opted out of the party, choosing to spend the night moving out of the Efficiencies into my new, gorgeous two-bedroom flat. The difference was night and day. Rather than that tiny room, I was now living with two and a half baths, two balconies, a huge kitchen and living room. It was only in moving that I learned that the TWN community had to live in the Efficiencies for their entire time in Saudi, whether it be one year or twenty; they did not get the nicer apartments.

Hitching a ride with Donna and Ahmed to pick up supplies, I bid them adieu and off they went.

The weekend came and went, and back at work, there was a familiar buzz. Donna was in prison. I felt nauseous, both from her being caught and my near miss.

Finally, three days later, I saw Donna again. She was trembling as we hugged. We went into the loo to talk privately; she looked exhausted and said it was the scariest thing in her life. Her eyes had a haze over them, and I tried to imagine what she must have experienced in that prison.

They had been driving friends home after the party, when a car of Saudis started following them, beeping, hollering, and ramming into their car, until it forced them off the road. This brought more unwanted attention, and within minutes, a huge group of Saudis surrounded the car, bashing at it and rocking it back and forth, trying to get inside. Donna said she was petrified and had no doubt that if, in their frenzy, the Saudis had managed to open the doors, she would have been beaten to death. The religious police—the Mutawa—just happened to be close by and came swinging their handcuffs in the air. Donna was taken to prison with no food or blankets but plenty of intimidation.

When we spoke, no charges had been filed, but if they were laid, she would be on the next plane out. It turned out that she had to return to the police station, compose a long letter of apology, and state her knowledge of breaking the rules of Islam. She was given a pardon. Nothing happened to her Saudi boyfriend.

We returned to my office, and Ginete brushed by Donna as if she were filth and started sniffing around. I knew she was furious that I had managed to move out without her—her anger was deliberate. Finally, she said, "I come to your office when I am observing and checking things out. I watch everything."

Sarcastically asking what it was that she was observing, I was all the time thinking, *you crazy evil woman*. She continued, "The doctors—and you, of course! My spies tell me that your secretaries are going for long breaks and taking advantage of you because you are being too nice. I tell you this: the nicer you are, the more they will abuse you."

I said nothing. Ginete hated that the doctors were happy, and the secretaries were smiling and laughing. I have no doubt that my treating them with respect and honour helped them to have respect for themselves.

My previous counterpart left behind quite a reputation. "Lethal-Letha" was her nickname. Misha, a party friend who worked next door, shared stories of Letha's ranting and raving, her belittling of the secretaries, her screams heard down the hall. No one, including doctors, was allowed into the secretary's office; everyone had to direct their communication through Letha who, not coincidentally, had been best friends with Ginete.

Another weekend brought another party, and again, the boy-girl ratio was even. I knew that I had to get out of that closet sooner than later.

I didn't know that my past was about to confront me.

Patricia, a Canadian nurse, heard I had been in Lebanon and got very excited because her boyfriend was Lebanese. She called me an angel. I was uncomfortable because I was not the same person that had been in Lebanon; there was quite a bumpy road between being born-again and being a lesbian. There was no time to tell her I was gay—everything happened so fast.

I was nervous for my blonde, blue-eyed friend because, frankly, I didn't trust Arab men due to my own history and what I had seen. So many women fall for these guys because they are dark, handsome, brooding, and exotic. It almost always turns out to be devastating when the man goes back to his three wives. So many of the ladies fell in love fast and hard.

The guys started asking me about Lebanon. They didn't quite look at me as an angel though. One man, in particular, challenged me and demanded to know if I was one of those Christians who came to his country. I tried to lie. He pushed the subject by saying that it was impossible to be in Lebanon during the war without an organization sponsoring me. I hedged.

He knew I was lying. "I know you. You were with those Christians in Nabetia and Arnoun."

I said nothing but felt absolute astonishment that he knew where I had been in Lebanon.

"I am from Nabetia. You people came to my country when we had nothing. Every family had lost a son, a father, a brother, their homes. You took a group of people who were down and out, desperate, trying to survive war, and you told them that what they believed in was wrong. You came to my people when they lost everything and you told them the one thing they had left—their faith—was wrong. You tried to take the only thing they had left. You tried to take their faith from them when they were most vulnerable."

I sat, horrified at the truth. Why couldn't we have simply

loved them and helped them rebuild their homes? I was ashamed. How could I tell him that I was sorry, that I was now a different person?

That party wasn't as successful as Patricia had hoped. I most certainly wasn't his angel, but I believe he was mine.

Back at work, needing to talk with Patricia, I went down to her office, only to find that she had just been fired—complete with a security escort placing her under house arrest. Patricia's boss, whom I had originally befriended until I realized she, too, was nuts, had caught wind that Patricia had a Lebanese boyfriend. From that, the crazy woman made up a story that she had seen him sleep overnight. Only I knew that her plans upon arrival were to get rid of the current staff, and hire "her people."

Patricia was allowed four days, rather than twenty-four hours, to pack up, but she was not allowed to leave the compound. Security took away her *iqama*. She was frantic because of having to leave her Lebanese boyfriend who, I might add, stood by her and supported her completely. Her friends managed to sneak him into our compound, and at this point, she had nothing to lose by his staying with her.

Patricia and her boyfriend eventually got married and lived in Canada. They were in love, and that gave me hope, not only for Arab men, but for men in general.

Already feeling a bit downtrodden over prison, firings, and runners happening on at least a weekly basis, I was attempting to pull back from Ginete's clutches. I now expected her regular phone calls for me to come down to her office. On this occasion, she informed me that my transcription was not very good. At this point, only about three, of approximately thirty, meetings had to do with her. When I asked which minutes she was referring to, she brought out the first. I reminded her that it had been my first day, plus it had been the entire medical staff. She proceeded to warn me that she had the power to dismiss me.

When Ginete's attempts at intimidation failed to impress me, she began getting quite deviant. Almost immediately after leaving her office, I was advised by Employee Health [E.H.] that

I was to see a Saudi cardiologist. The pretence was "concern" over my recent heart surgery and the desire to ensure I was fine. The fact that I had needed to pass a complete physical prior to my employment meant nothing.

The heat was a sweltering 125F as I sat in the waiting room, surrounded by women completely veiled and clearly distressed. One woman could hardly breathe, lifting her veil enough to get air from the bottom. I sat in sober silence watching this.

I was not happy that it was a male Saudi cardiologist in a country where there is such abuse to women. I didn't want him to see me naked or touch me. I didn't know him, nor did I know where his training was from. Granted, many physicians are trained in the West, but many are not and would not meet with North American accreditation. His assistant put my ECG cables on upside-down, which did not boost my confidence.

After examining me, he said my heart was fine, except that he could still hear a murmur. I told him *my* cardiologist had said there would always be a murmur and it was nothing to worry about. He was being insistent that I do nothing—no exercise, no lifting. This was from the old school of thought, which ended up killing patients because they did nothing.

I informed him that again, *my* cardiologist was very aware of my exercise regime and promoted it for the health of my heart. Thankfully, I managed to convince him that I knew how to be heart-smart. He sent an all-clear report back to Ginete. Nowhere else in the world would this be allowed! I just couldn't believe this was happening.

Calling me to her headquarters yet again, Ginete pushed the issue, stating that even though he said I was okay, I must be advised that should I have a heart attack, I would be completely on my own and neither she, nor anybody else, would help me. I would die! I'm sure my blood pressure went sky high; it was inconceivable that someone was talking to me as abusively and cruelly as my parents did. I didn't think it possible outside of my parents' reach, but here I was, being told that I could drop dead and nobody would care. I was looking at a she-devil who had no conscience.

I started hallucinating. *Dad, is that you?* I was talking to Ginete, but I swear I saw my father.

Sitting in the women's section of the cafeteria, trying to comprehend my new insane reality, I felt like a child who had just been reprimanded by her parents. Calm was quickly becoming elusive. Jan, the E.H. nurse, tried to join me, but I walked out. I glared at her, furious that a westerner was participating in this aggression. She later came to my office, closed the door, and started to cry; she apologized, saying she had tried to stop this. Jan informed me that she had been successful in something I would be happy to know about—she had refused to alter my medical records!

I was already contemplating doing a runner. Sadly, I knew that I had done a backwards runner from my family—right into this upside-down world. Now, I was already a bit panicked about where to run to next. I was feeling like a beaten, caged animal, and a visit from the director of E.H. unhelpfully reminded me, "Employee Health will still be watching you very carefully." Again, could my heart take much more of this? Did I have a death wish, or what?

Fed up, I wrote a letter of complaint to Dr. M. H. I sat in his office, aware that he was brainwashed by Ginete and doubtful about getting through to him.

He reminded me that he demanded perfection, and I stated that that was impossible—I could not meet his unrealistic demand. Inside, I was screaming obscenities at his insanity.

I suggested he ask the department heads how they felt about my work. If they were not satisfied, I would bow out of my contract. Barely out of his office, I heard him make the first call. I also heard his surprised response. The scorecard read one for the underdog and zero for the Mad Hatter.

One by one, they said I was wonderful, did my minutes to their satisfaction, was always happy and, above all, was an excellent supervisor. Dr. M. H. could do nothing but sign my evaluation. He admitted that he was comparing my work to a secretary in the U.S. who had worked for him for twenty-five years, and maybe, just *maybe*, he was being a bit unfair.

Ginete would not be silenced. "You are never safe. It may be one week. It may be two. We may not get you out in twenty-four hours, but we can get you out."

I stared back in disbelief. She was one crazy lady.

She continued, "You must improve. If you will not, tell me today and I will have you home tomorrow." I walked out, tears flowing down my cheeks.

Jackie worked in Ginete's office, and for that reason, I'd always ignored her. Usually, I had been able to contain my tears until I got out of the office, but this time, the floodgates opened. Seeing my breakdown, Jackie took my hand and brought me into the bathroom to see what was happening.

We soon discovered that neither of us had trusted each other for the same reason. I thought she was friends with Ginete just because she worked in the same office, and she thought I was friends because I was always there! My tears turned to laughter as I informed her that I was *always* there because I was *always* getting into trouble. We both detested Ginete, and on that note, a friendship was born.

Shortly after I returned to my office, Dr. M. H. appeared. "Why are you so paranoid?" was the first comment out of his mouth.

I could hardly answer him but managed, "You're joking, right? The way you and Ginete have treated me!"

He certainly looked guilty, but rather than give any degree of an apology, he said, "I'm not really the ogre you think I am."

I asked him why wouldn't I be paranoid with him, after how I was treated and what he was putting me through. He quietly said he knew why, and I took this to mean that he knew of Ginete's craziness. At the same time, he had yet to acknowledge his own willingness to participate.

"I like you very much, you know? I enjoy your sense of humour." He got up and left.

Man, this sure was the Mad Hatter's tea party!

My Tasmanian Devil

I needed a rest from the parties and wanted to explore Saudi Arabia. I didn't want to have just a western experience of parties, drinking, and dancing. I wanted to feel like I was living in the Middle East. I wanted to taste her flavour. In all its dysfunction, Arabia still held enormous fascination for me. I wanted to savour her culture.

Thank Buddha, we had Bob, our recreation coordinator whose job it was to organize field trips, shopping, and excursions for KEG staff. The bus would always be full, mostly with females because men, being allowed to drive, had their own cars, which allowed them much more freedom and independence for extracurricular activities. I needed a "legal" break from the compound.

It was on one of these trips that I met Tasmanian Tazzie. Although she had worked in the kingdom for two years, she still enjoyed hopping the bus to ride around and enjoy the city, and to hang out in the ancient sections of Riyadh, known by the names of Batha and Dhira. She was a girl after my own heart, because I also loved to get out and see how the world ticked.

Tazzie was private, eccentric—and she had become Muslim. I wouldn't find out why until she felt safer with me. Meanwhile, it baffled me as to why she would do that in such a strict country, but I only had to remember my own life choices.

She thrived on mystery and drama and loved to tell scary stories of Saudi. She made every event in the kingdom sound extreme and out of focus, which actually wasn't far from the truth. We became great friends, beginning with our first jaunt to the old 'hood of Batha.

Walking along the cobbled streets, we felt swept into their ancient world. Tazzie loved the mystique as much as I did. We treasured watching the live theatre surrounding us. Old men sat on stools in front of their souqs, smoking their hubbly-bubbly as they watched the world go by. In their own Arabian Piccadilly Circus, they twirled their prayer beads, argued with potential buyers, or if feeling energetic in the heat, yelled out to passersby to lure them in.

Hundreds of souqs selling carpets, textiles, spices, jewels, copper, brassware, handmade baskets—just to name some of the wares—all melded together, nestled side by side. There were blacksmiths, cobblers, butchers, and silversmiths all using archaic tools of the trade.

Carpets are very big in Saudi. Expats not only laid them on their floors but also hung them on walls as pieces of art. Dealers would speedily throw hundreds of carpets in a pile in front of any potential buyers, giving them barely a moment to see one before the next one came flying onto the pile. Lord help the poor worker if you asked to see that very first carpet, now lying under a hundred others! *Schwai, schwai!*

The tantalizing scent of spices wafted through the air and competed with their own equally brilliant mosaic of colours— rich blues, deep gold, dark reds—all showcased in ancient wooden barrels, sitting on display in front of the old, rustic shops. Frankincense, myrrh, cinnamon, eucalyptus, saffron, cloves, peppermint, lavender—oftentimes, we would see an old man sitting crossed-legged, with an enormous bowl of spice leaves, grinding them down to powder.

Ancient pistols and daggers hung off large hooks and along the walls. Tazzie and I liked to make up stories about their history. Mixed in with weapons were awesome displays of Bedouin jewellery, many too thick and heavy to consider wearing. Often, necklaces and anklet adornments were designed primarily of gorgeous turquoise but also incorporated semiprecious stones, such as amber, coral, and agate.

Gold souqs stood side by side in all their glory, creating a colossal allure of beauty. The front entrance to each souq is completely open, and only closed at night and at prayer time with a sliding iron and metal gate, secured at the bottom by one lone lock. Security is nearly nil because only the insane would consider stealing, a crime punishable in Saudi by chopping off the thief's hand.

Gold is 18, 20, and 24 karat, the higher the karat, the darker the yellow. Filipinos buy the 24K because it is a status symbol for them. Hanging from the walls and displayed in every nook and cranny were gold bangles, studs, dangly earrings, bracelets, necklaces, and puzzle rings. "Slave rings," indigenous to Arabia, were attached by a bed of gold designed to lie across the front of your hand extending and attaching to a ring. There were hundreds of tiaras, crowns, and breastplates for brides—all which sounded and looked like they were to be worn by a goddess warrior going to battle, rather than by a bride. Maybe the two weren't so different!

There was a silver lining in the clouds if you were a silver lover. Newer silver seemed almost second class—upstaged as it was by the gold, and priced at next to nothing.

The garment districts of Milan and New York would have wept at the beauty and inexpensiveness of textiles in Saudi. Hand-painted silks and linens, all flown in from Sri Lanka, Afghanistan, India, and Thailand, displayed colours, patterns, and textures of the kind seen on the runways of Paris. Their colours were rivalled only by the spices.

There is no shortage of tailors and seamstresses from third world countries. All they needed was a picture of a designer gown, and in no time at all, you would have an exact duplicate—including Demi Moore's famous black dress worn in *Indecent Proposal*, hanging in the closet of a friend of Jackie, along with a complete wardrobe of Laura Ashley knock-offs. The sewing was impeccable and their fees were far too low for what customers would have been willing to pay. Sadly, all that world of colour and design was hidden under a sea of black.

Another souq was for the exotic animal trade. Tazzie was aware that these birds were indigenous to Australia and New Zealand and had to be brought here illegally. By the look of this backstreet souq, I believed her. It was in a large barn-type building, chockablock full of the most gorgeous birds and reptiles. It was disgusting to see fifty little lovebirds in one cage. Reptiles were piled on top of each other. Seeing how they were kept was so disgusting, brutal, and abusive, I started gagging and had to leave.

Five times a day, everything stops in Saudi. The prayer call is heard on loudspeakers all over the city via the mosques, as well as on our hospital intercom. If you're shopping or dining at prayer time, you will be kicked out—Riyadh shuts down. Mutawa round up Muslims, making sure that everyone stops business and prays. You always knew when a man had gone on the Haj to Mecca because his hair or beard was dyed with red henna.

Women are not allowed to pray with the men, nor are they allowed to enter mosques. I know we see pictures of women at the back of mosques but in *my* travels, I have never ever seen a woman allowed to enter a mosque.

The streets are lined with women and their kids, all waiting for their husbands to return from prayer. Cars stop anywhere and everywhere, and the women are left at the side of the road, to sit and bake in the sun.

The few areas I saw that were allocated for women to pray were disgusting and filthy. In the malls, there is a filthy rag for a curtain with a sign for women to pray behind the curtain.

Tazzie educated me on the ways of the world in Saudi; in particular, she pointed out the inordinate amount of omnipresent religious police—the Mutawa. I had already been warned of their insane power within the kingdom, after seeing firsthand what they did to Donna. Riyadh, being the capital, was the strictest city with the highest population of Mutawa. People who had worked in Jeddah were surprised at the rigidity of life in Riyadh—at least, on the surface.

Spotting Mutawa was becoming easier: They all had long straggly beards and wore only a *goutrah*; their *thobes* were shorter than usual and showed off their ankles. I wasn't the only one who thought that they all had the "little man syndrome"— being Mutawa gave them much power. Mutawa formed the Commission for the Promotion of Virtue and Prevention of Vice; they held the right to harass anyone they chose to, especially the infidels, and *all* women.

Tazzie asked me to wear a black head scarf, rather than the gorgeous purple one with gold sparkles I had just bought. I said I would hide my hair, but I was wearing my pretty purple scarf. Poor Tazzie felt it was like a bull in a china store and that its colour was too eye-catching, but I loved my shiny purple scarf.

As we sat in Batha, three Mutawa and a few police in a van pulled up, yelled, and beckoned me over. I was already nervous, but feeling Tazzie's anxiety heightened the situation.

"Don't go near their car," she whispered. I motioned to them, as if to say *why are you speaking to me?* They started pointing to my bangs—or "fringe" according to most other western countries— and yelling, "Cover your hair. Cover your hair!" Of course, Tazzie reprimanded me—I had brought attention to myself with the purple scarf. I was ticked off because my hair was covered. The only visible hair was a small strand of my fringe, but that was enough to be harassed.

Calming down, we wandered over to the main square of Clock Tower, where stood the most spectacular mosque. Listening to the evening call for prayer, we shared one of those inspiring moments, feeling the magic of being in the heart of Riyadh. The sun was setting and it truly was an Arabian night, until Tazzie whispered that the square we were standing on was known as Chop-Chop Square. As she cautiously pointed to where executions happen, a Mutawa came storming toward us, indignant that we had the nerve to stand close to a mosque at prayer time when all the men were cleansing themselves. We scurried off; the moment of beauty had passed quickly as Saudi reality slapped us out of our enchantment.

I had been warned never to go downtown on Fridays, the Muslim holy day, because the executions take place after the noon prayer. Choice of technique: beheading with a sword! Those I knew who had witnessed executions told me that the person to be executed appeared drugged. Often they had some of their blood removed just before execution and entered the square delirious and staggering. Rumours abounded that the blood was reused for traffic accident victims, or so that the square wouldn't be so bloody. Mystical turned into barbaric. If westerners were found downtown, they were forced to the front of the crowd to watch the beheadings. Every week, East Asians, many of them Pakistanis and Afghanis, were executed. If you got caught committing a crime on Tuesday, you were beheaded on Friday—at least that's what it seemed like. Every Saturday, in its top corner, the newspaper would name the person executed and the crime, which appeared to be mostly drug trafficking. Often times, there was more than one person.

People from very poor countries risked death to smuggle in drugs. It was worth the cost of their lives because their families back home would be taken care of with the monies earned. Oddly, Tazzie and I would often smell marijuana in the older 'hoods. Turning up our noses for a sniff, we would see the men sitting on their carpets and smiling gingerly. There seemed to be no concern for the penalty.

I soon met people who had witnessed the horror. A nurse had snuck into a hotel overlooking the square and took pictures of an execution. She took them out of her bag, and I glanced momentarily then turned away in fear. Dr. C., a South African anaesthetist, said he had been one of those forced to the front to witness an execution of two men. He admitted to us that he could not sleep for months. He saw the executions every time he closed his eyes, and to this day, he confessed, he still slept with the lights on. This wasn't a horror movie but grim reality.

Suffice it to say, the executioner's blade was not always sharpened, and the death was sometimes slow and gruesome. Astonishingly, the Arabs would watch, screaming and cheering at each execution.

The Secret Underground—
Known to Everyone

Speaking of execution, I learned early on of the male gay subculture. If you are a gay man in Saudi, your life is wonderful. Although sodomy is punishable by death, that never stopped anyone, including Saudis.

Mario was my closest gay-guy friend. He was having a great life and had lived in Saudi for the past decade. Surrounded by so many gay brothers, I was surprised to meet only one other lesbian, an African American who told me point blank that she hated white people. So much for the sisterhood!

I had to come out. The rules of the road were the same for backpackers and expats. We were all just passing through, creating a freer, more immediate emotional reaction to life. People fell in love instantly; nobody waited until the third date to have sex; life was ramped up and in full throttle. There was so much sex and promiscuity that I just couldn't pretend any longer.

Happily, no one rejected me. I was "protected" if the guys came on too strong, and I was the dance partner for anyone who needed someone—male or female. It was fun to be the token lesbian in a closed society. My primary party dates, Donna, Misha, and Penny, all sweetly told me they had already figured out I was gay, and that's why they stuck close to me when the guys were on the prowl. Penny, whom I quietly nicknamed Shekel, would run over, hug me, and say, "She's with me." We had so much fun.

Mario and I holidayed and partied together, calling each other "wife." Mario had chosen to stay in Saudi during the previous year's Gulf War. Although many expats went home, he felt safe enough to stay. He and his boss, a Vietnam vet, retrieved a huge section of a bomb that killed Americans in the war and hung it on the wall in honour of their compatriots. It reminded me of Oscar in Lebanon—*a guy thing*, I thought to myself.

Mario owned a car and had several different Saudi lovers along the way; I was thus privy to the incredible availability of "man-2-man" sex in the *king*dom. A lot of the guys had affairs with married Saudi men, who took care of them, bought them gifts, and generally acted like their sugar daddies. It's true—many married men, including Saudis, have sexual relations with men.

Mario and I had vacationed in India together, and the sexual advances made to him were unbelievable. On a beach, we had just spread out our towels, and I turned to say something, but Mario was gone. Moments earlier I had noticed a man, woman, and baby headed down the same beach. Looking around, I could see the woman with her baby, but her guy was missing. A few minutes passed, and out from behind a rock came Mario, along with the stranger. Having exchanged that defining "gaydar" glance, the two of them had ducked behind the rocks, engaged in sex, and then headed back to their respective "families." It's not uncommon—I've seen it all over the world, and Saudi was not any different. I personally think it's male testosterone and the need for a lot of sex...

Back in Riyadh, Mario and I joined a party at Finnigan's—a very Celtic underground bar. With their traditional Irish tunes, beer, and laughter, the pub made you feel as if you were in the heart of Ireland. At the end of each night, a Celtic song would cry out, and the Irish would raise their glasses and voices, in unison, and become emotional, as if they were singing their national anthem. I expected U2 to walk in at any second. Those Irish sure know how to party!

As we drank our beer and danced the night away, I knew that I had missed curfew by a mere two hours. The other ladies were all having sleepovers on other compounds, but I had to crash through our security. How was I going to get home? Mario said it was so late, that I should just drive home with him and act like his wife. I did. Sitting in the front seat next to him felt sadly weird as I tried to remember "normal." When we stopped at red lights, Arab drivers would stare at me in disgust that a woman was out so late. It was nerve-wracking because any one of them could do whatever they wanted.

We stopped at Taco Bell, and I asked a little girl standing next to us what she was doing up so late. She told us she was with her parents, so no bedtime for her. All restaurants are divided into sections for women, men or families. The women are always jammed in the back, which is devoid of ambiance, and they order through a little peephole so nobody working there looks at them. There are private family booths where you close a sliding door so women can unveil. This was the first and only time I got to sit in the family section, with my husband. Our server whispered to us that this little girl was a princess, which wasn't so unusual in Saudi as almost everyone seemed to be a prince or princess. I looked at Mario. "I hope she can't smell the booze."

"Don't worry. She'll think we smell just like Daddy!"

We weren't being disrespectful; of course, Saudis drink as well. We were having fun with the rules that all this stuff is forbidden, but in truth, rules can't fully oppress human nature. Getting the giggles caused men to stare so we decided it was better to leave. We walked past three police standing outside by their car, and I hopped in the front seat with my wife—I mean, my husband. I could only hope the guard at the compound didn't care. Mario told him he drove me home because I was having trouble finding a limo. Security waved us in, glaring at me as we drove on. Being out so late, dining and driving with a man, it felt like my wedding night in Saudi.

Hospital Administration sent out one of their warning letters reminding staff to stay out of public places, such as the lobby, especially during prayer times. We were also reminded to wear minimal makeup and jewellery; women's dresses must be eight inches below the knee—this would be strictly enforced. Slacks were strictly forbidden. The letter ended with a "Do not laugh when together in public."

Shortly after the warning letter, a security person approached me on my way to work. "Look at you. Look at you! Go home immediately." He pointed toward my skirt.

I asked what he was talking about.

"Your clothes. This is not eight inches. Get out." I was sent home because my skirt was 7.5 inches rather than an exact eight inches. He must have been looking awfully close to determine his ruling; I thought *that* wasn't allowed!

In her paranoia, Tazzie warned me to be careful: Security might be watching me more closely than I was aware.

My attempts at escaping my family's abuses and degradations toward me should have had me wondering the obvious: Why on earth would I choose to come to a country that treated women with such disdain? Did I have a secret wish to be beaten down? Did I lead myself into the wilderness, intentionally to hurt myself? All that I was trying to run away from refused to stay in my past and remained very much in the present.

Making bread, drinking *chai*—Arnoun, Lebanon

Not quite as easy as she made it look!

Drinking from the well...

First of two bomb craters at school in Arnoun—our home

Lulu and me, hiding our faces—trying to get Noya to take a picture, but she wouldn't.

Secretaries Day, Saudi

All that glitters is gold!

Okay, I think we've got the message

A common Saudi sight—women sitting on the ground that men walk on...

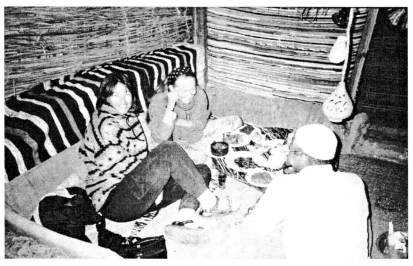

Ramses' bedouin eatery, Dahab—happy and high!

Stuck in Dahab…

Seen all through the Middle East

May the road rise to meet you; may the wind be always at your back... *Yella* my Irish gypsy friend... *Yella!*

What was I thinking???? *Yella!*

Walking a tightrope—UAE, New Year's Eve 1998

Me and my precious *habibti*, Lorraine

A Peek Under the Veil

Although Tazzie was typically serious and dramatic, she arranged a party in a friend's villa. That's where I met Mamma Aida and her three princesses. This was an all-women's party, respectful to Saudi rules, to celebrate Aida's birthday. Aida had befriended Tazzie while being nursed by her, which was rare due to the lines clearly being drawn in the sand between Saudis and expats. Aida continued the friendship, as she wanted her daughters to meet people from around the world.

After about twenty expats had gathered, Mamma Aida walked in with her daughters, Noya, Samira, and Lulu. Their *abayas* and veils hid stunningly beautiful young women.

Three distinct personalities emerged: Noya seemed to have the more reserved personality; Lulu, with her long flowing hair and sexy dress, was clearly the extrovert, while Samira, the youngest, had short black spiked hair and funky blue jeans; she looked like a lesbian. That wasn't my jaded opinion—Tazzie agreed with me.

The girls soon went from being shy to taking total control of the party. Off came the background pop music, and on came the Arabic tunes. With the volume turned up, Lulu wrapped a long scarf around her sumptuous hips and began to gyrate in unison to the beat. Her sisters and mother echoed their *zilagheet* shriek of joy—"lalalalala"—with their tongues, as they clapped to the rhythm of the beat. They looked surprised as I joined in, twirling my tongue and shouting, *"Yella, habibti, yella!"* This further encouraged them to let loose completely.

Lulu's dancing became sexier as she began shimmying her shoulders in front of her family, who responded with pleasure. Sexuality was being liberated. As in Syria, when women are together, they go wild.

The scarf was passed to Samira, then to Noya, who danced sexily but cautiously; it went back to Lulu and then to me. I joyfully wrapped it around my hips and began my initiation dance as they howled with delight. I shook my booty toward Aida, much to her delight. I was accepted.

The western women stood around looking slightly startled at my Arabian alter ego. Going by their faces, I thought it was the first time they were privy to the shenanigans of Arab women behind closed doors.

Uttering a few greetings and pleasantries in Arabic, Mamma Aida asked how, why, and where I had learned this. I told them of my travels but omitted the details of almost marrying a Syrian prior to actively evangelizing to save the souls of Muslims. Blocking more questions, I started singing a song I had learned in Damascus. They excitedly continued the song, saying it was a very old and famous love song. I knew only the chorus and let the daughters sing the rest.

After a nice lunch, I was sitting talking to Noya and noticed her mother staring at me, smiling. "This girl. This girl, I like very much. My daughter likes her and this is nice."

I went over and gave her a big kiss. She laughed, then jokingly slapped me on the head, a true gesture of acceptance.

"*Ana bahabick Mamma Aida,*" I said as she kissed my cheeks.

The rebel child came out in all of us—including Bev, a sophisticated socialite who was always the first to throw a welcome luncheon for newcomers. One weekend, she would be helping host an embassy party; the next, gleefully breaking the kooky rules. Like the rest of us, she had to find ways to survive the oppression. Together, we always managed to do something a bit "dangerous," by Saudi standards, anyway.

Being in a quiet part of the mall, we headed up the escalator to discover a mini-mosque. There were rows of prayer mats with a huge Koran sitting on a gorgeous wooden stand. I proposed that she act like she was praying while I took a picture, but she was afraid to. I knelt down and quickly fell forward in prayer while she snapped a picture.

Feeling like we had just committed the crime of the century—and, I suppose, in Saudi, we had—we ran so fast after that snapshot, then down the escalator, headed toward the exit. And predictably, Mutawa began following us.

"Cover your hair," they yelled as they picked up their pace toward us.

We began walking faster. Everyone around us seemed to be in slow motion, first staring at us, then all eyes moving to the onslaught of Mutawa. The only sound I heard was of my own heartbeat. Everyone looked suspicious. We got to the doors of the mall, only to see four more Mutawa and a policeman scurry toward us. "You must cover your hair!" they shouted.

Yeah, yeah, yeah! I muttered. Can't they see it's hard to keep a scarf on while running away from danger. They didn't understand.

To the surprise of the resting limo driver, we jumped in and I shouted, "Hospital. Hospital. Quickly. *Yella!*" The driver laughed nervously at our enthusiasm to get away. Clearly having a break from our Saudi reality, we willingly but unwittingly placed our lives in his hands. On a normal day of Saudi driving, an accident was always imminent—never mind that we were encouraging him to drive even crazier than usual.

Drivers in the Middle East drive as if they are all on a bad acid trip. I am sure there are no driving schools. Driving 4x4s is a bit different than riding a camel; I know, because I have done both.

Life is threatened each time you enter into traffic. If there was any attempt to have traffic rules, it was unsuccessful. Everyone is erratic, honking, speeding, and playing road games with each other. Kids are sitting on the dashboard when they're not crawling all over the car; there are no seatbelts and, often, five people in the front and eight in the back. It is nuts.

No one drives in a lane, but rather, cars are five-abreast, zigzagging in and out, gassing it in one breath, breaking furiously in the next, only to gas it seconds later. Jerk—uuurrcch; jerk—uuurrrrcchh; honk, honk, *honk*.

Along with the 4x4s are trucks loaded with camels in the back. With wild camels all over the surrounding desert, there are blurred *Yield to Camel* signs as cars whiz past them. My knuckles would have to be pried off the door handles.

I would yell at the limo drivers, "I'll bloody shoulder-check for you. Thanks for the freaking ride from hell!"

They, not knowing what I said would reply, "Thank you. You welcome. *Mafi mushkala*—no problem."

Drivers think the middle line is for passing. Two turning lanes will have six cars attempting to make the turn at the same time. It's like the Indy 500, seen through the eyes of the car-cam.

Here we sat, out of necessity—willingly jumping into the chaos and frenzy. "*Yella*," I shouted as we went from zero to ninety miles per hour in seconds, speeding off, supposedly, out of harm's way but, really, into the highway to hell.

Paranoia in, and out of, cars was constant. Hearing that I was typing daily entries about life in Saudi and then mailing them home, friends warned that I was signing my own confession.

A book written by a Saudi princess was banned within the kingdom and, of course, copies were everywhere, circulating amongst the women. I finished reading the book and laid it face down on the corner of my desk, for pickup by the next reader. Seeing it lying there, Tazzie was furious with me. I could be in serious trouble, she said, because it was a "banned substance!" It was also enough of a "crime" to get me kicked out of Saudi, Tazzie cautioned.

Nothing is private. Mail is opened at whim. I had received a statue of a small child sitting with her arms wrapped around her legs. *They* opened my mail, broke off the head, and then gave it to me. Upon questioning this, I was told that statues are idolatry and illegal, and I should be thankful they gave it to me at all.

The most important job in Saudi, scratching out all pictures of women's body parts—legs, arms, and faces—from foreign newspapers and magazines from around the world, is absurdly hysterical. It must take enormous concentration for these men not to stare at the body images before ferociously scratching them out with black markers.

And then there's the word *Israel*. Because Israel does not exist to the Arab nations, there *is* no Israel; therefore, that word is scratched out with more fervour than scratching out a pair of legs. Every newspaper, map, magazine, or anything that enters the country and contains the name *Israel* will get the offending word scribbled out.

Just as I first learned in Syria, the entire Middle East wants nothing short of Israel's demise. "Israel" is known as "Occupied Palestine."

Back in the office, Ginete continued to torment me daily. Even so, I somehow managed to run a successful medical secretaries department. Unfortunately, I was not always able to hide my tears from them, often returning from Ginete's bashings with red puffy eyes. My secretaries, whom I affectionately called "my girls," had been around for a very long time and not much came as a surprise to them. It made them uncomfortable, however, to have their supervisor treated so disrespectfully.

My girls threw me a surprise birthday party. They spent the previous night cooking and brought in scrumptious dishes from their home countries. They gave me flowers and cards that said they loved me. I loved supervising and learning from them as much as they learned from me, if not more. I certainly learned of their human cost in having to leave families and children and put up with prejudice and abuses, and yet, they managed to keep their integrity intact, to show kindness and gentleness.

Colloquial collisions and communication breakdowns were always entertaining and enlightening, with a near-impossible task of trying to explain.

Sharing a story, Bhama said, "I heard it through the wine root."

"Excuse me?"

"Wine root. You understand this? Someone telling me this story through the wine root?"

I laughed. "You mean the *grapevine?*" I tried explaining through my laughter, but it was another communication that got lost in translation.

In the relaxed birthday setting, she took the opportunity to find out about me, asking why I was not married and why I was a "spinster," a word I had not heard used for years. Although I was openly gay with my friends, I of course never told my secretaries or Ginete.

Bhama shared her Hindu faith, and as I tried to explain why I wasn't married, why I was not taking care of my family, why I had no relationship with my parents, her black eyes seemed lost. She was supporting her mother and her grandmother back in Sri Lanka. This was her "duty." She had an arranged marriage and never questioned it.

I tried to explain that in the West, if family relations are unhealthy, it did not make sense to have a relationship out of duty.

"But you have the same blood!" Bhama sounded confused.

Our two worlds had just collided. I couldn't explain to her about my family—it would be impossible for her to understand. I didn't even understand it. My family problems felt like they belonged only in our western world; I wondered if similar things happened in her world. How I would have loved to ask, but these barriers went way past language.

Our attempts to understand each other became even more heated when I later mentioned the ethnic cleansing in Sri Lanka by the terrorist group, the Tamil Tigers.

"I am Tamil!"

Embarrassed, I apologized, and told her that I had only heard of the Tamil in relation to terrorism. Bhama explained that the Tamil were simply trying to make better living conditions for their people.

Within a short time of this conversation, her grandmother had to be evacuated from northern Columbo due to an outbreak of violence. Her grandmother was on the last boat crossing into southern Columbo to escape this uprising. Her home was destroyed by Tamil Tigers, but Bhama still could not see this in any other light other than the Tamil helping her people.

I did not need more reminders that I was in an international environment and these were not just news stories. The people I worked with lived these stories—they *were* these stories.

Mamma Aida heard it was my birthday and invited Tazzie and me to her home.

Mohammed, her handsome son, along with the three sisters, picked us up. It was the first time they had been on compound and they were fascinated by life behind our walls.

Although their car still had very dark tinted windows, they were still afraid to take off their veils. It was strange to carry on a conversation with three women, all wearing black veils over their faces. Talk about lack of eye contact.

After arriving at their home, Tazzie and I were escorted to the guest room where women entertained their company. No male family members were allowed.

The evening was filled with conversations about our different worlds. Lulu would say, "I want my husband to have three wives. I will insist. Then he will not sleep with the western prostitutes." The fact that Tazzie and I were western went unnoticed.

Noya, the first girl in the family to have higher education, was training to be a doctor. When it came time for her practicum, and some patients were male, she literally felt sick to her stomach. Her veil was on, but she felt too close to the men and refused to work with them.

Noya was the most entrenched in her beliefs—and the most fearful. She would get very heated when discussing men and women. It made no sense to her that it should be men's own accountability for controlling their gaze and lust toward women. To Noya, women held that responsibility. I tried to say that women *shouldn't* be responsible. How the religious law convinced women that it was entirely their fault for men's lust is beyond me, but convinced they were. She had no doubt.

When asked why she should be responsible, Noya got quite upset. "Don't you feel like a whore when men look at your legs?" I didn't take offence, as she never meant harm. Personal accountability on a man's part was a totally foreign concept that she couldn't wrap her mind around. It reminded me of Christianity's foundational belief in Eve being responsible for Adam's choice to eat the apple.

Tazzie quietly brought up female circumcision. I looked at her in amazement that she had the *chutzpah* to ask; I was impressed. The girls glanced toward her for a second, and then simply decided the question had not been asked and moved on.

As we were driven home, I think we all had a sense of wonderment at our different worlds and beliefs. I'm sure we all went to bed that night thinking of what each other had said.

The next evening, Tazzie and I went to our favourite Turkish restaurant to continue our thoughts on religion and life. The women's section was in back by the kitchen with walls of plants all around the tables, to separate us from the men's section. Tazzie, having become a Muslim, was slightly paranoid in public and asked me to peer under the plants to see who was sitting on the other side of the wall.

With my head nearly resting on the table to see under the plants, I proceeded to describe the Saudi men on the other side. Our waiter snuck up behind me so that when I turned toward

Tazzie, he was right there in my face, and I screamed.

He pointed up. "No need ma'am. Look up."

We all looked up to a mirrored ceiling. Not only could we see the men behind the planted wall, they saw everything we were doing. We all had a great laugh, which was taboo.

A nervous manager appeared, whispering, "Sshhh. Quiet. Put on your *abayas*. Mutawa." They patrolled through the restaurant—staring at each of us, looking at my fake Saudi beer—completely intimidating. Meanwhile, Tazzie desperately tried to extinguish her cigarette because Muslim ladies cannot smoke in public. It felt like a scene out of *Casablanca* when the Nazis walked through the restaurant.

After they left, we settled down into a nice evening. It was clear that Tazzie, too, was a bit of a lost soul, looking for love, adventure, and drama. She asked me if I minded a personal question. "Did you ever have a baby?"

I admit I was very surprised. No one had ever asked that. I said yes and, very softly and quickly, told her the bare minimum of my story.

"How did you know that?"

"Just a feeling." She smiled. Tazzie confessed that she had wanted to know about me and sent my picture to a psychic in England. She wanted particularly to find out if I was leaving the kingdom. The psychic told her I had a lot of pain, had experienced much, had many secrets, and was full of fear.

I felt unable to tell Tazzie everything about what I was dealing with, and we chalked most of my fear up to my current situation. I knew in my heart of hearts that I was carrying a much deeper level of fear—of life, of death, of hell. And there we sat, two young women both in search of the seemingly unreachable state of nirvana.

Tazzie finally felt safe to tell me why she became Muslim. She was secretly "dating" a Pakistani Muslim limo driver. As it is forbidden for women to sit in the front of a limo, the extent of her relationship was sitting in the backseat, while he looked at her through the rearview mirror! From this, she fell in love with him. He and his marriage proposal were the reasons she became Muslim. She asked if I thought she was making a mistake, and I had to be honest. I thought it was kooky, and I was scared for her.

She, however, loved drama, and this was something to be excited about. Regardless of her quirkiness, Tazzie was a dear friend, and without her, I wouldn't have gotten to know the ins and outs of Batha or Dhira and other amazing places within Riyadh. We shared a common goal in our quest for love. I think we both knew that without ever saying it.

Near the doorway of the restaurant, there was a birdcage with two lovebirds, madly pecking away at each other. We could only assume the Mutawa did not know love or affection when they saw it, because they allowed the lovebirds to stay.

The manager said, "Cover your hair. Mutawa is waiting outside." He apologized for the abrupt end to the fun, which was the first time I realized these managers must fear losing business because of the Mutawa. They get temporarily shut down all the time for ridiculous non-reasons. We assured him we knew it was not his fault; we loved his restaurant and would be back, we said.

The Mutawa were just pulling away when we jumped into a limo. But they spotted us and did a u-turn back toward us. Our driver was scared, refused to speak to us, and kept looking in his rearview mirror. We were slightly paranoid, because we didn't know if he was working with them or not. We yelled for him to hit the gas, and he finally rocketed us out of there. Starsky-al-Aziz and al-Mohammed Hutch were left in our dust.

Sinking Relationships

I received only one Christmas card—from my mother. It simply said, *Love, Mom and Dad*. There was the usual *you can't hide from us* feeling, because we had not been connected for so long and certainly didn't write each other. It was like my mother was just letting me know that she knew where I was and what I was doing.

The only other family communication during my entire year in Saudi was a letter from Lorita, telling me she had been high one night and stormed over to Mom and Dad's to confront Dad.

She wrote that she could see his heart beating out of his chest as he stood there, demanding that she leave. Startlingly, those words disturbed me enormously. I felt such sorrow for him. I felt his weakness and his fear, maybe because I knew what it was like for my damaged heart to beat out of my own chest. I felt the pain, and it made me feel sickened that she did that to him. I had no satisfaction that someone in my family finally confronted him, because it was done in such a mean spirit—that's not what I wanted. I am so grateful that my spirit felt compassion rather than a sense of wicked satisfaction that he had been hurt.

Contemplating doing a runner over Christmas, I applied for my thirty-day vacation, only to be turned down by Ginete. She said I was not allowed to leave for that long, which was an out-and-out lie, because many people, especially if travelling far away, went for the whole month. I went as far as to say my father was very ill, but she didn't care, nor did she cave in. Choosing not to fight this battle, I just dropped it. I was more than halfway through my contract and could see the finish line.

I had always experienced sadness around Christmas, with the peace and love I desired seemingly elusive. The season always stirred my soul, and was a reminder of all that was wrong in my family. God, I missed Lorraine.

Somewhere buried in my consciousness, I understood that I was cocooning myself within everyone's "love" in Saudi. The friends, parties, and relationships were like a gift. I was accepted and felt, maybe for the first time, that I belonged. My soul-searching was giving me a small hiatus and allowing me to feel the warmth of belonging to a tribe.

But in truth, I wasn't really on a break. I was very distraught and couldn't help looking at Ginete and Dr. M. H. as parental figures. I was very angry at how men treated women. I wanted to lead a revolt and sometimes pictured all of the Saudi women shedding their veils and running through the streets free and happy. I had lots of heated discussions with women, some of whom were married to Muslims. Occasionally, one would return to work and say she had a fight with her husband and he slept on the couch because she had confronted him after talking to me.

I just wanted to shake us all up. We were allowing ourselves to be less than we could be, and I wanted us to change. Most importantly, I wanted *me* to change. I wanted to be so much more than what I had learned I was worth.

In my quiet times, I allowed myself to look at the different lives around me. Watching all the ladies fall madly in love with unattainable men, and seeing the extent to which we all went to find happiness, I would sometimes feel an overwhelming burden of sorrow. I felt like we were kids, left unattended to run amuck and look for love in all the wrong places. My playing hard was no longer filling the void. I didn't quite get it that we were all looking *outside* of ourselves for that elusive love.

In the Middle East, there is always a confusing build-up to the start of Ramadan. Rather than simply looking at the calendar for the crescent moon, they must see it with their own eyes—The Committee of the Moon-Sighting Men gaze into the heavens and only when they see the moon does Ramadan commence. If it's a cloudy night, there's a problem.

I had a difficult time with Ramadan. I already hated that women had to be responsible for men's lust, and now, we *infidels* had to stop everything so as not to be a source of temptation to the Muslims. There was no chewing gum, no drinking, no eating, no smoking in public places. I couldn't have a snack or chew a piece of gum or even have a drink of water in my own office. I had to hide water in a closet and sneak a drink behind my office door throughout the day.

The cafeteria windows were decked in black paper so no

Muslims would see in and be tempted. Muslim staff worked 6 hours while we continued our 9 ½ hour day.

I had a serious anger management problem with the lack of accountability. They were the ones fasting during the day, and I felt strongly that *they* should be accountable for their own actions. Wouldn't being strong in the face of temptation be more admirable?

Their laws about other religions exacerbated my anger. *It is forbidden* to celebrate, or even mention, Christmas. *It is forbidden* to celebrate any other faith other than Islam, and we were told not even to say "Merry Christmas." That didn't help my anger and I just didn't care—I said *Merry Christmas* to everyone. Everything seemed archaic and bizarre, and our mutual lack of respect for each other was blinding.

Ramadan is like working the night shift. After fasting all day, feasting and celebrations happen throughout the night, beginning at sunset. It's like having a Thanksgiving or Christmas feast every night for one month.

Eid Al Fitr is a three-day celebration of the end of Ramadan, where a feast of lamb is the main course. For Muslims, the lamb is symbolic of Abraham sacrificing his son Ishmael. Interestingly, the Old Testament and Judaism say it's Ishmael's brother, Isaac, who was sacrificed. The New Testament and Christianity announce the "sacrificial lamb" to be Christ.

I was so turned off by all the rules and what I perceived as the phoniness of religion. In one breath, I was trying to find peace in God, and in the next breath, I was in such an angry place. I felt explosive. We all seemed to be drifting, blinded by the sandstorm.

Muslim Tazzie mirrored my sense of being lost. Western women with a Muslim *iqama* were watched closely during Ramadan and Eid. This made seeing her Pakistani limo driver more difficult than usual, though not difficult enough to stop their marriage plans.

I was stunned. Tazzie sensed he had a wife in Pakistan—which he denied. She had never even looked at him face-to-face, and yet she was going to Pakistan to marry him. I understood wanting adventure and drama, but this seemed extreme. Tazzie headed to Pakistan to become his bride. But she wasn't gone for long.

Upon her return, she looked shell-shocked. Closing all the windows, making sure that my roommate wasn't around, she stuttered over her words, trying to keep control of her emotions.

Tazzie had waited in the designated Pakistan hotel for eight days and saw or heard nothing from her Romeo. It was on the third day that he was to meet her, and as each hour ticked by, she sat alone. He stood her up. She went to a Pakistani palm reader who told her everything without knowing anything. She told Tazzie that Romeo was married with a child. His wife had heard of Tazzie and, knowing that she might become wife number two, had put a hex on Tazzie. The palm reader warned Tazzie that she was going to become very sick, which in Pakistan, isn't a far-out guess because of the different food and hygiene. Needless to say, Tazzie got very sick while there.

Back in Saudi, she was more distraught than ever. Together, we spoke with a Pakistani female doctor at our hospital. Dr. Mahmoud took it very seriously, saying spiritual hexes and curses are very common in Pakistan—no one doubts their power. She gave Tazzie some Valium and sleeping pills to help get through her trauma. I couldn't help but wonder how I, or anybody, would have handled this in our real worlds. It seemed that something like this could only happen in this strange kingdom we lived in.

Tazzie struggled for a few weeks and then, on a trip to Batha, who should be her limo driver but Romeo. They would reestablish and continue their backseat relationship until the end of my contract. Where things went from there, I don't know. I had a habit of burning bridges.

Tired of the craziness, I was excited about a desert trek, organized through the hospital. Driving down the "Road to Mecca," we passed steep cliffs and hills on either side of the road, which narrowed as we edged our way further into the Red Sands.

Bedouins in their black tents dotted the landscape. This was their home. In the city of Riyadh, there are hundreds of apartments standing empty. The Royal family built them in an attempt to bring the Bedouins in from the desert. They came, didn't understand a toilet, and left, choosing to return to nomadic life. When they would come into the hospital, they had culture shock, standing on toilets, eating and sleeping on the floors, surrounded by a circle of family members who stayed throughout their time in-hospital. Nurses complained that they had to take more care of families than the patients themselves.

The dunes were a brilliant red. I walked up one in my bare feet but couldn't make it to the top—my heart pounded from the strenuous climb. I asked what the view at the top was and everybody laughed. "More sand!" they said in unison.

The catering staff laid out Arabic carpets on the desert floor, and we sat to eat a feast of shish kebabs, salad, rice, and desserts. Huge camel spiders, which are apparently deadly, would roll like mini-tumbleweeds across the carpets and food, and leave everyone screaming. The kitchen staff would beat them silly, laughing at our fuss.

I met Wanda in the Red Sands. She was fresh off the boat from America, and we all had a laugh at her hysterics over the camel spiders. Wanda was a flaming bottled redheaded Miami goddess, complete with makeup, nails, jewellery, and hair bigger than Texas. She was asked to tone it down, take off the fake nails and calm her hair down. Wanda did not take well to that. She was a divorced, mid-fifties woman who was stepping out of normalcy for something exotic.

Enter her Arabian knight. The fact that he was married—to three wives—meant nothing. She met him while he visited his sick father in hospital, and the affair began immediately. His exotic features next to her flamboyant looks proved to be so opposite, the differences met around the other side.

Having passionate affairs was nothing new: men with men, women with men—those Saudi men got lucky anyway they wanted. Because the women in Saudi are treated so cruelly, there seemed to be no need to get ethical about one man's cheating. I think a part of me liked that he was leaving his wives alone for a while.

As being in Saudi magnifies life's dramas a hundred times over, Wanda was in love within days. She would feel weak at the knees as he stood there in his *goutrah* and white *thobe*—her own Ali Baba.

Mr. Ali Baba had mentioned the camel races were coming, and Wanda thought of it as a date, temporarily forgetting that she could not be seen in public with any man, never mind a Saudi. Still wanting to attend, Wanda asked me to go. She was very angry when I said absolutely not. Did she not remember Recreation Bob telling us that he refused—on ethical grounds—to take staff? The camel jockeys were all very young, little boys—*all* TWNs—with no provisions given to them for protection during the race—not even proper helmets. Every hospital within the kingdom had seen their share of brain damaged little boys who fell during the race. Their lives were disposable; never would you see a Saudi child riding in a camel race—but Wanda still desperately wanted to be close to her lover. My answer remained the same.

I realized I hadn't seen Wanda in over a week and decided to pop in, sure that she was still angry at me for not going to the camel races. I found her lying on the couch crying. She was very distraught and confessed that sex was not as exciting as she had been pretending. He would only have intercourse with her from behind; he would never face her during intimate moments. And he insisted Wanda shave her pubic hair, because it was unclean.

I lost it. "What about his bloody hairy body?" I cried out. "Why isn't *he* unclean? Don't you see this is abuse toward women?"

Wanda snapped out of her sadness and quickly started defending him. It was his custom and he loved her, she insisted. I watched her turn her back on herself, and again, it felt so familiar. She declared to me that she respected Mo's wishes and directed her anger at me, accusing me of being upset and hating men because I was gay. She ended by saying, "How could *you* possibly understand?"

With that, it was hopeless to explain that I knew what she was doing. It was impossible to tell her that I had often stood right where she was standing. One moment, I would be abused by Ferzat, and by many, many others; in the next, I would dismiss the event and continue to deny how I was being treated. How I wanted to tell her that I *did* understand her and her need to pretend that she was being loved.

I did manage to spit out a judgement, though. I let her know how sad it was that in such a short time, she had accepted the abuses thrown at women. Needless to say, that didn't go over very well. We had a huge fight and never really spoke again.

Life after life seemed so sad—the western women were putting themselves in such painful situations. Tazzie and Wanda were only two samples of the chaos. Why were we all struggling so hard? In that sense, I didn't feel alone.

Trying to find respect for Saudi men was proving even more difficult than finding a soul in Ginete. My anger was always bubbling not too far under the surface. Even the little things were getting to me. I was at our grocery store, the Euromarchè, asking a limo driver a question when behind him, a carload of young Saudis began honking and yelling for the limo to move and for me to get out of the way. I screamed at them, "Just wait a bloody minute!" Thank Allah, they started laughing at me and bowed their heads in mock apologies to me. I could have been imprisoned.

It felt like everything was crashing in and my coping skills were disappearing. Even a simple outing to an open-air flea market turned hostile. Recreation Bob told everyone to meet back at the bus in two hours. People dispersed in pairs, and Carolyn and I went off to shop.

About fifteen minutes later, a group of young Saudi men—not Mutawa—surrounded us and yelled, "Get out! Cover your hair and get out!" As usual, my hair was covered except for my fringe. We were a bit frightened because their yelling drew attention, and I was aware of how easily a frenzy could be created. Insanely defending our right to be there, I tried to talk to them because they were just young punks with no authority—not that that mattered to them. The ringleader stepped up to within inches of my face, furiously spitting, "Get out. *Now!*"

Carolyn and I turned and walked away, furious that their behaviour was acceptable in this culture. We scurried to the other end of the market and felt safer there, but the band of bullies soon followed us. As I knelt to look at something, I saw sandals gather all around me. I stood up to find myself encircled by them—again. The leader of the pack started to scream in Arabic, as he flailed his arms in my face. As we fearfully walked toward our bus, we wondered how the other women had fared. The bus was locked, and we had to stand outside with nowhere to go in the heat of the desert, not willing to endure any more humiliation at the hands of young, power-hungry men with the cultural right to intimidate any woman they saw fit.

My tongue was getting bruised from biting it.

The Chief of Medicine dropped by to see how I was doing. We talked about the stress of all the firings, and about the anxiety I was feeling from my work situation and Ginete's constant bombardment of abuse.

He confided to me that he had also experienced Ginete's and Dr. M. H.'s wrath. He had previously been told that his wife had to quit her nursing position immediately, or he would not be recontracted. His wife had dared to confront Ginete, and now, she was being punished. Sixty years old and near retirement, he'd swallowed his pride, and his wife quit her job. It's a day-by-day contract here.

He happened to mention that the American base had a counsellor, whom many of the staff utilized. I was ready for help. For the first time in my life, I was off to lie down on the leather couch. I had no idea my past was alive and well in my present. At this point, I had no contact with my parents, not even an address. I was about to realize how much their presence remained active in my life and my relationships at work.

I needed to talk with Lorraine. To make a long distance phone call was anything but spontaneous. You had to submit a request in writing at least twenty-four hours before, and then the hospital operators would make the call for you—maybe. I could not have dialled an outside number, even if it was an emergency. Often, switchboard forgot and said, "*Bukra. Bukra. Insha'allah*— Tomorrow. Tomorrow. God be willing." I had to contain my anger when hearing this again and again. I knew I was being told, "If I bloody well feel like it tomorrow." Everything they did not feel like accepting responsibility for was an "*Insha'allah* moment." Allah certainly took the blame for a lot of choices they made—or didn't make.

Lorraine was so supportive and happy that I was getting help. Neither of us knew it would be life-altering. We both just thought I would learn ways to cope with my anger over bosses, men, and even the women and their crazy love affairs. This kingdom was so backward in terms of western-world reality that I wished I had been more sensitive to what I wrote in my letters to Lorraine. I'm sure they sounded frantic and a wee bit crazy—all the more reason why she strongly supported my seeking guidance.

I was collapsing under the hostile attacks from Ginete. Friends would try and help me. She wasn't worth it, they'd say, but I wasn't able to cope. She just got under my skin.

I had another nightmare. Again, my "self" was divided into two people. I was locked in the basement with my father. I tried to get up the stairs and made it halfway, but Dad got in front of me and blocked me from the door. The handle was only a few feet from my grasp; the basement was black and ghostly, cold and scary. The door opened a crack. I stood there, peeking from behind the door, and urged the "me" in the basement to come up to the light. My dad slammed the door shut.

I woke up with anxiety. Everything felt so real. I felt my dad's controlling power over me; I felt my fear and hopelessness; and I felt the darkness of the basement entombing me. My dreams often showed me as two separate people, yet the same; one was either dead or held captive while the other was free. I wanted to become one with the free me.

The Other Side of the Door

Pacing outside of Dorinda's office, nervously awaiting my first session, I could hear the voice of a gay brother. The door opened and out walked Mario. We both flushed with embarrassment. It's such a close environment—there is no hiding anything.

My nervousness soon washed away, as Dorinda turned out to be very gentle and easy to talk to. A social worker by trade, she told me she had a full-on counselling business in Saudi, which came as no surprise.

I naively thought counselling was going to be all about Ginete and how I could deal with her. When Dorinda changed the subject from Ginete and asked me about my family and upbringing, I felt a lump form in my throat. *Uh-oh... did we have to go there?*

The office lighting was very bright, and I wanted to hide. I asked if I could dim the lights, and Dorinda allowed me to turn off the overhead lights and turn on the softer lamps, making it dark and cozy. I felt a bit safer. I would begin each session this way, always surprised that the previous clients endured the "spotlight." Dorinda said I was the only one who changed the lighting.

Other than opening up to Terri just prior to heart surgery, this was the first time I had ever talked in a counselling session about my parents, or gone into details about my incestuous-type relationship and the subsequent wrath of my family. I shared my fears about my dad dying and me not having closure. I mentioned that I felt an internal hysteria that once he died, I would be forever lost in a madness of unfinished longing for things to be different. My dad had been dying of emphysema for years now, and time was running out.

I gave my history of how I tried getting married, became a born-againer, which led to an exorcism to expunge the devil from me, which then led to my mother and brother kidnapping me. I tried to laugh at how being born-again wreaked havoc in my life. I had difficulty telling Dorinda that I'd had a baby, because that subject was off-limits to everyone—including me. I buried it as deep as I could.

Dorinda said it was very clear that I was reacting to Ginete and Dr. M. H. as authority and parental figures. I could have just as easily put my parents in their place, and, in fact, I had. She felt I had a form of post-traumatic stress disorder.

When asked if I ever thought to look up my baby girl, I abruptly said no. I finally admitted that it was my biggest fear to find her; I was petrified that my parents would be right and she would be mentally retarded or insane because of me. Throughout my pregnancy, my parents told me repeatedly what a monster my baby would be, and I think somewhere, not so deep inside, I felt akin to the young mother in *Rosemary's Baby*. The way my parents talked, they convinced me—I had, on more than one occasion, been told I was a child of the devil. I shared with Dorinda that I checked my baby out completely upon her birth, to make sure all limbs were there—at least that would be a fighting chance for normalcy. Because it was such a closed subject, I think Dorinda decided to refocus on my parents and me. After all, that's where my problems started, and I needed to work through why I was making the choices I was making.

She began to teach me about responding versus reacting, but at that time in my life, it did not come easy. For me, not reacting was a sign of weakness, passivity, and cowardice. It made no sense to sit quietly while being attacked, to walk away, or to say nothing. I *had* to attack back. In hindsight, I now feel like a stranger to that belief system, but at the time, I had clearly developed my own survival code.

I was being introduced to new concepts and learning about perceptions. Whom did it hurt? Did Ginete get hurt by my crying endless hours of grief over her? Did her day alter in any way by my being so angry and explosive inside and feeling such hatred? Whom did it hurt? I admitted that it made me even more furious to see her smiling as I sat wounded in the corner. I wanted her to feel my hurt.

I learned not only about my own energy circuits but also about other people's energy—positive and negative. What I had always referred to as a "vibe," I now understood was really an energetic vibration that existed within every living thing.

The concept of *choice* in what I did with my energy and power was introduced but took a while for me to understand. Did I want to give my power away? Did I want to keep it? Did I want to consider redirecting it? All of my reactions were my choices. At the time, I never thought I had a choice—I was too busy defending myself by attacking back and then crumbling at not being loved.

Dorinda was very skilled at revealing my insecurities as reflections of the chaos in my life. I saw how I allowed authority, parents, and men to embed turmoil in my internal dialogue. I allowed the behaviour of others to define who I was. Although I appeared tough on the outside, I was really a frightened, angry, insecure little girl who had not yet developed self-worth, self-esteem, or self-love.

I was being shown and taught how to detach myself somewhat in order to observe my feelings in action. In practicing this and reviewing my experiences every week, I learned to step out of the heat of the battle and evaluate what I saw. If I stepped out of my body to *escape* reality, why not step out of my body to *rewrite* reality. These were my first baby steps in breaking old, familiar habits.

During our next session, a breakthrough happened. As I wandered through my past relationships, I admitted to seeing a darkness within me—a rage. A memory played before me, as if I was watching an old movie, and I shared it with Dorinda.

While waiting for heart surgery, Frances had come back into my life as a friend, but inside, I had an unresolved anger toward her—it was palpable. It jumped out during a brief conversation. It was quite a surprise to hear that she was now on a spiritual quest of her own. I believe that's what triggered my fury.

"I feel I came into your life to help bring you back to God," Frances declared.

"*Really?* I've always blamed you for taking me *away* from God!" After all, I was trying very hard to be a born-againer, fending off her constant advances until my defences wore down—at least—that's how I saw it. And now, she was being "religious"!

For the first time, I saw how my blaming *her* for "taking me from Jesus" was a way of losing my personal power. I was beginning to grasp how I owned my own choices—this was a first for me.

Dorinda was impressed. She knew that every person, every situation gave us an opportunity to choose.

In ending our session, I mentioned that a few months past heart surgery, Frances had invited Lorraine and I to The Centre for Spiritual Living—their mission—learning to live from *Spirit*. I hadn't been inside a "church" in years, and so, when invited to attend winter solstice services, I walked through the doors in fear, but I walked out with a small sense of love—my trepidation of God was still overpowering. I had written a list of things I was working on—especially forgiveness toward my father. The ceremony involved burning the list, and surrendering it to Spirit. Dorinda enjoyed how Lorraine just loved everything; she simply didn't carry fears of God and punishment, and so for her, this was just a beautiful celebration. It was clear to Dorinda why Lorraine was such a gift in my life. I never did thank Frances for introducing me to Spirit in a tangible way—although at the time, I wasn't fully conscious of what the depth of that introduction would hold in my future.

Dorinda asked me if I could see how much anger I was bringing from my past into my present, leading us into deeper discussions about my mother and father. She noted that I was so angry at my mother but not so much at my father. My only explanation was that at the very least, he showed some kind of affection, but my mother had only shown anger, rage, and hatred toward me.

The impact of my father's letters had not yet penetrated my soul. In reading them, I would go into shock, which helped absorb my grief. Because I never went back to reread them, it would be several years before I really saw how horrible they were. If I had realized how horrific they were in this moment, I doubt that I would have been so gentle with my dad. I told her that although he stopped drinking when I was born, his behaviour was like a dry drunk.

In Dorinda, I had someone with whom I could communicate and who wouldn't call me a liar. I finally shared the reason why I was so angry at my mom. I explained how I had been so nonchalantly told of my mother's hatred, how Dad had raped her, and how she turned on me. Even as a little girl, I was desperate for my mom's love; I told Dorinda about the card I sent, asking if Mom loved me, and about how my mother had laughed. My dad, on the other hand, never said he hated me. I was so angry at my mother for not protecting me. It was back to the Stockholm Syndrome again—the abused attempting to bond with the abuser.

Being so far away and in such a strange land made my relationship with my parents seem surreal. It all seemed distant, just the way I liked it. As I would talk about my parents, I viewed my relationship with them in an almost out-of-body mode. I felt like I was peering into a looking glass, observing another life, another girl. My life outside of Saudi felt like a dream but was smouldering internally as I brought my sorrows, anger, and fear into my current relationships. It was becoming clearer that I emotionally and physically blew up when dealing with female authority figures, but with male figures, I internalized my rage and redirected it toward myself.

This whole counselling was getting a bit overwhelming for me, and anxiety attacks were not strangers. At the end of each session, Dorinda would skilfully bring me back to the present moment and ensure that my psyche wasn't stuck back in a memory. Sometimes we would sit for a few minutes and just chitchat, until she felt I was clearly present.

Dorinda suggested I write to my dad but said I didn't have to mail it to him. She just wanted me to get out my emotions. She tried role-playing with me, saying she was my mother or my father. She wanted me to yell and get angry, but I just couldn't. I may have saved her life by not jumping into that game! Who knows what rage would have come bubbling up?

She also suggested that I join an Incest Survivor's Group, but my quick retort was that I didn't do well in groups.

"Have you ever been in a group?"

"No."

We laughed and she said to think about it. I never went.

I did, however, write a letter to my father. In it, I confronted him about his feelings toward me, asked him a bunch of questions, requested that he answer them in truth, seal the letter, and arrange for me to receive it upon his death. I tried to explain to him my pain and how he affected me. I pleaded for his truth, feeling that if I gave him the out to give it to me after he died, then he would be honest. I went as far as to tell him I was told of the rape—I felt nervy being on the other side of the planet. I mailed the letter and, as it left my fingertips, realized that he was now going to hear a little bit of my soul crying out—directly to him:

I'm attempting to write this to cleanse my soul of years of pain and anger, and eventually, I would like to be able to forgive you and Mom. I find that when I say the word "forgive," I immediately get angry—it's like I need to hang on to my anger to protect myself. I dare not reach out anymore to you.

I ask you for once to acknowledge my feelings and the truth—before it's too late. I want you to be forced to hear my side, where no one is able to cut me off or you're not able to storm out of the room, like you have done every other time I've tried to seek truth. I do *not* want this letter to be like when I was *forced* to tell all after being kidnapped and you turned it all around, putting it on my shoulders, and then walked away. You did not ask forgiveness, nor feel you needed to be forgiven, for falling in love with your daughter.

Don't you realize the hurt and pain you've caused me? What have I ever done for you to be so mean and cruel? How can you blame me for all the wrong you did—don't you see I'm a person with feelings? All I ever wanted was a normal relationship and to be able to say, "This is my dad." But you destroyed that, and yet I keep loving you *as a dad*.

Sadly, I have to add "as a dad"—isn't it pathetic that I have to feel dirty when I say I love you?

You've blamed me, but how can I be blamed for the way you feel? You're the dad! I want you to know my feelings, but I feel like if I expose them to you, you'll just destroy me.

Your letter after my heart surgery showed no compassion, just anger. I wonder if I died, if your mourning over me would come close to my mourning over what we never had? You've blamed me for going on and on about the past, but guess what? It's not in the past: it's right now—it's never stopped.

You and I know that you attempted to get into bed with me, that you fell in love with me and acted toward me as you would toward a mistress. You pushed Mom into the background and brought me into her role—and on and on. Dad, this is, at the least, emotional incest.

I know you don't have the empathy to support me. I know you will say I am insane. You must know in your heart of hearts that your actions as my father would have a profound effect on me—as a child, teenager, and young woman—right up to today.

As I write, I go from anger to pity to sorrow. And you just want both of us to forget it all. Dad, people can't forget a lifetime of hurt and violation. Everything has created how I feel, think, act, react, communicate, love, and hate.

You've been in Alcoholics Anonymous but I've never heard you say its pledge:

To be accountable for your actions;
To make right all the wrongs;
To admit you have a problem…

Can't you do it before you die? Or can't you just write all the truth in a letter, and I won't read it until you're gone? *Please* don't leave this planet without finally being honest. *Please* don't leave me with the pain I carry—*please* don't.

I began to recognize within me how I felt *personally* attacked by Ginete, Dr. M. H., and other authority figures. I observed my reactions to even simple situations. If someone didn't hand me an attachment in a meeting, but handed it out to everyone else, I would become internally irate and feel that they were personally attacking or ignoring me, because they felt that I was nothing but a secretary. I started to understand that I perceived everyone's actions to be against me because of my own personal hatred of self and complete lack of self-worth.

Dorinda helped me to see and turn away from that damaged perception, to feel my energy changing as I reacted or responded, and to start rewriting my internal dialogue. It was finally beginning to feel silly that I needed to attack back or sabotage situations in order to feel strong and powerful. My perceptions of becoming passive and cowardly if I didn't fight back were changing to an understanding that assertive versus aggressive was a much more powerful and non-abrasive tool.

Up to this point, if Ginete flipped out, my reaction was like pouring fuel on an already burning fire. It was a surprise to both of us when I began to quietly walk away. I learned that my calmness imploded her weapons of mass destruction against me.

During my time with Dorinda, I also discovered my wounded inner child—a lost, needy, insecure little girl who sat right in the centre of my heart and cried out to be loved. *Out of the mouths of babes...* It was her little voice that would be the catalyst for the opening of my heart to forgiveness. I finally heard her torment and her tears. On the suggestion of Dorinda, I went out and bought her a present—a cuddly teddy bear.

That night, as I lay in bed, I pictured her trapped inside me, all alone and crying for someone to come and pick her up. I scooped her into my arms and told her how much I loved her and that I would never leave her alone again—she was safe. I could tangibly feel her tiny body in my arms, which felt so full of strength and love for her. I would take care of her from now on.

In my mind's eye, we went for a walk together, into some of our old 'hoods. I held her precious little hand as we stood together, looking at various houses we had lived in. There was no need to remember all of the sordid details, but only to remember that we were very sad. At each house, I would look down at her and say, "I'm here now and you are safe with me." We would walk to the end of the block and not look back as we turned the corner—letting everything go from that house.

It was very powerful, very intimate, and very safe. "Our" poor little teddy bear was squished to bits from all that hugging.

With sleep about to overcome me, my visions turned to something beautiful: As I had stretched my arms out to scoop up my inner child, I flashed back to when Mother Mary appeared, with her arms outstretched to me, while I had sat, so frightened, on that plane. I never understood it then, but now, I felt her divine mothering come through me to "us."

Dorinda helped me to see both my adult self and myself as a little girl, and to interpret whether a reaction was the child's or mine. I had also returned to the place where I could open a door to God again. Dorinda always said I sounded like a Buddhist and slowly, slowly, I began to talk with God. I told him how afraid I was of him and of being damned to eternal hell. It was another beginning, with lots of bumps and falls along the way.

Dorinda was such an extraordinary, wonderful, gentle and supportive counsellor. When the time came for us to end, she gave me a painting. She had laid to rest her artist inside, she said, but through me felt a stirring to draw again. Her painting was in an Australian aboriginal style, because she had spiritually learned so much through them while living in Australia. It was of footprints through the desert, wandering full circle and coming to rest at a mirage of water—representing life force within a parched desert. She couldn't have expressed my journey more beautifully.

My journey in this desert became less barren as I began to have clarity about why I was behaving the way I was. I have precious Dorinda to thank for that.

I no longer had such an intense need for partying and superficialities. It was time to become more introspective again. I became much happier, even though Ginete never changed a follicle!

Travels Through Time and Spirit

The deserts were always full of magic. I am so thankful to Jackie and her husband Grant, because if not for their friendship, I would never have experienced journeys back through time.

On one occasion, Grant came to pick me up—without Jackie. It was only on his way through the security gates that he realized he was meeting a woman who happened *not* to be his wife! I had to sneak into his car and hide while we went back through security.

With check stops and roadblocks to monitor movement, you cannot travel two miles in any direction without a security check. I decided just to act like his wife and hope for the best. We were both giddy with nervousness as I crawled into the front seat, next to my new husband. I would have landed in prison if I'd been caught. Up to that point, I had never heard of a man being arrested; it seemed always and only to be women.

Throughout the year, I spent the occasional weekend having a sleepover on Jackie and Grant's compound, which was a treat in itself. Not only was this compound beautiful, with no Saudi nationals, making for complete freedom to walk around in shorts or bathing suits or whatever, but they also had real alcohol. It wasn't that I drank a lot, but when you know you can't is when you want to do it even more. Compounds housing military, oil, or diplomatically immune staff, supply alcohol for their personnel. The rule was that every bottle in must equal every bottle out. After one party, everyone was on hands and knees looking for a lone beer bottle, and the search didn't stop until it was found; they took this very seriously.

They joked with their friends, whom I dubbed the uppity British aristocrats of Saudi, that they had pulled me off the streets to befriend me in order to keep them well-rounded and in touch with the "people." I said I was actually an heiress but wanted a taste of life with the lower classes. I was their Eliza and they were my Henry Higgins.

There were always social functions, sit-down dinner parties, formal dances, none of which were part of the daily repertoire in my real world. Jackie and I loved playing dress-up; I tried on her gorgeous gowns and she put makeup on me. It was nice to feel sexy, and wear something that fit, rather than a baggy outfit hanging eight inches below the knee.

Some of the party-goers had top-secret jobs, and hard as I tried, I couldn't get anything out of them. I spent a weekend shortly after Baghdad had been bombed and was impressed that none of them discussed it, war, or anything to do with their jobs. Off duty was off duty. I admired how they were able to disassociate from their work and enjoy their lives to the fullest while on their tour of duty in the kingdom.

Jackie was cheerily knocking at my door within a few hours of my head resting on the pillow, after a very late evening of dancing. "We're off for a desert trek. C'mon. We've got us a convoy!"

Once the Tylenol kicked in, I was thrilled. Coffee and real toast later, we were off to the Najad desert. The ride was so bumpy I wished I had a crash helmet on—and a back brace. Our 4x4 crashed over rippling sandbars created by the winds; it was like hitting wave upon wave on a stormy sea. There were wild camel herds everywhere. Nomadic Bedouin tribes, with their black tents, tended to their goats and dotted the otherwise barren terrain.

The convoy followed very strict rules. No one was to question the lead driver. Everyone's mileage was set to zero. Compasses pointed to true magnetic north and exact coordinates were followed: N28° x SW7°—drive exactly 7.5 miles south, turn left, drive 1.2 miles west, and so on. These directional charts were "classified" and "top secret," because once the Saudis found out, they would attempt to catch people in the desert. It would often feel like we were spinning endlessly around in circles, but suddenly, we would arrive.

There stood Pinnacle Point. If there had been any clouds, her reach would have pierced through them. The panorama of desert, and this secret place standing in solitude felt thrilling, eerie, treacherous, inhospitable, and incredibly beautiful all at once.

The challenge, should I choose to accept it, was to climb the tallest of the two pinnacles. I was petrified but Jackie would have none of it; she grabbed my hand, insisting that we were doing this together.

There wasn't enough ledge room for us to be side by side, so I was forced to walk behind her, trying not to look at the drop-off immediately on my left. After the ledge, we scrambled down one escarpment and climbed up the backside of the pinnacle. The top was like a flat pancake with enough space for only twenty people to stand. The view was breathtaking.

The only sound was of the wind. My spirit was soaring, and I felt like dancing a native Indian dance, for I sensed that their spirits were present. *Was there a connection to this land and our native Indians?* I wondered. One thing for sure, this was a spiritual experience.

As I imagined myself, dressed in feathers, dancing to the sun and the wind, I remembered a story that Myrna—Frances's partner before me—had told a long time ago. Myrna and I had always had a love/hate relationship, and oddly, I felt like I had always known her. Even before I met her, there were things I seemed to know about her.

One evening, after a few drinks, Myrna shared her experience. She was into past-life regression and various spiritual quests, which of course, at the time, I believed all to be satanic. When I saw pictures of her walking over fire, she got my attention. Myrna was put in a trance and went back in time to another life, in which she was an army officer in the 1800s, when North America was at war with the native Indians. I was an Indian princess and she had fallen in love with me. Another Indian band kidnapped me, and Myrna, along with her troops, attempted to rescue me. In the confrontation, she was killed.

I said, "So, you died for me," at which Myrna got very upset, because in our present day life, we almost never got along. She'd rather kill me than die for me. My friends joked, saying that even in this lifetime, I was treated, and acted, like a princess—maybe I had been an Indian or Arabian princess in a past life, and that's why I was always called back to the desert.

Standing there on top of Pinnacle Point, the closest I've ever been to the heavens, already feeling native spirits around me, I recalled that I had also been kidnapped in this lifetime. And right now, military personnel surrounded me. I knew that my feelings and senses were being exposed to a mystical correlation that far surpassed any previous beliefs and allowed me to savour this mixture of alchemy and spirits—and me. *Yeha-Noha*—Sacred Spirit.

It was wonderful to be outside of my body and back into spirit.

Jackie and I were last to start the climb down. Grant kept shouting, "Watch the hole." We were expecting a small hole where you could turn your ankle.

"Do you mean this hole?" we laughed. You couldn't miss it. Looking into a hole the size of a crater, I felt like I was about to free-fall into eternity.

Other weekends brought equally glorious adventures. From the Empty Quarter, to desert roses, to an ancient petrified forest— these vast, uninhabitable deserts allowed us to peek into the window of time.

I would get such a rush as I touched wood, or rocks or stones, from a forest that grew millions of years ago; and I would marvel as I lay searching for shark's teeth on what was once the bed of the ocean. Talk about feeling the energy of life. Could there be a better way to enjoy Saudi?

As with any archaeological dig, it took us a while before that first tooth was found. Lying on our bellies, our sun-screened faces becoming gritty, catching millions of granules of sand, the 120F sun beating down on us, we were kids in a big sandbox, as we held up our finds. Mine met with laughter as we compared a real shark's tooth to my dry ball of camel dung. I was sure I had a molar! Coming from a shark-tooth dig into a petrified forest all in one day was nothing short of phenomenal.

We drove by a wind-carved rock, shaped like a lion, that stood guard at the entrance into the supernatural petrified forest. I just knew angels and spirits were there amongst the ruins. I felt them. This forest stood in the middle of the desert and was covered in lava from a volcano millions of years ago, and it wasn't easily accessible. The passageway up the gorge, which we were expected to conquer, looked impossible. It was inspiring how the 4x4s got through the ravines. Allah help you if you got stuck.

Driving straight up to the heavens through a narrow crevice was both frightening and exhilarating, and it became a sexual experience between driver and assistant. As Grant commandeered the vehicle, Jackie would scream out, "Come on.

Come on, Grant. Keep going. *Don't stop.* Yes. *Yes.* You can do it. That's it. Keep going. Brilliant. Dig in. Gas it. Full throttle! C'mon. Push. *Puuussshhh!"*

I found it hilariously funny to be a backseat voyeur on this excursion. I would try and join in as Jackie motivated her husband, but it was much more fun just to listen. Besides, two women telling Grant he was brilliant might have been a recipe for disaster if it overstimulated his motor skills. After getting out of our 4x4, we all hugged; he stood trembling with excitement at the thrill of conquering the mountain.

I performed my sexual experience re-enactment while my audience roared with laughter. Someone stood by, filming me on a camcorder, and as the day went on, various people had quite a giggle watching the mini-film.

Jackie had invited two doctors from her office to join the trek, which originally made me a little nervous, as both were closely connected to the Mad Hatter. As our day progressed, they laughed and said they had no idea how much fun I was. I shared a little of Ginete being an albatross around my throat, and they admitted that they also had their problems with her and tried to avoid her at all costs.

Letting go of work, I joyfully accepted their invite to go climbing. The shale hill was a bit difficult and very slippery, as we staggered our way up. Once we reached the top, our group appeared a long way off; we tried yelling down to them but to no avail. Walking along the top ridge, we stumbled across what appeared to be a native Indian burial ground; there were two adult graves with stone markers and one tiny grave in the middle. The three of us stared in amazement. How long had these been there, and who were they?

The guys went off exploring, and I stayed behind. I could see our camp, although no one there could see me, and so it was safe to be alone. This time, I danced.

This could not be a coincidence. Each of these deserts was enigmatic; each felt connected spiritually. The wind blew softly over my face and through my hair, the sun shone so brightly, and everything felt in such perfect harmony. I danced to the music of the hills, mountains, valleys, the forest, and the seabed from antiquity—it had all been here forever! My heartbeat was my drum. All of this energy surrounding me had born witness to the beginning of life itself. I wondered how long my spirit had been here?

By the time I rejoined the docs, I felt like I had been travelling through time and space—floating through the cosmos, dancing on the moon, sliding into the back of beyond, until suddenly I was deposited back into my body and into the present moment. My astro-travels had made me thirsty and hungry. It was time for a cool one!

At work a few days later, I told a doctor about my belief that the deserts had native spirits present. He got excited and said that he had been scared to mention "spirituality" to anyone because it was forbidden. He proceeded to take out of his pocket what looked like arrowheads that he had found in the desert.

Ginete began to show cracks in her armour. I had been too busy dodging her bullets to notice how paranoid she was—until she started speaking of her fears about men. A patient had been sexually assaulted, and security had become even tighter than usual. Ginete usually showed no emotion in any given situation, but this time, she was really afraid. It was the first time I saw her vulnerability and her humanness.

Penny suggested we try and befriend Ginete by inviting her out. I made the effort and she accepted our invitation to go to Pizza Hut.

Our timing was off—it was ten minutes to prayer time and they were closing the doors. I suggested we hop in the limo and get a falafel to go, but Ginete became agitated and angry that Pizza Hut "refused her business." She had been in Saudi eighteen years and knew that everything shuts down for prayer, but interestingly, she seemed to take it personally. There lay another subtle lesson about looking in the mirror and seeing my reflection in someone else's behaviour.

As Penny and I began walking down the street to hail a limo, Ginete became quite neurotic and admitted that she had never walked anywhere but in the compound. This was unbelievable to me. *Extremely institutionalized* came to mind. She was close to agoraphobic. I saw the fear she had when she went beyond her own mini-kingdom. Outside, no one cared about her passport and she felt like a TWN, an East Indian—and a woman: she had no power to wield.

This trip allowed me to unravel my anger at her abuses and gave me the opportunity to see past them, into her soul. Ginete did have a soul! She, too, mistook events as a personal attack on her and felt enraged. She, in all of her pseudo-power, was really a scared, insecure, fearful girl who hated being in her skin. She berated, and was prejudiced against, those whom she wanted to have beneath her, but in truth, she was also looking in a mirror.

I was getting it. Ginete and I were very much the same and had many similar life lessons to learn. We were two broken, hurt women, allowing our wounded child within to rule our emotions. Could I dare go as far as to thank Ginete?

I came out of my thoughts to the voices of Ginete and Penny arguing about going home. "Ginete, if you're that upset, take a limo back to the compound and we'll see you tomorrow," Penny said, tired of the battle.

That silenced Ginete because she was afraid to be in a limo alone. The three of us finally ordered delicious falafel sandwiches at my favourite takeout, and to compromise, we took them back to Ginete's apartment and ate them around her table. It no longer felt like I was sitting with the enemy. Ginete was soft and giggly, asked Penny about her boyfriends and, for the first time, looked relaxed. She never asked me about my boyfriends.

Secretaries Day gave a great reason to celebrate gratitude and feel happiness. It had never before been celebrated at the KEG. I bought flowers and a small gift for each of my secretaries and typed a diploma of recognition for each of them; the diplomas listed wonderful qualities about their work and personalities. I arrived early and put their gifts and bouquets on each desk and made a sign for their office door: "It's Secretaries Day. Have you told your secretaries you appreciate them lately?"

They arrived together, and I heard them reading the sign. They were confused because they had not heard of Secretaries Day. When they saw their flowers, they were overjoyed, and as each secretary read her personalized diploma, they tearfully giggled like little girls. The doctors started coming in and thanking them and, throughout the day, brought candies, cakes, and flowers. Ginete appeared and tried to pretend she was happy and appreciative, but her phone call to me moments later to remind me that we were not to show excessive joy almost popped my bubble. Ginete warned me that the girls would now think they were important and would become unmanageable.

I refused to let her rain on our parade. This was one of my happiest days as supervisor. I was elated at being able to show appreciation where it was lacking before. There was such joy in giving love. Secretaries Day sealed a relationship of respect, integrity, and equality between my girls, the department heads, and myself. Lord, it would have been nice to keep the happiness going.

Those Who Have Not Sinned—Cast the First Stone

Rumours started to circulate about a stoning in Chop-Chop Square. An unmarried girl was accused of premarital sex, and her sentence was death. Everyone was talking about this. It was thick in the air. She would be brought out in a bag, so that she could not see anything, and all the men would throw stones at her, starting with small ones, until she died.

Friday, the Muslim holy day, arrived. The call for prayer came at noon, and then it was as if Riyadh stopped breathing. Every woman knew that after prayer, this girl would be executed. I sat in my flat, my heart pounding, as I sensed her fear and torture. I sent her love and angels, and prayed for her to lose consciousness immediately.

I had always enjoyed the lament of the call to prayer; it always felt mystical. But on that Friday, I hated it. I thought of men cleansing themselves before entering the mosque, leaving their women and babies wherever, regardless of the heat, and then walking into the square to cheer, as they stoned to death an innocent soul.

Out of all the executions that took place throughout my time in Saudi, this day was the worst. It was all but unbearable to know that fathers were allowed to do honour killings: they could kill their daughters or wives if they even just suspected some misdeed. Stories abounded about girls being drowned by their fathers, girls being put into a locked room to starve and go crazy, and maids being raped. Even outside the hospital, there were Saudi women begging, forced to sit on the ground and ask for money, while the men walked by and ignored them. These women had been beaten and kicked out for offences mustered up by crazy husbands, and now, their families refused to take them back.

I had always felt in my heart that if I could touch one woman, my time there would be blessed. Touching *me* still didn't quite register in my consciousness.

I spent many evenings at the pool—it was exercise and an escape. Being in the water, under blue skies with palm trees, felt soothing to a tired soul. This night, a young American lady joined me. We talked about the execution, and she had tears in her eyes. She had married a Saudi who had become a religious fanatic and then a Mutawa. She was in her early twenties, with two babies, and knew her freedom was over. Her husband had recently brought home a second wife and now spent most of his time with the new wife. But he would never let her leave the country, especially with the kids. She was in prison for life.

Listening to her helped me to balance my emotional outlook and calm down about work and trivialities. Knowing that I could have been this woman if Ferzat had managed to marry me in Syria brought me to a place of gratitude. Although I had endured many hard lessons, my life was blessed.

Ma'arsalama means good-bye. Several *ma'arsalama* parties were arranged for my farewell to the kingdom. They started with my last banquet with Aida and her girls. We ate a magnificent feast, danced, laughed, and felt free for one more night together. It was so clear that Mamma Aida loved her daughters and would protect them as much as she could. No matter what their fate, she would always support them.

I shared my horror stories of working with Ginete over the course of the last year. Aida was furious and wanted to come to the hospital and speak with Ginete, without Ginete knowing she was my friend.

Aida's husband was a fairly high-ranking man in Saudi, and she said they could get rid of "this Ginete." I kissed her and told her I believed Ginete would stumble when her own karma kicked her in the butt some day. A part of me half-expected to see Aida walk into Administration and have Ginete removed.

Aida held my hand throughout the evening and seemed to watch out for me. I asked her in Arabic if she wanted a cup of tea. "*Sub chai?*" and they laughed as I served her.

Aida was very cool. She was an only wife and told her husband that if he ever came home with another wife, she, Aida, would kill him in his sleep. He never did. Aida attempted for herself and her girls to be as free as possible within Saudi society. She loved watching her girls talk about boys, act sexy, dance, and joke about husbands. Her home always felt like a small cocoon where Aida would allow her girls to become butterflies.

As we sat drinking *chai*, Aida nudged my arm, "You? You have the boyfriends?"

"No." I hoped it wouldn't go any further.

Aida grinned. "Oh. I think you don't like the mens. I think you love women."

I sheepishly said, "Mmh mmh."

She smiled, and that was it. Tazzie heard this and was amazed at how Aida wanted to let me know I was okay. I wondered if she suspected the same about her own daughter, Samira. It seemed so obvious that she was gay, and perhaps her mamma knew and loved her anyway. Wouldn't that be something! I really loved Aida and appreciated a mother being so desirous for her children to be happy.

A knock on the door quieted the girls. Noya motioned for her mother to go to the door. "It's my father," she told us. We had never met him—this relationship was strictly ladies only.

With the girls momentarily unsupervised, Lulu appeared to be bursting at the seams with excitement. "I have met a boy!" she exclaimed. I was shocked and asked how it was possible. Lulu quickly divulged her secret. A favourite pastime for teenagers was, of course, shopping. Lulu and a group of girls would go to one of the malls, see their male peers watching them, and quickly, each girl would walk by and lift up her veil for the boy to see her face. This, I was told, was very common amongst the young. I was thrilled to have a sense of their future—a rebellion against being covered. I asked if she was scared of being caught, but she was too excited at showing her beautiful face to the opposite sex to care of consequences. Lulu and Samira giggled and made me promise never to tell their mother. I loved it. Go girls!

Aida returned and we all settled down. "My husband wishes to tell you that because his family loves you and accepts you as a daughter, he too wishes to accept you as his daughter. He has just returned from Pakistan where he purchased for you this gift. Take this as an offer of love from your Saudi family." She gave me a beautiful hand-painted marble plate.

I was so moved. I'd never met this man, but I felt such a family love from him. A complete stranger showed me more kindness than my own father.

This one family and their genuine love momentarily eased all the horror stories and events that occurred within Saudi Arabia. They were so generous and loving. We were intrigued by our different customs and beliefs, and we enjoyed experiencing our two worlds collide. Through it all, we still saw the similarities we shared and felt love and respect. At least, we tried. I wondered where the girls' lives would go from here. I secretly wished that Aida could protect them forever.

My old rebel socialite friend, Bev, and I took Nedra, a new administrative assistant at the hospital, out for dinner. She was nervous about Saudi and its culture, and we joked that it was easy to adapt—wrong is wrong, and right is wrong. If that got confusing, I recommended just relaxing into her personal "normal," so as not to lose herself completely.

Nedra was already afraid of Saudi and the Mutawa because it appeared stricter than she had imagined possible. It didn't help when our Filipino waiter told us he was afraid—a Mutawa had slapped him in the face on his way to work, for no obvious reason. He was young and just wanted to go home.

I told Nedra she had to stand strong, or fear would conquer her; she must walk with her head held high, with a sense of empowerment and a belief that she was all right.

After dinner, we left the restaurant and went for just such a walk. Nedra stood tall, pretending to have a book on her head, as we proceeded to walk the runway of Riyadh with pride and a few giggles. A whole week had gone by, and we were all so happy because it had felt like no one had been picked up and dumped in prison for ages.

That was all about to change.

Penny, Misha, and I were making plans for the following weekend, with Misha arranging a transportation request for us to go to an underground bazaar. We joked with Misha that she was lucky to find two friends willing to travel with her. While many of us managed to duck out of harm's way, trouble seemed to find Misha.

In the airport at Jeddah, on her way back to Riyadh, a Saudi man approached her, yelling at her to cover her hair. Jeddah was much more relaxed and women only had to wear *abayas* and not head scarves. She continued on her way to board the plane, choosing to ignore the man, but he stormed after her and spit in her face. She was so taken aback, her immediate reaction was to spit back. He then punched her in the nose and broke it. That, sadly, wasn't going to be the last physical violence for Misha.

After arranging transport, Misha invited us to a house party that night. Penny and I decided to opt out.

Misha, Nedra, and Sheena hitched a ride with a married couple, Khaled and Kara. Tony, the compound Casanova, followed in his own car. Unbeknownst to anyone, the house was being watched. Mutawa surrounded it and an all-out lynching was about to unfold.

After leaving the party, Khaled and Kara again drove the three ladies back home, with Tony following in his car. Stopped at a red light, they were ambushed by the Mutawa. Tony and Khaled, Lebanese and Egyptian, were severely beaten up, and Tony sustained broken ribs. This was the first time that I had heard of men getting hurt; even more shocking was that they were both Arabs!

Kara had her skirt ripped off her. Nedra and Sheena were thrown into the back of a police car. Misha was not so lucky.

Mutawa picked her up and sent her flying head first, into the back of the police car. This was after they had kicked and beaten her. While she tried to sit up, a Mutawa leaned into her and slammed her left eye with a right hook. Misha, holding her eye and severely beaten, kept repeating, "Here is my *iqama*. I am American. Take me to an American hospital. Take me to a hospital."

They laughed at her, and she went crazy with fear. She removed her hand, which had been holding her eye in place—the blood began pouring down her cheek. She pointed to her eye, shouting to be taken to the hospital. Seeing all the blood, the Mutawa may have been afraid she was going to die, because they raced her to a filthy clinic—they dared not take her to one of the accredited hospitals, run primarily by westerners. Misha was petrified and would not allow anyone to touch her. As Nedra and Sheena sat in handcuffs, Misha demanded to go to KEG. When the Mutawa finished their *chai*, they first threw Nedra and Sheena into prison and then brought Misha to KEG, leaving her at the hospital entrance and taking off. Fortunately, they forgot to take blood tests for alcohol.

As the news circulated through the hospital, Catering called me and asked what to do with the luncheon goodies. Nedra had ordered a luncheon for me to celebrate my EOC (end of contract) with my secretaries. Needless to say, the luncheon was cancelled. The sick feeling in my stomach was palpable. Where were they? Were they okay? This felt like the day of the stoning.

Tony's job on compound was to immediately find out what prison women were in and to secure their release. Because he was now in prison, we were all the more afraid. Everyone knew that women prisoners were always in danger until they were found. The rule was to locate them sooner, not later. Because of Tony's serious injuries and subsequent hospitalization, the girls stayed in prison for five days. Nobody could replace Tony's skill at communicating with the jail keepers and getting quick releases.

Word finally came that the hospital found the girls and they were okay. There was a collective sigh of relief.

When I finally saw Tony, he was driving through our compound. I stopped when I saw him; he put on the brakes, backed up, got out, and embraced me. I felt his heart pounding. All that was needed was the warmth of a hug. No words were spoken.

Tony and I always had a fun and flirty relationship. At the beginning, he had tried to make me his zillionth conquered love squeeze, but alas, his charm fell on a gay soul. Tony was bisexual and certainly loved his women. After the gay thing was out, we continued flirting, dancing, and partying together. After he got beaten up, I felt like I loved him as a brother. That moment together was so quiet and still and beautiful. Although he had been in Saudi for over ten years, he was now talking of leaving, even though he didn't want to return to his life in Lebanon. Saudi, for so many, offered a bizarre type of freedom.

Misha was in seclusion on the ward. The nurse said she was in shock. I brought her my teddy bear to cuddle but wasn't allowed in. I was told she slept at night cuddling the teddy. Her eye was severely damaged, including a fractured orbit, and she would require several surgeries. There was a sense of grief on the compound as we waited for Nedra and Sheena to come home.

When I saw Nedra, she told me she kept hearing my voice in prison, telling her to just stand tall and be empowered. She didn't feel so empowered. Nedra was devastated and never left the compound again. I would visit her and try and get her to come for a walk in the Diplomatic Quarters where it was a bit safer, but she wouldn't budge.

This gang of thugs—the Mutawa—went on a rampage and nothing came of it. They destroyed people; they destroyed Misha's eye; it was irreparable and would eventually permanently droop down. A beautiful young woman was devastated. And all of it was because of a house party. Yes, there were married people, single men and women, and alcohol. What does that really matter, anyhow?

This event so impacted our hospital that the other women who had previously experienced prison seemed to unravel. I was swimming and Mary came to the pool, her expression anxious. I knew she had previously been in prison and asked how she was handling all this. She was not okay. She had been picked up for prostitution for saying hello to a male friend while standing outside of a hotel. She needed to vent, and so, we sat by the pool, dangling our feet in the water.

While in prison, she was hooded to induce fear, sleep deprived, and given no food. When she, or any other expats were in prison, they would take names and addresses of relatives of the other female inmates—mostly TWNs—who weren't lucky enough to have sponsors to get them out of jail. These ladies, who endured rapes, beatings, broken limbs, and cruelity beyond imagination, all seemed to share a common capacity—compassion and empathy, but more obvious, they still had hold of their spirits. All of them said their families back in the Philippines or other third world countries did not know if they were dead or alive. Each of our imprisoned KEG ladies promised to write the families once they themselves were released.

Nedra, Sheena, Donna, and every other woman who had been in prison, all said that many women were permanently maimed from having broken bones that weren't repaired. Mary confirmed this. Her own experience was equally frightening but at least, her bones were left intact. The Mutawa gave her two choices: be flogged sixty times, or leave the kingdom immediately. Fortunately, our man Tony found her and got her out of prison.

No charges were laid. No flogging and no deportation.

Mary had previously dated Tony and fallen madly in love. With him getting beaten up so badly, she had reached her limit on life in Saudi and decided to go home. Within two weeks, I saw her sobbing as she said good-bye to Tony and the Middle East.

Donna had landed in prison twice. And now she, too, had come to the end of her sanity. She put her notice in, broke her contract, and, forfeiting a large amount of money, left the kingdom.

I received a phone call one evening from Misha. Still in isolation in hospital, she was scared and lonely. I walked over to the hospital, past the front desk, and into her room. We sat together for three and a half hours. My God. Misha still had an imprint from the Mutawa's sandal on her thigh. She had been haemorrhaging behind the eye and had two fractures. She was trembling with fright. I just listened, letting her get it out; I hoped that just being together in that quiet hospital room was some comfort to her.

Misha said the Mutawa were out for blood, like crazed animals on crack. They had blood all over them as they sat drinking *chai* and congratulating each other—while the girls were in handcuffs, and Misha lay bleeding profusely. Rumours flew that the king's son was coming to formally apologize to them.

Usually, women out of prison just dealt with it amongst their close friends. I think there was a previous need not to complain because they landed there by doing something "illegal or immoral." Not this time. These ladies broke down, saying prison was a nightmare.

Jan from E.H. set up a group counselling session with Dorinda, who first met just with the women, and later added Tony and Khaled to the group. As they met in Jan's flat, she and I visited together, rehashing our history. Jan had been the one who refused to alter my medical records, and over time, we became wonderful friends. Jan told me that the girls were sobbing at the beginning of the session, and she felt it was appropriate to leave them alone with Dorinda. After this initial session, each person made a decision whether or not to continue with individual counselling. The women continued.

Not surprisingly, nobody went home right away. Nedra felt she needed to finish her contract for the sake of her boss. I also think they needed time to go by before leaving this world of insanity and merging back into their real worlds. The jump back into "real time" would have been too much for them at this stage.

We found out that Khaled was a black belt. Even as his wife was being stripped of her dress, he never raised a hand, although he could have easily hurt or killed several of their attackers. Khaled said it took 100 percent discipline not to use his black belt. He knew that if he did, he was well outnumbered by a frenzied group of madmen. Although he could have done damage, the group would have taken control and probably killed them all, or at least, the women.

News of the violent incident hit North America and was on CNN. *They were coming from a party and there was alcohol*, was the report. Misha was furious, because it sounded like CNN was blaming them for getting beaten up.

Rumour had it that there might have been a precipitating factor in this extreme violence. A U.S. female soldier was on her military compound and a Mutawa was trying to get in, which was off-limits. The soldier warned the Mutawa that he was not allowed and if he insisted, she would shoot him. He insisted. She shot him. She was out of the country within the hour. A friend of mine, a squadron leader in the military, confirmed the truth of the story.

It was a reprieve to hear the good news from Lenora, one of my secretaries, that she was pregnant. She wanted to tell Ginete herself, perhaps because they were both from India, and she wanted to share her excitement, but she soon returned to my office crying. Ginete's response was to tell Lenora to go to Personnel to see when she would have to exit Saudi. Within the week, an official policy came down from Administration stating that pregnancy would now be grounds for automatic dismissal. There would no longer be an allowed maternity leave. Women would be given two months to exit the country.

Lenora decided to stand up for her human rights and went to Ginete, stating that this rule should not affect her because she had become pregnant before the new policy was created. Ginete said that she was in full control and would choose whether or not to keep Lenora. "I know people like you are desperate for money," she said. At a time when women were holding each other up, and violence was so intense, it was an enormous disappointment to hear Ginete berate a fellow Indian woman.

Lenora's husband, who also worked in Saudi, phoned the next morning. "Lenora is not coming in today." Asked if she were ill, as she'd never had a sick day, he responded, "Yes. She's sick and tired!"

Lenora made a decision that she was not waiting for Ginete to decide her fate. She quit. Nothing less than a revolt followed. I lost another secretary, Ivy, who had also decided she'd had enough. She had worked for over a decade in Saudi and now felt she had enough money to enjoy a good life in the Philippines with her children. Three of four secretaries working in Ginete's office also quit, all tired of being degraded, insulted, and constantly abused. Jackie was one of them.

Ginete soon hired one westerner to replace my two, stating out loud that one western secretary equalled two TWN secretaries—a callous reminder of the socially accepted racial prejudices held within the kingdom. The idea that a woman spoke these words left me deeply saddened. I wondered what Ginete saw when she looked into the mirror.

It was time I had a meeting with my secretaries, prior to their leaving. I attempted to explain what a mental health day was, and told them I wanted them each to take at least one mental health day off per month—they were to call in sick. They were overjoyed at the prospect of being able to take time for themselves without fear of losing their jobs. They worked so hard and had never dared to call in sick before. I took a few mental health days myself.

It felt like Saudi was imploding. Everyone was leaving. There was a rumoured assassination attempt on the king again. The country was saying they were running out of money. Many hospitals, including ours, were concerned about meeting payroll. The Mutawa were becoming more and more aggressive. My trip into wonderland now left me in a purple haze of confusion.

Dr. M. H., the Mad Hatter himself, held tea parties strictly for the medical staff. Never had there been one for any other staff, until me. As word spread that I was ending my contract, the doctors began to speak out, requesting that I stay on. They went as far as to make a statement at each meeting where Dr. M. H. chaired. Dr. M. H. would listen to them declaring their sadness that I was leaving, and he would quietly say, "Let the minutes note Dr. Wafai's comments," or "Let the record state the reflections of the medical staff..."

I was embarrassed and thrilled that the department heads were going out on a limb for me and being so bold as to confront Dr. M. H. in meetings—with Ginete sitting on one side of him, and I on the other, taking the minutes. A memo soon appeared: "The medical director cordially invites the medical staff to attend a farewell tea in honour of Edna..." My secretaries, having worked at the KEG for years, knew it had never happened before; they cried for joy and said they felt so proud of me—one of my most precious delights in Saudi. The memo also noted that the farewell was not only for me, but for my two secretaries who had just quit.

My girls went one step further—they had a *ma'arsalama* party for me as well, inviting their circle within the Filipino community. I was so honoured. Everyone made food, dressed up beautifully, and had a blast. We ate, danced—including line dancing—which Filipinos love, and we cuddled all night. Although I'd invited a few western friends, only Mario came with me—it was the two of us with everyone else being Filipino, but nobody cared. There were no borders and no judgements—just love.

Needless to say, *ma'arsalama* party planning took on a much quieter tone. Penny decided that she would rather have a low-key pizza night with our friends who had been in prison and beaten up. We would just have a night of laughs at her flat and forget about any illegal partying. It turned out to be a fantastic night. Everyone's humour was full-tilt, and we laughed and laughed all night. It was glorious to see Misha, Nedra, and Sheena having fun and feeling safe.

A doctor offered his villa for another party, which would include alcohol and music if we wanted. Feeling relatively safe in our compound and behind the walls of a doctor's home, the party planners decided it was worth the risk. Anyone was welcome, and I understood the reasons of those who did not wish to come. At first, there were rumbles amongst my co-workers that we were crazy to plan a party but as everybody talked, we began feeling we had to recapture *normal*. Too many ladies had succumbed to unhealthy brainwashing to be so upset and fearful about a lousy party.

It turned out that everyone came, except Nedra, who was too scared. Even Tony, Khaled, and Kara dropped by for a drink. I was so happy. I think it was medicinal for every one of us to be together. Nedra sent flowers. It was so sad to think of her, new to Saudi and holing up alone in her flat. In our real worlds, the situation would never have been so dramatic. It was just a house party.

Misha constantly trembled and glanced up nervously every time the door opened. She had been so viciously attacked and was temporarily emotionally crippled with fear. She seemed frail, and I just kept hugging her all night, as she repeated, "Please don't go—*please* don't leave me."

I would hear later that Misha returned to the U.S. and had surgery, but her eye would never be the same. I don't know how she's doing emotionally and spiritually. Sadly, we lost touch.

Everyone who was beaten up that night left Saudi within a few months of my EOC. Some had worked there for years and years, and in many ways, their lives were better than they would have been in their home countries of Lebanon and Egypt. It was both sad and ironic that the Mutawa cared so little about their fellow Arabs and Muslims.

The night of my flight out of the kingdom, everybody came over to dance and sing and say *ma'arsalama*. I was manic. I was so excited. No one, including me, thought I would make it to the end of my contract without being imprisoned or fired, or both. Someone said I must have been exercising my intuitive skills to know when not to go to parties. I had always felt I was just lucky, but the coincidences were too many for me not to wonder if it really was intuition.

Mohammed, who had picked me up upon my arrival in the kingdom, interrupted our final good-byes by calling to say he wanted to take me to the airport three hours early. I said *no way* and hung up. Everyone warned me that Mohammed might well not show up at all. On the suggestion of my friends, I then called Security and thanked them for sending me a car in three hours, a bit of a passive/aggressive nudge for them not to forget me. Mohammed was just being lazy and wanted to avoid driving me later in the evening; he would rather I sat in an airport full of men, restricted to a corner for three hours. Forget it. I was not being bullied by anyone anymore. This was my last night in the kingdom.

Mario gave me a beautiful gold bracelet, which I have never taken off. Tazzie gave me a gorgeous hand-stitched quilt from Pakistan. She was very quiet that night and found my manic high difficult to handle.

Jan took me aside and started crying as she said how proud she was of me for maintaining a sense of humour and happiness, despite all that was done to me by Ginete. She felt I was a young woman trying to find my voice, and she knew that I had touched women in Saudi and helped them.

Jan had heard of my helping Hoda, a Chinese Muslim girl married to an abusive husband. Ali would not give Hoda permission to leave the country. Hoda packed up and we made a plan. She would go on vacation with her husband and then just leave—just walk away. I would mail her belongings to her immediately.

After running into his fist and breaking her nose, as well as being raped by him, Hoda found the courage to confront him. Then, by a miracle, Ali signed documents allowing her to leave. He assumed she would return, but she never did. Hoda went from a meek, frightened young woman to an empowered goddess. Unable to seek asylum in her own country, she had the courage to go to Singapore alone and start her own art gallery.

Jan also knew of the many times I sparked debate and conversation over the roles of women in all societies. We laughed at how I used to get upset over television shows because they always had fat, bald husbands with gorgeous sexy wives—we never saw the opposite. Didn't that bug anybody? I was knowingly radical, but for the most part, it always opened up a great conversation and was food for thought. Jan's words to me were such a blessing.

Both of us were crying as she gently put a native dream-catcher into my hands. It was very special to her, she said, but her heart was now asking her to give it to me. "May all your dreams come true," she said as we cried and embraced. Jan didn't know about my interest in native spirituality, and when I told her, her gift was made even more sacred. I still have my dream-catcher.

"Listen, Edna. Listen. One more time." The party got quiet as we listened to the ominous call for prayer at sunset. I would never see the sun rise on the Kingdom of Saudi Arabia again.

Two months later, I heard that Queen Ginete had been fired, with a personal security escort off compound. She had stepped on one too many toes. And soon Dr. M. H., the Mad Hatter, followed on her heels and was not re-contracted. *Hum'da'allah* for karma!

1995

An Answer to My Letter

I missed my siblings and returned to Canada for two weeks to see them. Afterward, I planned to travel Europe with Lorraine.

Throughout my year abroad, faithfully once a month, I would write long letters detailing life in Saudi and send a copy to all my siblings. I had a habit of "overkill" when desperate. I also bought my siblings presents. The ones whom I wanted to love me the most usually got the most expensive gifts.

I always knew when I was acting from a place of fear because, as I shopped or frantically wrote, I would hear that voice inside asking me to settle down. It was like something would possess me and I would go temporarily crazy, getting all hyper in my need to find a perfect gift. The fact that my sibs barely said good-bye, never mind wrote, and weren't actively interested in my life, should have been a loud drum roll for me. But I just kept trying to win, or buy, their acceptance. I wasn't easily letting go of what I so wanted to possess—their love.

Upon my arriving home with all my prezzies, not surprisingly, no one really responded. No one was interested in my stories—it all felt unmistakably familiar. I couldn't wait to give my brother an eighteen-karat gold puzzle ring only available in the Middle East and Asia. As I tried to present it to him, he kept interrupting to yell at the kids or make a phone call. I finally just handed it to him and left—I never saw him wear it. I had known all along that my gift giving was a desperate cry for acceptance, and when not accepted, I only berated myself. After all, I had heard that voice telling me not to set myself up. Rather than taking this as a lesson to listen to my intuition, I just beat myself up for being a stupid idiot. I had a ways to go.

My siblings' coldness toward me seemed to be more pronounced than before. It was as though I had been physically gone long enough for them to get over me. I felt dead to my family.

I didn't know that they had already received a letter from Dad in response to what I had written him. It began with a preamble:

> I'm pleased that Edna did write her letter to me because it opened my eyes to what has really been going on in the minds of my children. It has also provided me with the opportunity to review my past and to respond to

her in a sincere and forthright manner. And to this end, let me stress that there will be no further discussion or correspondence with any of you in respect to these matters. Edna has stated her concerns and I have responded. That's the end of it as far as I'm concerned.

Uh-oh, it didn't take much to realize that he had no intention of speaking from his heart in an honest way. Or maybe, this was his honest way. Deception and denial are very powerful when one needs to survive. His entire letter ran to forty-five pages. Addressed to me, with copies distributed to my siblings, it in part said:

> I have read your letter several times—not in anger, but to reflect and determine if I really was the mean, cruel, heartless, lying, stealing, inconsiderate, mentally and sexually abusive father you suggest I was.
> I am not from the generation that says *I love you*. That's a new phenomenon, part of the sham created by the love culture of the "flower people," the hippies who started tearing down the establishment, introducing our children to L.S.D. and the rest of their crap, including free sex, common-law, etc. They spent their time saying, "I love you"—those huggy-wuggy, lovey-dovey founders as they jumped to their deaths, believing they could fly...
> You wrote *that I attempted to get into bed with you*. Do you honestly believe that's a true statement? I did lie down on my back next to you to watch TV, but we were clothed. Your statement suggested that it must have been nighttime and you were in bed, and I was probably in my pyjamas and tried to get under the covers with you. That's exactly what your statement would suggest.
> You also wrote that I was telling everyone that you were my mistress. I believe I did make that statement to a young man—jokingly—on the aircraft, as he seemed to like you.
> Now, I have a question for you:

Have you ever had or shown in any way a greater affection for me than you should have? (You don't have to answer this—it's just food for thought.)

Certainly, my behaviour in Montreal was bizarre—my whole life was bizarre at that time. It was a midlife crisis. It's too bad I didn't think of this when I was confronted by you and your sisters.

You dated a man who worked for me—and you slept with him. And then you would come to church with your mother and me, and take communion, even though you'd had sex with him. I commented that this was sinful, and you rationalized it by saying you loved him. God doesn't accept reasons for sinning!

Picking myself up off the floor, I wondered if I could get through the rest of his letter. There just aren't words to explain what it's like to have your father spew venom and gasoline all over you and then light a match, only to continue spewing lies while you are frantically burning to death right before him. His descriptions of what *didn't* happen creeped me out—he was almost describing what *did* happen. Saying I was nineteen, when I was seventeen, probably helped him pretend I was more of an adult. Did that make it okay to him?

The next part of his letter was highlighted:

Most important of all—if you were so concerned about me, why in the name of anything logical or sane would you ever want to go to Montreal with me? And I might add that you were extremely elated about the trip. I also remember that you and your Mother had a bit of an argument at the time. She was not happy about the situation. But you still went. Why? Makes one think doesn't it?

You've always been treated like a little innocent child, needing to be taken care of. When we went to Montreal, you were no child. You were a woman who was already a mother and certainly knew her way around the gay bars, the straight bars, knew where the dope was, and much, much more. You were very mature, like nineteen going on thirty-two.

And you say your mother didn't love you—what a stupid, ignorant, and ungrateful statement. If she turned against you because of Montreal, it's because she was of the opinion that you provoked me on occasion. You say she rejected you. She rejected your lesbian lifestyle, and so did I, and so did other family members.

What a complete and utter disaster half of my children have been: sex, drugs, lying, cheating, stealing, rebelling, gay bars, prostitution...

After your question regarding my raping and beating your mother, it took me several days to get my reasoning back... and then I confronted your mother. Your mother mentioned that I forced myself on her at one time—or words to that effect—which she says was rape! And she said I beat her, but it must have only been a few times. Hopefully, what your mother said is a misinterpretation or stretched a little. There is no doubt that I pushed and pestered her until she gave in during my drinking years, but I would never force and attack her.

Edna, you need a therapist—they would have a field day with you. For a while, this was all the rage: women everywhere being sucked in by these quacks and destroying families as hordes of "victims" came forth.

Edna, I hope and pray every day that you will turn back to the Scriptures before it's too late. Even if homosexuals say they are born with "it," they know it's perverse and against God's laws, and should pray to remove these sinful desires from their lives.

If you should drop dead of a heart attack, do you really believe you would want to face God?

Love,
Dad – June 16

Ahlen wa sahlen—welcome home! June 16 was coincidentally the date my baby girl was born. I crumbled in silence, with no human expression available for my emotions. As I lay on my bed, I heard moaning—I knew it was my soul.

And, with that, Lorraine and I headed to Europe. Eventually, we landed in God's country. Israel.

An Angel, a Rose, and Jesus

The only way to cope was to put the letters and emotions away, and move on. Lorraine and I seldom discussed my family, and I was able to tuck all the dysfunction away and get on with my life. I must have forgotten that my heart had already broken down from trying to contain a toxic dump. But I just didn't know what else to do—yet.

Enjoying the financial gains from Saudi, Lorraine and I had spent the past several months backpacking and camping throughout Europe. With December weather getting colder, I suggested we take a three-day cruise from Rhodes to Israel.

I wondered how I was going to react going back to Israel as a gay woman with my partner, and still fairly fresh from the last nail in my coffin from my family. I needed to implement all that I learned through Terri and Dorinda. It was time to move up the chakras into God-energy. Did I dare? All of my thoughts remained internal—I never shared any of this with Lorraine.

Pulling into port, I had a spiritual anxiety attack, feeling as if I had willingly walked into the heart and soul of God. I was now on his turf. I didn't know it at the time, but I had made an "unconscious" decision to enter the dark shadows of my soul and face my fears about God, religion, and judgement. What better place to "unconsciously" set in motion my journey than in the Holy Land!

Lorraine had no spiritual angst. Her family had never made religion a big deal. She had no fear of God, didn't know the Bible, and learned all the "rules" through my stories. Lorraine's peace about life and death was my strength. She didn't know it, but she carried me through my fears.

When we docked in Haifa, I had rehearsed Lorraine in preparation for Israeli customs. I reminded her not to get her passport stamped. If you have an Israeli stamp in your passport, this automatically bars you entrance into all Middle East countries, excluding Jordan and Egypt. Israel is quite prepared to stamp a piece of paper.

I forgot about my various and sundry Saudi stamps. Lorraine went first. As the stamp came down into her passport, I exhaled a deep *oh, crap*. She later said she had gotten nervous because they were so serious, and there were soldiers with machine guns everywhere. My turn.

A customs official opened my passport, his eyes widening at the multiple stamps from Saudi. Before I could exhale, I was surrounded by security, who escorted me to a side area. They were speaking with each other in Hebrew, each taking a turn to look at my passport.

And then the questions: "What were you doing in Saudi Arabia? Why did you go there? Did you have Arab friends? Did you speak to your Arab friends? You tell us you spoke to *no* Arab peoples? What was it like? Were you happy? Why are you in Israel? How long do you wish to stay? Why would you want to stay in Israel more than one week? You see things and you leave. Why do you wish to stay longer? Who are you with? Please point to her?"

I told them I did not befriend any Saudis and that our two worlds did not mesh. I had to point to Lorraine, already through customs and sitting on the other side watching me from a distance. She looked worried.

Assuming they couldn't touch her, I cockily noted that she had already cleared customs. Three security people promptly escorted her back to where I was. She looked very frightened, and I said to just speak the truth.

Everything was unpacked, scanned, squished, and dissected. In my increasing paranoia, I began wondering if I had anything illegal or Arabian in my backpack—a throwback to my drug days, perhaps. I was afraid that they would find out I had also lived in Lebanon and had already had a customs fiasco in Israel.

After what felt like an hour, someone returned with my passport, motioned for us to repack the mess they created, and we were cleared to go.

"I told you I have trouble getting through customs!" I said sheepishly to Lorraine as she picked up the panty-liners and tampons strewn across the table, all having been scanned one by one!

We hopped a bus to Jerusalem and Lorraine's eyes opened wide at all the soldiers with machine guns sitting on our bus. It was common to have the butt of a gun dig into your thigh as you stared into the nozzle facing you. She had to politely ask a soldier to stop resting his machine gun against her hip. I told her this was the norm in Israel. There are soldiers and guns and check stops everywhere.

In the Old City of Jerusalem, we passed through the Damascus Gate and entered—surprise—the Arab section. We walked through the crowded streets, and the souqs buzzing with activity, the smells of hummus, pita, falafels, and spices all, once again, created that old familiar feeling of stepping back into time. I was excited to share this world with Lorraine.

She seemed to have no culture shock, after our initial baptism by fire at customs and on the bus. Together we took in the smells and tastes and feelings of the Old City with ease.

Did I have Arabian blood in me? Was Lorraine so comfortable because her bloodline descended from Russian Jews? Were we a completely out-there representation of how the two nations could love each other? Being gay on top of it all felt like God saying, *Everyone, just come from a place of love—that's all you need.* I wondered.

We heard about a family who rented the upstairs of their home and went to meet them. Along the Via Doloroso, I told Lorraine she had just walked the path that Christ had taken to his crucifixion.

Tamir, his pregnant wife Angel, and their daughter Rose were Christian Palestinians living in a 2,500-year-old home. Each spoke varying degrees of English. The entrance to their house was a thick black cast-iron door, surely borrowed from a dungeon. Lorraine, who was taller than me, sadly hit her head on that bloody door a number of times—I guess humans were much shorter in the days of old.

The house had no windows at all and felt very much like a cave. Dome-shaped ceilings and archways separating each room enhanced the cave-like effect. Fresco wall murals covering several of the large walls added to the primeval ambiance. These beautiful murals of ancient Arabian women by the sea—many of whom were naked—had been painted in bold, bright blues and vivid colours. If my sister Naomi had seen this "pornography," she would have fainted—and all of it within a family home!

Tamir had added an upstairs to house tourists, particularly during Easter. These were two adjoining rooms with a window, small balcony, a kitchenette, bed, and television.

I asked if we could rent the room for a few days, but Tamir wouldn't budge on renting it for a minimum of one month. I knew Jerusalem got cold in winter and wanted to head to the desert climate, but Lorraine wanted to make this a home base where we could store our things, and from which we could travel on day trips. We paid in advance and headed upstairs.

We quickly became like family members and enjoyed the

company of our hosts. Rose and I bonded immediately. Tamir did not care for his daughter or his wife, was furious that Angel was pregnant, and did not hesitate to say so. He was always throwing things at Rose and saying she had such opinions for a girl that no man would ever want her. Naturally, I became very protective.

One night, Tamir had far too much to drink and, in slurred words, admitted his true feelings about his wife and daughter. He left nothing out. When he said that he'd married Angel as a favour to her father, because nobody wanted her, I became angry. "Then why did you have sex with a woman you despised?" I shouted.

Lorraine hit me on the arm. "*Don't* ask that! He's drunk."

I was disgusted and told him so.

We retreated to our room, and Angel and Rose soon joined us. Angel confessed that Tamir beat her, which was no surprise. He always threatened that he would put her on the street with only the clothes on her back. I told her she should not put up with this. Leave him. Go with her parents. Don't let him be like this. I didn't overlook the coincidence of having a conversation with yet another beaten woman, as I encouraged her to empower herself and begin to have a voice. I knew I was also preaching to someone else who needed to get the message: *me*.

Angel was afraid. She knew her husband was going to marry Rose off in a few years, and Rose was petrified, as she nodded her head in agreement. She wanted me to take her back to Canada. She was thirteen and wanted to get educated, but Tamir thought education for a woman was useless—women were useless. Lorraine and I would later join mother and daughter on trips to visit Angel's grandmother or other relatives. It was always a lot of fun to be with just the ladies, who, of course, were anything but useless.

Tamir would often come home and complain about the Israeli checkpoints—as a taxi driver, he encountered many. The family always referred to Israel as Occupied Palestine. Tamir would talk tough about the soldiers, but as we came to witness, when dealing with them, he was clearly nervous and beaten down. As in Lebanon, Israeli soldiers all seemed to speak Arabic, but the Arabs did not speak Hebrew. Watching Tamir change when stopped at the various checkpoints was quite sad. I could understand how, with no freedom in their own birthplace, people's blood boiled.

Christmas was fast approaching. Lorraine and I were saving Bethlehem for Christmas Eve. This was to be the first year Bethlehem was "open" for celebrations under a Palestinian flag. The last time I had been in Israel, it was illegal to have a Palestinian flag, and now, they were flying everywhere.

Christmas Eve, we took a city bus and spent the afternoon in Bethlehem, in anticipation of the evening's celebrations. I took Lorraine to one of the supposed spots where Jesus was born. We found a balcony overlooking the valley and hills of Judea, as I told the story of Joseph and Mary riding up on the donkey to this very stable. She loved my Bible storytelling. With the Judean desert wrapping the outskirts of town, it was such a contradiction of magnificence and relentless poverty, anger, and hatred. Did anyone ever sit overlooking this vista and just be still?

All the flags signalled that we were now on "official" Palestinian turf. This did not bring with it a sense of peace, however. This was the first-ever Christmas celebrated under the Palestinian flag in Bethlehem, and who knew what might happen? I had talked with many Palestinians and Muslims, and I knew that outside of conquering Jerusalem, nothing else would stop their war. I wished in my heart that Bethlehem and other territories would be enough to bring at least a moment's calm.

We headed into a part of town where the tourists don't go. There was such poverty. Two young guys followed us, ducking behind walls as we turned to look—we got nervous. As they started throwing stones, we picked up our pace back to a more populous area. This was daytime. What was the night going to bring?

As daylight turned to dusk, the Israeli security forces were out in full force. Israeli soldiers were on every rooftop, visible in every direction. Security barriers were put up in all entranceways into Manger Square. Bulletproof vests, machine guns, army fatigues—this didn't feel like Jesus' birthplace, and it certainly stopped feeling like it belonged to Palestine.

Evening brought thousands of people into Manger Square, which was becoming claustrophobic. As a hand grabbed my crotch, I screamed, but nobody cared. There were too many men coming and going.

Little kids were constantly approaching us to buy old, sun-bleached postcards or sticks of juicy fruit gum; most spoke English because of their interactions with tourists. Some had tears in their eyes, and an older boy told us that they were not allowed to go home until they sold everything. It was child labour, but as in so many other places we had seen, it wasn't out of the ordinary. We bought several items and did our bit to help, but eventually, we had to get tough with them and tell them to leave us alone. We didn't want to become their easy targets—we knew some of it was a scam.

Lorraine was getting brushed up against, and it was time to get out of the throngs of mostly Arab men. The majority of tourists were close to or inside the Church of the Nativity.

Momentarily forgetting that they were the targets, we naively thought we'd be safer if we stood by the Israeli soldiers. Their young faces contradicted their army fatigues and machine guns.

Lorraine had to go to the bathroom, which was in back of the square, closer to the homes where we had been earlier. As I waited, a commotion broke out. Israeli soldiers are trained to take all sorts of abuses and never cock their weapons unless they are under personal attack in a life threatening sense. Two soldiers shouted as they looked upward into a window. As something was thrown out of the window, the guns were cocked. I was petrified. They were in firing position and ready to shoot.

The Palestinians around began chanting and hounding them. Everyone was looking up to the light in the window. Something came flying out again. It looked like garbage. The soldiers flinched but did not shoot. They began shouting louder for the crowd to move away. One soldier was radioing for help, one had his eyes on the window, and others were pushing back the crowd. This was in a corner where nobody would be aware of the events unfolding unless they were right there. I stood frozen in fear. My girlfriend was on the other side of these soldiers, innocently going to the loo. One of them pushed me back.

I kept yelling, "Please. Please. My girlfriend is in there."

He didn't react. Everything seemed to happen in slow motion. As something else was flung out of the window, the guns pointed upward, again cocked for shooting.

Lorraine came around the dark corner, fixing her pants and tucking in her shirt. A soldier grabbed her and pushed her toward me. Startled, she looked around.

"Just walk this way," I said grabbing her arm and thanking Yahweh. We walked to the nearest exit and got out of Bethlehem as I blurted out what had just happened.

It was very late and very dark—not the best time to be in the labyrinth of the Old City. We briskly walked past the stray cats, up the Via Doloroso to our home.

"Merry Christmas," I ironically whispered.

Lorraine quietly replied, "Some things should just remain a fantasy, like 'Oh, Little Town of Bethlehem'." It was Christmas morning in Israel.

You couldn't help but run into Christian groups touring the Holy Land. Some days were more difficult than others for me. Especially because of the nightmare I just had...

In my nightmare, there were guerrillas firing machine guns at each other, commandeering the street I happened to be walking on—in the dead of night. Bullets were flying past me and I was petrified. I ducked into a bathroom and hid behind a door; suddenly, a machine gun was pointed at my head. The man made me get down on my knees and was about to murder me. I looked at him and asked if I could have one minute to pray to God to save my soul. He gave me one minute, but did not lower his weapon from my temple. I closed my eyes and began praying, knowing that I had just heard the "click" of the trigger. I wasn't able to finish my prayer.

Waking up, I remembered every feeling as if it had actually happened. I would just reach a cusp of understanding, of allowing myself to believe what truly resonated within me, but then, all those years of indoctrination into fear and damnation would creep back in. Being in the land of Jesus stirred up all the gloom and doom. My soul still held fear that I had to be born-again to get to heaven. This was not a peaceful place to be in, considering all the death around us.

I was so tired of running from God but I was even more tired of being scared. I spent much of my quiet time internally talking with God while visiting the sites. I whispered to God that it was good for me to be open and accepting about my sexuality. I explained to him that it was more than a sexuality issue—it was my essence as a human being. Maybe if I just explained myself to God, maybe…

I was thankful that I wasn't preaching to others and dismissing their personal beliefs. It was time to look inward, to separate religion from spirit. I would watch the Christian groups touring and praying, and a part of me would feel angry. I wanted to yell at them that they were phoney. They never accepted me as I was. I would shake my head in disgust as they sat in their prayer groups. I felt hatred toward them. I refused to allow myself to see that I was simply looking into a mirror at my own reflection—again. I had to forgive *me*, not them.

Bombs and war never disappear from day-to-day life in Israel. Throughout our stay, there were innumerable incidents. We always seemed to be only a step away from terrorism. Phoning overseas to say Merry Christmas to Lorraine's parents, we were told that a bomb had exploded at a bus station we were very familiar with; many people were killed.

We spent the day outside of the Old City, had a nice brunch in Zion Square, and walked around the Jewish section of Jerusalem. This part of town was visibly more well-to-do with no signs of poverty. Zion Square would sadly be the site of several suicide bombers during our stay.

Lorraine's primary goal when entering any new village or city was to find the marketplace. She loved this. Jerusalem's markets were home to fresh picked fruits and veggies from neighbouring kibbutzim.

We were enjoying pizza and a drink when a man came running up to us, flailing his arms in the air. "You must move. You are not eating kosher. This is a kosher restaurant beside you. You are *too close*. You must move!"

An onlooker was kind enough to explain that we had mixed meat with dairy, which equalled a not-so-kosher meal, and we were sitting right under the sign "Kosher Food Served Here."

Oy vey, schmeckena tourists! Lorraine giggled and, in her best Jewish accent, admonished our "stupidity" for not knowing. Did God really demand all this?

Only a few days later, suicide bombers blew themselves up in the middle of this wonderful marketplace; there were several deaths and many injuries. I didn't feel "spared" by God's wrath and I didn't blame God. It was a human act of violence; hatred or love were all random choices we made—they weren't done *to* us, but *by* us. This seemed huge to me. Wow, I felt a breakthrough coming.

Just after entering back into the Old City through Jaffa Gate, we were stopped as officials blocked off a package in the road. The bomb squad came, imploded the package, and life went on. This was more than common. Watching the bomb squad, I wondered who the people were under those protective suits. What kind of a person does this for a living?

And so, this was Christmas.

Back at our home, Angel had prepared a feast. She was puzzled why we weren't helping her, but I just couldn't. I am close to a vegetarian, and I don't fare well in a kitchen at the best of times. Looking at almost an entire lamb sitting on her counter did me in. As she started chopping, I started gagging. I knew we were insulting her. I felt the same as when Ferzat's mother expected me to help. What was second nature to these ladies was completely foreign to me.

Seeing the finished dinner, neither Lorraine nor I could bring ourselves to eat it, which added further insult. For Lorraine to not even try meant it was clearly uneatable, because she would try anything. Angel started crying, saying she cooked all day and nobody would eat. She laid quite the Muslim-mother guilt-trip on everyone. Muslim-mother guilt is equal to Jewish-mother guilt. How do I know? I was raised Catholic! The genetic guilt-tripping code did not divide and separate! All mothers have it!!

Eventually, we put the music on and started belly dancing, which brought joy to the house. Rose and I danced and cuddled up to sing songs. My Arabic song delighted everybody as they sang along, filling in the blanks.

We spent the next couple of weeks touring the various sites of Israel. We were sitting up on the Mount of Olives, overlooking Jerusalem and listening to a tour group hear how Jesus wept over Jerusalem while he stood here. Suddenly, a Palestinian man whacked my can of juice and sent it flying, scaring the be'jesus out of all of us. I didn't have time to react, because he went into a rage, yelling and pointing his fingers at me. Lorraine told me to stay quiet but she didn't have to. I was scared and had no idea what had set this guy off. As the tour group disappeared, we followed, afraid to be left behind.

A bit unnerved, we proceeded down the mountain. I sometimes felt light-headed and thought it was anxiety. All the spiritual sites got to me. My internal confusion heightened as we went and sat in the Garden of Gethsemane, where Christ had called out to Father God before he was betrayed. Again sneaking a listen to another tour group, we heard that several of the trees around us were four thousand years old. I felt their energy, fascinated that they had stood witness to that moment in Christ's life. I have always had a love of trees and their majestic beauty. I love to watch them sway in the wind, and I sometimes hug them to feel a sense of grounded-ness and oneness with nature. I sat in Gethsemane for a long time, quietly talking to God and asking for an understanding.

Being an observer of the various religious beliefs and behaviours surrounding me, I felt separated; I did not want to be part of any organized religious group. With holy sites being disputed—two different locations declared to be the birthplace of Jesus, two different places declared as his burial site, and on and on—it began making more peaceful sense that all this was symbolic. It was the symbolism that held meaning, and not location, location, location.

Based on my study of chakras, I wondered if my dizziness was from feeling overwhelmingly insecure and fearful, from not being grounded. All the energy of God around me was overpowering, rather than *em*powering me. I finally saw a doctor and he diagnosed an upper sinus infection that was throwing off my equilibrium. Several shekels' worth of antibiotics later, I was physically fine; all I had to do now was transfer that into my internal balance, and I would be healed.

On a bus ride home from the Jerusalem Mall, which in itself is a security shakedown, our bus driver kept flirting with Lorraine. "You don't remember me? I see you together at Bethlehem on Christmas. You stay by soldiers and watch people. I was soldier." It was a bit creepy to hear that someone had been watching us so intently.

Giving us a tour along the bus route, he noted that Israeli settlements were always on the hilltops, in "dominant" positions, while the Palestinian 'hoods were in the valleys. He asked Lorraine if she wanted to go for coffee, and in my best Jewish accent, I said, "What am I, chopped liver?" Only Lorraine laughed.

Back on our own turf, we spent a lot of time at the Wailing Wall, sitting in the square observing the comings and goings. Hundreds of tourist groups, mostly with a Christian religious affiliation, pray at the Wall, on "the trip of a lifetime," as they put it. I loved that I had been able to travel numerous times throughout my life. The money that many tourists spent on a one-week all-inclusive would have lasted me through six-months of travelling. *Maybe I should become their tour guide*, I thought. Lorraine enjoyed my tours and my stories. I could give them a trip of a lifetime.

Orthodox Jews, with a small box full of prayers resting on the front tip of their black hat, came often to the Wailing Wall. With their white and black shawls, and long curly ringlets dangling down their cheeks, they stood in front of the wall. They rocked back and forth, back and forth, all the time twirling a ringlet through their fingers while they prayed. The rocking seemed to put them into a trance as they lamented with fervour. The Wailing Wall is full of tiny pieces of paper stuck into every nook and cranny; these are prayers that people have left there for God to answer.

A very small section of the Wall is for women to pray; again I fantasized about leading the women over to the main section of the Wall. Apparently, God did not think women were worthy to pray with the men.

I was surprised that Jewish women shaved *all* their hair—body and head—upon marriage. Muslim women shave only their body hair. Christianity's apostle Paul told women to sit quietly in church, off to the side; he told them to cover their hair as well. Christian women thus dodged the shaving rule.

Catholicism also used to insist a woman cover her hair while in church. I remember being a young girl and having to pin Kleenex or handkerchiefs on top of my head. I thought God should love our hair. Why does he feel women's hair, which he gave us, is unclean but man's hair is not? It's all a bit conflicting because God *says* in Islam that a woman's hair is "unclean" and should be seen only by the husband; meanwhile, our "same" Christian God *says* a woman's hair is her crowning glory. It all sounds so trivial, yet it is so disempowering to women.

Palestinians share the wall where it heads into the Dome of the Rock, which is directly behind the Wailing Wall. We spent a few hours in the beautiful gardens but were not allowed inside the Mosque.

Watching Christianity, Judaism, and Islam merge on this one corner, I thought it might all seem silly—if it hadn't been so serious. Each religion had declared this exact, tiny spot to be holy and significant. That one wall—the last remnant of the temple connecting Judaism to Christianity—was also coincidentally where Islam's Abraham sacrificed Ishmael, *and* where Mohammed's ascension into Heaven took place. Doesn't that seem like an awful lot of activity for one little corner on an entire planet? And that's what the war and hatred is all about? No other piece of land will do. Couldn't they just share, with Israel owning one side of the Wall and Palestine owning the other?

There is a belief that is often overlooked when people talk about the Middle East. The Arab nations all share the same message: *Jerusalem is their Holy City and Israel must be destroyed.* With that being their ideology, no other piece of land is going to appease them—not Bethlehem or Jericho or Gaza. Israel cannot exist and nothing short of her demise is going to stop the war—ask them. They tell the world but we're not listening.

Did God really *allow* for significant religious events to sit juxtaposed in one location and cause such hatred? Shouldn't *we, the people*, be accountable for our choices? Maybe we need to leave God out of this.

Deep in contemplation, my mind's eye zoomed out, peering into the cosmos. I wanted a view from the heavens. An attempt to grasp the magnitude that there are billions of galaxies, each with billions of stars gave me butterflies—what a colossal vision. My imagination travelled down through our own galaxy—the Milky Way—as I danced from star to star, saw the expanse of forever, and finally zoned back in on our little planet, back to Israel, back into my body, to rest in this one, small corner—in a city named Jerusalem.

Refocussed on all of our various rituals, I felt like we were bringing God into our 'hood, rather than expanding our beliefs into *his* 'hood. God felt so much bigger than all of our beliefs. Couldn't pure love and being the best we can, be the answer? For a moment, my fears seemed so limiting. It was wonderful to step into love and out of fear, even if for only a heartbeat of time.

At the top of the wall surrounding the Old City, there is a boardwalk patrolled by Israeli soldiers, who look down and watch everything. I could see why the Palestinians felt like caged animals, but I also understood that Israel was protecting herself. Having empathy for both sides added to my sense of sadness over the seemingly never-ending conflict.

My thoughts were interrupted as soldiers once again began pushing the crowd back. A black pouch was sitting unattended by the Wailing Wall. The soldiers quickly set their well-rehearsed imploding process in motion.

In came the bomb squad, a man dressed in a space suit walked slowly toward the pouch. I heard ticking in my head; or was it my heartbeat? Nobody moved. Nobody spoke. The package was wired, encased, and *boom*—imploded into bits of nothing. False alarm. The spaceman walked toward the now shredded pouch and lifted it up to indicate the all-clear. Someone had left a camcorder unattended, and it was now history. We waited around to see if anyone would admit to owning it and leaving it by mistake. But no one dared walk up to the bomb squad to claim this purported lethal weapon. It was just another day in Israel.

Tamir was entertaining a Greek tour guide passing through with a busload of tourists. They were headed to Egypt, via the Sinai, and we hitched a ride. We stored our stuff at Tamir's and made plans to come back to see Angel's baby, who was due within the next month.

We had no idea there were a million Greek Orthodox churches dotted all through the desert. We stopped to visit every one.

As they dropped us off at yet another, it was time for us to bid adieu. We were about to learn why people get stuck in Dahab.

The Sinai used to belong to Israel but was given back to Egypt in 1979. It was nice to see Israeli tourists with no visible animosity; this indicated peaceful relations between the two countries. It felt natural to see them sitting side by side, even though only a few years ago, they were at war over this land.

Dahab is a small village in the middle of the Sinai, which the locals refer to as Lower Egypt. They still refer to Cairo as Upper Egypt, just as the Pharaohs did millennia ago! Dahab was the only place in all of the Middle East where you were allowed to freely and legally smoke marijuana. And there was never a shortage, as the plants grew everywhere.

We stayed in a $1.50-a-night cement room with a slab for a bed. Our landlord, Ali, loved us and treated us like goddesses. We would sit in marijuana heaven for the next thirty days.

Dahab was a magical carpet ride. Daylight's natural high came from snorkelling in the Red Sea, desert trekking, sunning, eating pineapple pancakes, reading, playing backgammon, napping, and more napping—all of which fused nicely with our nighttime highs, full of laughter, music, getting high, and munchies.

Ali seemed taken with Lorraine and me. I think he enjoyed that we were "lovers." He was always snapping photos of us together, or with him. He was never sleazy with us—it was more like he had a crush on us. We could tell that his friends teased him in Arabic.

Ali supplied us with endless amounts of pot and offered us a free room for another month. He was never overbearing or in our face, probably because he was too stoned to muster up that kind of energy. Lorraine and I spent more time with Ali and his band of thieves than with the tourists passing through—some of who seemed unable to pack up and leave. It was easy to fall into the groove of Dahab, with its bohemian rhythms. We were invited to a private "restaurant" as Ali's guests.

Ramses was the proud owner of this eatery, a Bedouin tent with the front opening up to the sea, the shore only a few yards from where we sat. Handmade colourful carpets hung on the "walls" and were scattered randomly across the floor. Seating consisted of cloth-covered foam running along the ground, hugging the walls of the tent. Big comfy pillows were scattered everywhere for backrests, and a fire pit built into the ground sat in the centre of the tent; it gently warmed us as the desert night turned cold. Candles were lit and soft melodic Arabic music played in the background.

The mood could not have been cozier. We were a group of peaceful hippies and Bedouins sitting together, breaking bread, getting high, and passing the hubbly-bubbly around like a peace pipe. There was a sense of eroticism in the air, and I imagined myself doing the Dance of the Seven Veils. That night was a special night, with nature about to unfold another enchanting moment.

It was already 2:00 a.m. and the sky was blacker than black. Ramses, Ali, and a few others grabbed our hands, saying, "*Yella Omi. Yella!*" And we all gathered at the sea. With anticipation, we looked up to the stars and the darkness. Then, as if appearing from the depths of the Red Sea, the most spectacular golden full moon rose, lifting out of the water, quickly rising upward toward the heavens. As if watching fireworks, we oohed and awed at this Arabian moonrise never to be forgotten. The vibe of the evening was perfect, until our conversation turned a dark corner.

Only a small handful of foreigners were ever invited "in" to this dining experience, mostly a girlfriend here or there. I imagined these young, gorgeous Arabian knights enjoyed their lives, charming the western ladies. Ramses certainly seemed to take after his ancient predecessor. That night, the centre of his attention was Geezala, a pretty German journalist who was living in Israel and covering the Palestinian/Israeli struggles. Petite, blonde, shy, and quiet, she was obviously quite taken by Ramses' charm. Tall, dark, and handsome, he had enough charisma to lure many a woman to his tent.

"A girl was executed in Upper Egypt today because she was having sex with a man." Ramses threw it into the conversation. Ali and the other men nodded, a silent understanding passing amongst them.

"What happened to the man?" I asked. Geezala looked nervously at Ramses, as we all felt his hostility toward the question.

Ramses replied, "Nothing of course. What a stupid question."

This opened the floodgates to a very intense conversation with three western women and a group of Arab men.

Geezala quietly responded, "It's not so stupid a question. You are implying this girl was wrong." It was obvious Geezala was feeling betrayed and somewhat dirty. With everyone knowing she was involved intimately with Ramses, she shrunk before our gazing eyes.

In a deep, thundering anger, Ramses raised his voice. "Even if she were my sister, she would still need to be put to death!" he said with arrogant conviction.

"If you believe that, then what are you saying of Geezala?

And what about you? You also are having sex out of marriage." It flew out of my big mouth.

"She should not have been with this man. She shamed her family. She *must* be put to death!" he declared, wanting to end the conversation.

"You have just called your girlfriend a whore!" I screamed back.

Geezala looked stunned and devastated. Yelling in Arabic, flailing his arms, Ramses jumped up, cursing women no doubt, and stormed away. Geezala and I exchanged glances, deep into each other's souls. No words had to be spoken.

The next day, Lorraine and I decided to get away from the thick tension lingering in the air. Very much aware that I had upset the natives, we retreated to the mountains in back of our Bedouin village.

To the south of our Bedouin camp was the Red Sea and to the north were barren, rugged mountains with rough, jagged peaks that shot up to the sky, then obliquely crashed into the desert floor. Sandwiched in between the roughness was the occasional mountain of smooth, soft sand.

We began the morning climbing and sliding our way upward, each footstep sinking into the red sand. As it got steeper toward the top, I began to slide back down the mountain. Lorraine was much higher than me; I looked to one side and saw a drop-off into a gorge. I was much too close to the edge and felt a bit panicked as I tried to hang onto the sand with my fingernails. I called up for Lorraine to come rescue me; she started coming down the mountain on her bum. The sand turned into a magic carpet and off she went, right past me, unable to stop. Flying by, she shouted, "Just slide. Use your feet as braaakkkeeeesss."

Although she didn't appear successful in braking, I had no choice. Dropping and rolling as if putting out a fire, I fell inward to the mountain and began my own sail down. I managed to slide uncontrollably right into her and wrapped my legs around her as if we were on a toboggan for two. We glided to the bottom, painfully out of control, as if flying through the air. Laughing hysterically, we lay there for a long, long time, our hearts pounding from the adrenaline rush. "Again!" Lorraine laughingly yelled as she tried dragging her tired and sore butt back up. Exhausted, she collapsed only feet from the base of the mountain.

After further climbing over rocks, through crevices and valleys that travelled deep into the desert, we found ourselves in a dry wadi; it called to us to trek through its snaking path up into the mountains. As tempting as it was, it seemed all too possible to get lost within those mountains, and the hot, searing rays of the sun were beating down on us. Desperate for cover, we found the desert's lone tree, standing with its branches withering in the heat. Within the tiny circle of shade, we plopped down in gratitude to our little tree. Smoking a doobie and lying within the tree's shadow, we felt distant from the unravelling of our Dahab paradise. After a month of laid-back happiness, everything had changed.

Back at camp, Ramses continued to be angry. We never had any more splendid nights in his tent. Other than being cordial, Geezala never talked with us, but it was clear that she was suffering internally. She never got to know that I deeply understood her pain. The moment never presented itself to share.

Shalom Israel

Sensing that I was leaving Israel possibly for the last time, I prolonged our trip back up to Jerusalem. Due to excessive marijuana use, we had only minimally enjoyed the Red Sea and snorkelling in Dahab. I couldn't imagine going right through Eilat without getting our toes wet.

After coming across the Egyptian/Israeli border, we put up our tent just outside of the town of Eilat, at Coral Reef campground. At the entrance was an Israeli military tank, supposedly watching over the Sea of Aquaba, which separated us from Jordan. The two soldiers didn't appear concerned as they lay back in their seats, sound asleep in the heat of the day, machine guns resting on their shoulders. Lorraine snuck a picture of them, and I laughed at how angry they would be to get caught napping while holding machine guns and operating a tank!

We had a fantastic time, complete with trekking to the top of Mount Yoash in time for sunset over four countries in one magnificent moment: Egypt, Saudi Arabia, Jordan, and Israel were at once bathed in golden red light.

Snorkelling for hours, we floated past coral walls holding hands throughout our amazing odyssey. The only sound was our steady breathing, in and out. Royal blue, yellow velvet, polka-dotted, striped, green, sky blue, cobalt blue, orange, pink, and lavender—fish of colours I have never seen before all swam around us. The coral and sea life danced, moving and swaying as part of a symphony. This was an underwater Mozart festival.

We couldn't stop. I was freezing from being in the water so long, but it felt impossible to get out. There was too much to see.

We snorkelled over to "moon crater," a circular wall of coral that dropped into the depths of the ocean. The coral, very much alive, opened and closed, as it swayed back and forth within the current. Deep in the coral were two octopuses, enough to scare me momentarily until I saw they were busy eating with their tentacles pulling in food. Huge stingrays swam by, along with what we called tutti-frutti fish because of their rainbow colours. Directly below our tummies were a school of lionfish, which we later discovered are deadly. We saw heaps of sea urchins, sitting quietly within the coral.

Such a gloriously different world—a parallel universe underwater! It was so intimate to be with Lorraine, holding hands or resting my arm on her lower back as we swam side by side. Time sailed by. Being in this sea, in all her majesty, made the desert feel a thousand miles away. This was the Promised Land. The dolphins were still to come.

As soon as my body slid into the deep, all I could hear was the sound of dolphins underwater, harmonizing with my breathing. It was mesmerizing—I had always been in love with dolphins and this was beyond my wildest dreams. I couldn't see them, but I could hear them talking and laughing with each other. It was early morning and they sounded chipper. It all felt surreal as, looking everywhere, I listened to their sounds, anxiously excited that dolphins could appear out of the deep waters at any second. And appear they did. There were eight of us in the group but this was an individual experience.

The dolphins danced under us, came shooting up from the deep toward us, gliding by us and under us on their sides, first to the right, then to the left, then diving down to the deep and shooting back up gleefully. They seemed to be performing for us, saying, *Watch me! Watch me!* I would cup my stomach with my hands, feeling like I was protecting myself. I felt so open and vulnerable with the deep ocean and her dolphins all around. I would be floating and looking straight down, trying to see the sea bottom, feeling like I was suspended in air when, up from the depths, shot a dolphin, her nose coming right for my tummy. Only feet away, she rolled on her back, swimming directly beneath me, smiling and looking up at me as she performed a forward somersault, with three twists, then plunged headfirst back down to the depths.

At the end of the day, we went over to the floating pier where the staff fed the dolphins. We were told that dolphins can see sixty miles ahead and their sonar can tell if women are pregnant. The instructor said he always knew if a woman was pregnant by watching the gentleness of the dolphins with her; sometimes he knew before she did. He also said dolphins are very sexual and flirtatious.

Lorraine was playing with a tiny piece of seaweed. A dolphin, swimming backward in an upright position using her fluke, kept nodding and making noises directed to Lorraine; obviously she wanted something. Lorraine threw the seaweed into the water; then we watched the dolphin dive down and come up directly to Lorraine with the seaweed on her nose. Taking it from her nose, Lorraine was able to cuddle the dolphin. They played the game over and over; the dolphin loved it as much as a dog fetching a stick.

Soon we were both caressing and cuddling the dolphins. Their grey backs felt like velvet and their tummies like thick rubber. When they had enough human contact, they simply swam off, and that was that. Having always had a love affair with dolphins, this was one of the biggest thrills of my life.

The world of chaos was distant in memory. It would have been a perfect ending to our vacation if not for the morning newspapers reporting an honour killing in Jordan. A father, believing his daughter had been with a man, took it upon himself to uphold the family honour by attaching his daughter to a heavy boulder and dropping her into the sea. He watched her sink and drown. I prayed that the dolphins would rescue her, and quickly and peacefully bring her to the Sea Goddess and into her next life. Such would be honour indeed.

It was time to travel back to Jerusalem, collect our things, meet the new baby, and say good-bye to our family. Then we would head back into Europe, and finally, home. Hitchhiking was permitted on this stretch of road, and we caught a ride with an Israeli man. I discovered that he had done his tour of duty in Lebanon the same time I was there. He had been in charge of interrogation as part of Israel's Mossad, and I could only imagine the things he had seen and the death he had known. I didn't want to think about how they interrogated anyone. The Mossad, Israel's secret service, has a veil of mystery to them. He said he had not been allowed to discuss what he did until after his discharge from the army. Even then, he decided not to say anything, because no one would understand. Having to carry war secrets for years, having no one to share with, or no way to purge the memories, seemed cruel.

As we said *shalom*, there was a heartbeat where we quietly looked into each other's eyes—a momentary pause on such a beautiful word. *Shalom.*

Hopping a bus, we passed by the Dead Sea and Masada. I was saddened to see that there was now a massive resort, and you no longer had to climb Masada—a cable car now took tourists to the top. I loved my memories of being there when it was still in its raw natural form. I recalled having to climb it the hard way, one step at a time, all the way around the mountain. Our bus continued through the Negev, past Jericho and into Jerusalem once more.

Back with our family, we were introduced to the new baby, Catherine. We could only imagine Tamir's reaction to having another girl. It wasn't long before Angel confided that the moment we left, Tamir had beaten her up badly. He kept punching her in the stomach, trying to kill the baby. She was taken to the hospital and told that if the baby's head had been on the side he was punching, the baby would have died. I felt responsible—me and my opinions and open disgust at how men treat women probably had Tamir fuming under his skin. Man, I needed to learn not to be so aggressive when trying to protect women.

When Angel proudly said she had stood up for herself for the first time in her life, my guilt subsided somewhat. She told the police to take Tamir away. He spent a few days in jail while Angel recuperated, spoke with a lawyer, and then confronted him. She told him she had learned that this house was hers and he did not have the right to kick her out, but she, in fact, had the right to kick him out. Tamir then became very quiet and promised he would not hurt her again. I was so proud of her—she had found her voice.

Saying good-bye to Rose was the hardest. She was the only one of us who was not yet able to have a voice. She stood in the kitchen and wouldn't look at me.

I put my arms out. "Rose. Please?" I motioned for her to come. She ran into my arms and we cuddled for the longest time. I felt her tears fall on my heart and I wanted to steal her. Rose very seldom had stepped out from the protection of her closed-in city; she was literally and spiritually walled into the old ways. Here was a young teenager, knowing that education was available, wanting to have a career, but her father ruled her life and said no.

I had taught her the chorus of a song—altering it slightly—which we often sang together. We sang it one last time; "Run to me, whenever you're lonely. Run to me, whenever you're scared. Darling, you run to me" by the BeeGees. She was so cute because her pronunciation of "ing" was "ink," no matter how much we practiced. I still sing that song and think of her—I wonder if she does the same.

It had been three weeks since we left Dahab. We were walking through the Old City for the last time, when a girl came running through the crowd toward us, calling our names. It was Geezala.

She threw her arms around me. "Thank you. Thank you," she said. "I opened my eyes and saw that I was going to be making a terrible mistake." She had realized that her Pharoah Ramses still believed that women were not equal to men and they needed to be controlled. If he could inflict an honour killing on his sister, how could he possibly respect or love Geezala? One moment, one night, and one chance conversation had the power to alter the course of her destiny. *Hum'da'allah!*

When we left Israel after three months, security was even tougher than when we had entered. Answering the same questions about Saudi, and the fact that we stayed with a Palestinian family for so long, led to another intense search. An Israeli female guard frisking us was the only entertaining element. Lorraine had every inch of her bust squeezed, lifted, and kneaded like dough. Then I stepped behind the curtain; the guard took one look at my small chest and dismissed me.

After we again refolded our knickers and repackaged our tampons, we had our own security escort past the crowds and lines. We drew much attention to ourselves as we were ushered right to our seats on the plane. Shalom Israel.

1998

A Cup of Tea with a Spoonful of Forgiveness

Whenever I returned to Canada, it usually took about three years for my wanderlust to creep over me again. Although Lorraine and I now lived in a gorgeous little flat, had great jobs, and were overall happy, that unsettled need for travel would inevitably take hold of me. Lorraine would have loved to buy a home and settle down, but to me that meant prison. Every time she mentioned a house, I felt handcuffs being slapped around my wrists.

The Christmas holidays had begun and Jimmy's partner, Verna, decided to invite the entire family for both Christmas Eve and Christmas dinner celebrations. Although petrified to be with my entire family, including Mom and Dad, I promised Lorraine we would go together, to honour my sister-in-law's effort.

I've had my share of physical illnesses, but the flu was not typically one of them. I hadn't had the stomach flu in years, but on Christmas Eve morning, I woke up with a fever and felt nauseous. By midday, I was throwing up. Lorraine went by herself. My family agreed that I was faking it but, come Christmas dinner, and Lorraine there without me, they opened to the possibility that I was indeed, sick. Coincidentally, my father was also sick. He and I were the only members of our family not to make an appearance on Christmas Eve or for Christmas dinner. It would be the last chance for a family get-together.

The seasons came and went, each bringing sadness surrounding my family relations, which had ground to a halt. I had not seen my parents in years. I once saw my dad sitting in a park by himself—on Father's Day. I cried for hours at the waste. Eight kids, and he sat all alone in a park. Things had gotten so bad that my own mother would pretend not to see me on the street.

It was becoming increasingly hard to live in the same city. I was planning on getting out of Canada again and applied to the United Arab Emirates. The thought of moving to another city within Canada must have been too simple a plan, because it never entered my mind. If I were leaving, it had to be on a grandiose scale—nothing short of the other side of the world.

On a dark, wintry evening, less than two weeks before flying away, I heard a small, unmistakeable voice inside my being. It was not the voice I normally heard, not the one constantly chattering away, oftentimes negatively. No, this voice was different. It felt like it came from a floating area around my heart centre, as opposed to coming from my head. Quietly, it told me to go see my parents.

It was time. I had come a long way from the days of absolute fear of God and now felt more in tune to spirit, angels, and intuition. My new understanding allowed me to feel safer in the Divine's love, believing that I was part of God and this universe, just as I am.

I still, however, debated with that intuitive voice. My parents would be out, I argued, but it quietly said, "Go."

I had to forgive my father, my mother, and myself—to release each of our souls from my entrapment of hatred. Mostly, I had to forgive me and release me from all the blame I put on my shoulders. This was killing me.

Lorraine never questioned what I was doing. She instinctively knew it had to be done. We looked up their address and drove in silence. My dad was very sick with emphysema, and I was soon going to board another plane.

"Mom. It's Edna." The buzzer let me in. As she opened the apartment door, we guardedly greeted each other. Sharing a cup of tea and one of my mom's homemade biscuits, I commented on how many years had passed since I had the pleasure of her cooking. I don't remember much of the conversation—it was all idle chitchat and improvisation.

After about twenty minutes, my dad appeared; he had just gotten up from a nap. There we sat, my parents and me, alone together for the first time in forever. I talked about my upcoming job overseas, and then we moved into the living room. I took a deep breath in.

"Mom. Dad. I came here because I wanted to talk with you both before I go overseas. I want to tell you that I forgive you for the hurt you have caused me. I also ask you to forgive me for any time I didn't come from a place of love."

"We forgive you. We also are sorry," they harmonized.

My dad continued, "I have prayed for this day to come. Your

lifestyle has alienated you from our family, and I fear for your soul and that you will be spending eternity in hell."

Mom added, "The Bible says you are an abomination to God. It's just not natural."

So much for forgiveness and being non-judgemental.

Watching their mouths moving and their eyes still full of anger and disgust, I began a conversation in my own head.

I looked at them sitting there condemning me, and I wanted to blurt out, *What about your other kids? Among my siblings, there was another teenage pregnancy by my oldest sister but that seemed to have gone off the radar, appearing not to have happened. Drinking excessively, drugs, manic depression, bisexual relationships, children "out of wedlock," abortions, anger management problems, prostitution... What about these? Why was my life so drastically wrong?*

As I sat yelling in my head, I knew that my siblings had known their share of being disowned, but as times changed, so did my parents. When it suddenly wasn't so bad to live common-law, they changed with the times and became accepting. Not so with me.

As my dad, in particular, continued to tell me how much he feared for my soul, how my lifestyle had alienated me from my family, and how I would be spending eternity in hell, I tried to get him to look at the whole picture. "I don't mean to bring up old stuff, but Dad, the way you were with me and all that stuff. I've been so abandoned by this family." I didn't rehearse that line. It just seemed to come from within me and took even me by surprise.

Mom jumped in, sounding baffled. "Abandoned! It's *you* who abandoned us!"

My mother started crying as my head began swirling in a daze of confusion. *I abandoned them? Is she crazy? I've been kicked out of this family for years.*

Zeroing in for the kill, she continued, "Do you know there is not a day that goes by that I don't think of Tamara-Lynn? Do you know how much I cry for her and long to find her and worry about her?"

Back inside my head, I stared at her in utter disbelief. As I talked, I knew no words were coming out. *Tamara-Lynn! My baby! You told me throughout my entire pregnancy that I would be giving birth to a monster, a freak. You both kicked me out and only visited me in that home for unwed teenage mothers a few times during the whole nine months. And you now speak of my baby—and you even know the name I gave her!*

My mother continued, but I wasn't listening. My anger was consuming me.

Tamara-Lynn. You brought up her name like it was nothing to me. As if I had no emotion, you are sitting here throwing her name at me and crying tears of sorrow. You have never ever, ever asked me how I felt. What is going on here? It's as if it's your baby.

I couldn't take it anymore. I had nothing to say in response to my mother. No way was I going to expose my feelings about my baby girl. I continued struggling to breathe. "Mom. Dad. Stop. Since I have been here, you have said over and over that I'm going to hell. If you say it one more time, I am leaving. Dad. You can never, ever, ever say those words to me again. If you tell me I'm going to hell one more time, I will get up and leave. As for Lorraine, she is the one person who has loved me unconditionally, and I love her and you can't condemn me for that. You have told me my whole life I'm going to rot in hell. What about the things you've done?"

Not hearing me, Dad said, "I have made my peace with God. You must make yours. He wants you to return to the fold. You will rot in hell if you continue this lifestyle. Your mother and I are concerned for you..." Blah, blah, blah, blah...

Praying for my angels not to abandon me, I knew that the moment had come to stop their abuse and to speak my truth. I needed to tell my father what I knew deep in my soul. Finding my voice, I looked into my dad's eyes.

"Dad. I have always felt that I would be totally alone when you die. I have promised myself not to share my sorrow with anyone in our family. No one can see my pain. I have it all planned. I would go to the funeral home alone and talk to you after you died, because then you couldn't hurt me anymore. For your funeral, I am going to sit at the back of the church. Nobody in my family will ever see the pain in my heart over your death or know how my life has been so destroyed. My pain is a very personal sorrow."

Sitting quietly and saying nothing, my father lowered his eyes to the floor. My mother sat, staring at me. They were both quiet. I had been heard. My angels were visibly in the room.

After moments of silence, my dad said, "It's your sister's birthday in two days. Why don't you come and surprise her?"

"Only if Lorraine can come. No matter how you feel, she is the best person in my life, and nobody has loved me like she has. We have been together for almost a decade, and I love her. You both have missed out on having me as a daughter and knowing her. You would have loved us both if you had only given us a chance."

Dad said okay, but Mom said nothing. I said good night and left to meet Lorraine at the coffee shop; she was surprised that we were going to dinner. I had no energy to rehash the evening and Lorraine was gracious. She knew that when it was the right time, we would share everything. She gave me the space I needed.

Lorraine had met my parents years ago but when we arrived for dinner two nights later, they said nothing to her. *Oh no.*

Both Naomi and Lorita were already there with their kids, which helped redirect the tension. There was no surprise—they had already heard I was coming. There were a few surprises for me, though.

Naomi and Lorita were now living in the same house. Lorita had turned to Jesus. Although she still believed in her mystical experiences and the native truths she had discovered, she was more and more turning to the born-againers. When I talked with her, she said she wanted to believe me, but now had doubts. The things I told her about my spiritual journey made sense to her, but they weren't exclusive to finding Jesus, and that was now confusing her.

I knew I was losing her. Even her kids, after being put into Sunday school, were suddenly afraid of everything. The whole world seemed dark and of the devil to them. Nothing was blessed—everything was cursed.

It was very subtle, but Lorita began questioning why I had so many physical problems. I could hear it in her voice—she was calling me an attention-getter and a fake. She had become like the rest of my family. I was already struggling with understanding why illness and injury happened so much in my life. I felt guilty and believed that maybe I was a fake.

Within moments of that conversation, Lorita dropped a thirty-pound rock on her toe and was in a lot of pain. Looking at each other, we both knew the gods were talking. If only we could have our own beliefs and accept each other in the process.

The kids were drawing a picture of me, and Dad said, "You can go into my bedroom if you want. I have pictures of Edna on my wall."

My heart sunk. Lorita and I jumped up and went into his bedroom. It was eerie and alarming. There on the wall was a frame full of pictures. Several of them were of me, at the height of Dad's craziness. In one, he had his arm around me, and I remembered the exact moment because I was panicked and afraid. Lorita thought the pictures were creepy too, and we left his bedroom. Mom said nothing.

Back in the living room, I became very quiet and fought the need to run. Lorraine had been uncomfortable since walking in to a deafeningly silent welcome.

Finally, my mother's voice rang out, "Supper's ready—everybody self-serve. Get your own plates and load up."

I was in the kitchen alone when my father appeared. "Hey, baby. You can eat that in my bedroom if you like."

Time stopped. I just couldn't believe it. Silence overtook me again. I said nothing. I looked into his strange eyes, spiritually thrown into a tailspin. He stood there, smirking.

Returning to the living room, I felt life around me was going on without me. I just sat there, eating in silence, looking to Lorraine, pleading that she read the hidden fear behind my eyes.

The night went by, and everybody bundled up to go home. We were gathered at the front entrance, and Naomi started to tell a story. As she talked, Dad began to do what he used to do when other family members talked: he singled me out and made fun of the person talking, all the while directing his comments to me. I wondered if anyone had a clue as to what was going on.

I hugged my mother, told her I loved her, and thanked her for dinner. I turned to my dad, hugged him, kissed his cheek, and said, "I love you, Dad. Good-bye."

I would never see my father again.

After all these years, he showed me no dignity or graciousness.

How could he do that? How could he not have changed? How dare he have those pictures of me on his wall? How could he make a come-on to me again? And again, I had no witnesses. I went there to forgive him and then he acted the same as before. Oh, Lord, what do I do now?

Finally, unable to hold things inside, the dam burst, and I spewed out all that had happened. Lorraine had felt something was terribly wrong and had just wanted the evening to end. Hearing for the first time what happened when I went over by myself, and now this, was too much for her. She found their cruelty despicable.

With only two weeks left in Canada, I called on Terri again, desperately needing her skill to see past the physical and connect the dots into the spiritual. Over the last three years, she had been deeply inspirational and tried to guide me to find my own truth and my own self-love. Terri understood immediately that I went having an expectation behind my forgiveness. She helped me see how I attempted to forgive. But when I was slapped with the reality that they hadn't changed, my forgiveness lost its intensity. I had never imagined forgiving them *without* their changing.

This was my greatest opportunity to finally let go of expectations. I had spent my life expecting and hoping for something different from my parents. If my heart were to truly forgive them, it must be with no expectations attached.

As I struggled to understand, I found out serendipitously that I now had high blood pressure. Could God have yelled at me any louder?

Terri asked, "Would you feel angry if someone beat you up?"

"Yes."

"What if someone raped you? Or abused you?"

"Yes."

"What if your boss tells you that you are useless and stupid? Would you feel anger? Weren't you extremely angry at Ginete?"

"Yes, I was. I get your point."

Finally, sensing a way to break out of my "Stockholm Syndrome," I went off to talk with my dad—spirit to spirit. There was no more talking face-to-face. For the first time, I felt that having anger toward Dad would be an okay emotion. I first wrote down and then spoke these words out loud, as if he were sitting in front of me:

Dad. Seeing you, seeking to forgive you, and then finding out you haven't changed at all has been devastating to me. I know that we will never see each other again, even if you live a long time. I must absolutely let go of any last fantasies about having a dad.

After leaving your apartment, I pulled out a handful of letters written by you. As I read them in horror, I realized how I have protected myself all these years. When a letter would arrive, I would read it once, go into shock, fold it up and put it back in the envelope.

Only now have I dared to reread them in an attempt to get some understanding of you. Did you know that counsellors and every person who has heard about you have had a similar comment? They all say I need to redirect my anger to you. I only now realize I have spent a lifetime being angry at Mom and the world, but I have never had the courage to be angry at you. I always justified this by saying, "At least he showed me some kind of love." It felt logical and safe. But not anymore. Dad, I am so angry!

Spending all morning reading your letters gave me an insight into your thinking that I had not previously had. I cannot believe the running theme in all of them: I seduced you?! How dare you say I seemed to enjoy the attention and that I came on to you. That I was thrilled to go to Montreal alone with you. That I never tried to stop you and that, in fact, I encouraged you! I am so angry!

You know something, Dad. I wrote to you, asking you to speak the truth and be honest for once in your life. I suggested you write the truth and give it to your children upon your death. Instead, you wrote lies, lies, lies, while you were living, and you sent a copy of my private letter to you, along with your forty-five page response, to all of your children. You told our entire family that it was my fault and that it was I who seduced my own father! It was I who desired to become my father's mistress! You even called your own wife a liar when she said you raped her. Oh, my God! You were given every chance to be accountable and you chose not to be.

I fear death. Why? Because you ripped my soul out of me by telling me I was useless, a sinner, a whore, a slut—and that I would rot in hell. I am so bloody angry. My mouth is spewing with curse words, trying to spit out this venom I've carried inside me.

I turned my anger toward Mom because she didn't protect me, and she turned her anger to me. But we have both been looking in the wrong direction. How the hell could she protect me when she was your victim as well?

The truth is you were a filthy pig to your daughter. You ripped out a piece of my heart. You choked my spirit.

I know in my heart of hearts that I saw you for the last time. It was the very last time to look eye to eye, and what did you do? You had the nerve to sleaze out on me again and invite me into your bedroom to eat my dinner! How disrespectful, when you knew we would never see each other again.

Collapsing, I felt emptied, drained of all feeling. I heard my still voice: *Forgive them and let them go. Let the weight of sorrow be lifted from your heart. It has caused enough damage. Have you not had enough of a broken heart? Your healing does not depend on external expectations--it is your internal change to outside forces that will bring you healing. Forgive, let go of expectations, and forgive again. Surrender what is not to be and embrace what is.*

Terri thought I was using my angels because I was afraid to say God had spoken to me. I was avoiding direct communication with God because it did not feel safe. She asked me to begin talking to Father God and Mother God, which I had a very hard time doing. I realized how I put God and parents and not being loved all in the same basket. The image of the Mother Mary on the plane to Montreal crept back into my memory, along with Lourdes and, again, the night I met my inner child. She had been trying to get my attention all this time, but it was a new concept for me to undo my image of God/Goddess as authoritative parents. Although I had been shown so many beautiful signs, I needed time. First, I needed a connection to a Father—that was my priority.

Going through my chakras, envisioning their energies radiating divine love, I prayed as my plane helped me escape.

> Father God, I choose to no longer have bloodstains dripping on my path from my leaking heart. No more. I take back my power. I am a child of God and of light. I am worthy to be loved. I am empowered within myself. I am. I am safe. Thank you, Lord, for leading me to peace.

Mother God would come into my life later. Meanwhile, destination Persian Gulf took care of my immediate need to distance myself from the throes of that last night with my father.

My Vision Quest

The native spiritual definition of a vision quest means to separate oneself from the tribe and go into the wilderness—alone—in search of your spirit guides to help prepare for your soul's journey through life. I was on my way.

The medical director and I had both worked at the same hospital in Canada. I had asked about him but regrettably did not listen to doctors and nurses telling me this man had a huge ego, and I needed to be careful not to tick him off. Many administrators working in the Middle East are very dysfunctional people, able to wield power that they are unable to have on their home turf. I ran away from the best job I ever had. From working for a wonderful female administrator at a woman's health centre, getting paid nicely, and always being happy at work, I went willingly into the clutches of someone I had been warned to stay away from.

Lorraine understood my need for travel and distance from family. This time, she would be able to join me within a few months—I would not have left her for a whole year again.

My contract and airline ticket for the United Arab Emirates arrived one month prior to my agreed-upon start date. Before signing my contract, I added a clause stating verbal approval had been granted for me to have a new flat, and faxed it back.

Tawam Hospital is in the garden city of Al Ain, in the Emirate of Abu Dhabi. On arrival, I was expecting to be set up in the all-new, female compound, but instead, I was put in a slum, complete with shanty flats, rats, and cockroaches. The couch and bed springs popped up, and the linoleum floors were peeling. Not even the efficiency flats of Saudi were this derelict. Apparently, they ignored my approved request. Knowing the process and length of *"Insha'allah"* time, I took matters into my own hands. In my exhausted state, I felt that I would be fine to turn around and fly home again. Having brought my trusty camping mattress, I lay on the living room floor for the four hours before work; they expected me to begin orientation at 8:00 a.m., after arriving at 4:00 a.m. I don't know what it is about Middle East contracts, but they expect you to fly across the globe and appear for work promptly upon arriving. Nothing impressed me thus far.

I very quickly realized that again, I was reacting in anger immediately upon arrival. I had brought my anger with me. On the one hand, I had a pull toward the Middle East, and on the other, I resented and hated it. Maybe I was just tired.

Sleep deprived, I walked to the personnel offices, dressed for a Canadian fall. A clerk kept urging me to sign my contract and give it to her, but I refused. I told the recruiter, Andrea, that there was no way I was living in that dump. She said everyone must stay there for the first while. When I questioned why my roommate Sylvie had been living there for eight months, Andrea took me to Housing where I met with Mohammed. On hearing "Blah, blah, blah, blah... *bukra*... *Insha'allah*." I leaned over his desk. "No *bukra*. No *Insha'allah. Today!*"

I knew that if I unpacked my bags, I would be there forever. I simply refused to work. I told Andrea she could let me know the hospital's decision, and I would wait at home. I couldn't understand why westerners accepted this. As I walked back, I saw the new female compound in the distance. The apartment complexes looked luxurious in comparison to my present flat. I did notice, however, that there wasn't a tree in sight. The buildings stood in the middle of an open barren field of sandy desert—not a tree in site. I was a bit scared of what I had gotten into.

Andrea called me a few hours later to see how I was doing. I reminded her that I had written on my contract that I wanted the new female compound; surely I was not the only person who felt this way. I asked if Dr. Tirón, my new boss, was willing to help; in his position, he could move mountains if he chose. He chose to stay out of it.

"Wow. What a nice guy! What a nice beginning to know he doesn't care to help!" Andrea agreed that it was odd. The warnings I had received about him were now echoing in my head. I was tired, cranky, and hot, as I was still wearing my winter clothes in desert heat. I told Andrea she could phone me with news of a move or news of a flight.

Realizing that my reaction was offending my roommate, I apologized. After all, this was her home, and she was making the best of it. Sylvie was dating a Pakistani named Azam, who worked in "Administration corridor," where I was to be working. He came over to see who the new troublemaker was. Azam was a friendly, polite, handsome Muslim man. At first he just stared at me, trying to figure out my problem. I suggested that rumours were flying about me and he said, "Edna, everyone is speaking of this. They are thinking you are some big-shot lady from Canada."

How could I explain that I had been through this *"Insha'allah"* before and was not going to settle? Maybe it was a panic attack. The phone rang. It wasn't Andrea. It was Housing—I was moving in two hours.

My new digs were nicer but no comparison to Saudi. Although the building was new, wires hung from the beams, paint was already chipped, and it was freezing inside. There was no shade, no grass, no flowers, no fountains, and clearly, no groundskeeper. The new female compound looked like Saudi's Empty Quarter, its surroundings totally inhospitable. Considering Al Ain is the garden oasis of the UAE, it was shameful to see that not one tree was left standing within our compound walls. It felt insulting and cheap.

Meeting Dr. Tirón was odd, as I was already unimpressed by his reputation and lack of concern toward me. He laughed at my troubles and said he wouldn't live there either. I sat wondering why he chose not to help and felt like thanking him sarcastically.

Andrea had told me that women in Tawam wore uniforms, and so, I brought no other work clothes. Dr. Tirón said that my position was one of prestige and I should dress accordingly in nice dresses. I was surprised at his candour when he said there were a variety of seamstresses in town to make me nice clothes. My first thought was that he had become Middle Easternized in his thinking of women and felt comfortable saying whatever he wished. He was very arrogant, but I felt much more equipped to deal with him than I had with Ginete. I wasn't yet taking his remarks personally. *He* could buy my pretty clothes if he wanted me to dress up. I wore the same uniform as everyone else.

My office had the most beautiful view, with huge windows looking out to a mini-oasis of palm trees, weeping willows, and green grass, complete with tropical birds—a stark contrast to our housing compound hidden in the back.

Tawam was an acute care hospital, with four VIP wards and two royal suites. These were special wards for the elite or royalty, of which there were many. Nurses working the VIP shift often did nothing except serve *chai* to patient's families; it was part of their duty. Even the regular ward patients, regardless of status, all expected VIP treatment, and the nurses had a hard time dealing with this. Health care was free to nationals and staff.

Signs posted throughout the hospital urged visitors to turn off their mobile phones. Attempts were made to explain how the phones interfered with equipment, but it was to no avail. Everyone walked around talking through their headsets as if they were appendages they couldn't live without. It became a joke that in every car, every mall, and every café, there was a constant hum of various ungodly computerized tunes to ring in call after call. There would be five men sitting around a table and each one of them would be talking to someone on their mobile. I began suspecting that they were talking to the guy across the table.

The old compound housed the recreation centre and outdoor swimming pool, but western staff did not run it, and there were no organized tours, trips, or barbeques—we were on our own. There was no sense of community. Staff formed cliques very quickly, usually with people from their particular orientation group; a general sense of camaraderie was visibly missing.

Alcohol was not forbidden, and Tawam had a small liquor store on compound, with staff allowed to spend a percentage of their monthly income on alcohol. We each carried a booklet that had to be stamped every time we bought booze. Men and women could be together anywhere, anytime. Women could drive, and did. Western women did not have to wear *abayas* or cover their hair. They were asked only to wear modest clothing out of respect. There were no Mutawa to fear. There were even Christian services every week.

A hierarchy of nations still existed but the mix wasn't as divided: Some third-world nationals—still referred to as "TWNs"—lived in the same flats as westerners. The clerks, housekeeping, and food workers, all from India, Pakistan, Bangladesh, and Sri Lanka, as well as the outside workers from Afghanistan, all lived together.

Afghanis were again designated to work "the yard." They "mowed" the sand, built houses, installed plumbing, electrical work, and air-conditioning, all with no experience whatsoever, and all regardless of the heat. Metal rods hung from ceilings because they didn't know what to do with them. I was afraid of the electrical wiring. Not knowing the politics of their country, I was confused why this was better than Afghanistan. It must have been bad if this was considered a good life for them. In winter, when the temperature dipped to a bone chilling 65F, they would don scarves around their faces. I was told not to talk with them but felt uncomfortable walking past them every day, as if they didn't exist. I occasionally said *"Marhaba,"* as I passed by, but they would just stare back at me, talk amongst themselves, and nod their head toward me, not sure what to do.

Azam, carrying himself with a sense of pride and an educated body language, was the head of the clerks working the Administration corridor, running errands, copying, handling mail, and serving coffee and *chai* to administrative staff. Being Pakistani, Azam would treat the Indian staff, particularly the cleaning staff, as if they were his servants. There was visible tension. He showed such a kind heart to everyone, except those from the country at war with his.

Azam's group sat in a small room next to my office. A bell would ring and they would race down the hall to the office of His Excellency, Sheikh Mohammed, often only to serve a cup of *chai*.

All the TWN men lived at the back of our compound, in what looked like prison blocks. One big room with bunk beds housed eight to twelve men. As I got to know them, they told me they were served the same meal everyday—chicken, chicken, and more chicken. Maybe the prejudice wasn't so hidden. I wondered how they managed to be so clean and well-shaven each day, always immaculately dressed and primped; they had outdoor sinks and took turns shaving. Many of the guys were skilled tailors and made their own suits.

After seeing where they lived, I was embarrassed at my outburst for what I called a dump. It was humbling to see those with little earthly riches display such beautiful spirits—for the most part. I was grateful for them in my life because they taught me grace and dignity.

The TWNs had arranged their own day out. They were allowed use of a hospital bus and organized a picnic, a visit to a camel trading post, a round of machine-gun firing, a camel ride, and a swim in the river. I saw the notice on the hospital board and signed up, assuming there would be lots of staff going. I did not know that it was really designed for the TWN male population. Neither did Christine, an Irish nurse. There we were, with about fifty dark, handsome men, all curious why we had come along. Only one other woman was present, a Sri Lankan lady with her husband. She wasn't allowed to talk with us or participate in the activities—she was just there. Christine and I gravitated toward each other. She had been in the UAE for a few months already. All of the guys who worked in the room next to me were on this trip, including Azam. They were very friendly, and I saw them laughing as they watched us. They never once made us feel we didn't belong. And then there was the camel ride.

This wasn't a riding stable with trained guides and camels with saddles made for westerners to enjoy. No. This was the desert, with Bedouins, their herd, and no saddles. I watched the guys attempt to ride, fall, hurt themselves, but try to laugh it off as they limped away. Of course, they began to prod me on and offered to ride with me. Azam said he would get on behind me.

I was going to accept his invitation before I realized that there really wasn't a "behind me." I would be sitting on the butt of the camel and Azam would be sitting a bit too close to me. I felt a stir in the crowd and decided this felt too uncomfortable. Azam and his buddies helped me on the camel. He became like my protector. I begged them not to go far from me, in case I fell. This they loved. They were going to be my heroes, and everyone was shouting, "Lean forward, Madam. Lean forward."

I had no choice but to lean forward. I was, for all intents and purposes, facing toward the ground. The camel was sitting down, with all four legs tucked under him; he raised his hind legs first, which in turn, lifted his butt higher and higher, thus making me the highest thing in the air. As his hind legs stretched out completely, the angle from back to front was a steep 90 degrees. And then he lifted his front legs. This camel must have been thirty hands high, and compared to a horse, he was not a gentle soul and had no graces about him. Allah, I was high.

As my brothers cheered me on, I saw the Bedouin laugh with his black eyes. He was going to have fun with me. He had a group of camels behind him and I was on the outside. There were five other guys on each of the other camels. The guy in the middle had camels on both sides of him, slurping and dripping gooie-yuck from their fat, fat lips and tongue, all over the guy's legs and hands. As the camel rested his large chin and slobbered away on the poor guy, I could feel his fear. I got the giggles and thanked Allah I was on the outside and in the back!

As the Bedouin hit his camel and shouted, "*Yella,*" I saw my life flash before me. Looking at our captor, I pleaded, "*Schwai, schwai*—slowly, slowly." Mr. Bedouin laughed and yelped, "*Yella. Yelllllaaa!*" I hung on for dear life. Every camel hoof that came down against the desert floor penetrated through each vertebra in my back and neck, crashing my teeth together as my head bopped recklessly. I already had back problems and thought I was going to break my back.

Having no saddle meant hanging on to the camel with my thighs. And hang on I did. I sat on his bum with his hump in front of me; the reigns stretched from his mouth, over the hump, and reached back to me. The leather penetrated my palms as I held on for dear life. I decided to call Mr. Bedouin's bluff and started to holler the women's "lalalalala" and shout, "*Yella,*" myself. The quiver in my voice was a result of the camel's stride. As he looked back surprised that I was encouraging the camel to go faster, he laughed, called my bluff, and hit the gas pedal. My teeth were crashing down on each other. My boobs were aching as they tried not to rip away from my chest from bouncing so violently. I thought, *Holy crap, just don't fall off. Don't panic.*

All the guys surrounded my camel and helped me off. I ended up falling off and a few of us had to roll away as the camel's tush came down to the ground for a rest. I was trembling and shaking. This time I accepted the guys' offer to get me a drink of juice.

Christine was petrified but decided she had better get on this camel now or never. She had wanted to first watch me, insanely thought I was having fun, and decided to get brave. She only lasted a minute and was screaming to come back. Mr. Bedouin had to turn the camels around and she got off, saying, "Jesus, Mary, and Joseph." I laughed and laughed. I had just enough time to snap the most brilliant picture of Ms. Christine on her camel looking like a pro. I framed it and gave it to her for her birthday, and she was prouder than proud.

Off to the rifle range. I abhor guns but for some crazy reason, I decided to try and shoot with the guys. The Arabs who were teaching us devoted their time to me; my brothers sat around as I lay on my stomach with a rifle in my hand. It had the makings of a porn movie. We had so much fun trying to hit targets. By lunch, I was starving.

The meal was set on silver platters atop carpets laid out all along the floor. Everyone ate with their hands. I was uncomfortable dipping my hands directly into the food along with everyone, so I used the pita bread. It was such a nice picnic, full of Asian foods.

I wanted to go swimming, but of course, with every Asian man on compound present, there was no way I was going to put on a bathing suit. They had assumed I would not and pointed to an area where Christine and I could lay by the water and relax. As the men became boys, throwing each other into the water and having a blast, Christine and I went off and lay on the dock, napping and laughing about our great adventure. Throughout the day, many of the guys would come, stand beside us, and take a picture.

Back at work, I was surprised to see pictures of our trip on the bulletin board. That day broke all barriers between us, and from then on, we had a wonderful working relationship. How sad that no westerners joined us for the day, which turned out to be the happiest I had all year.

Compound life was very isolating and lonely. Without phones or television—never mind satellite—there was an incredible sense of loneliness. I could count my friends on one hand. I often looked out to the vast emptiness surrounding me and wondered what everybody did on weekends. My recreation was swimming, and I had brought heaps of self-help books on energy and healing. I hoped that I would turn this bleakness into a time of peaceful solitude to read, meditate, study, and heal. But the silence could sometimes be deafening.

Mattie and I would have been in orientation together, except that I missed it due to my revolt. She had heard about me and asked for help. Her voice cracking with emotion, she spoke of living in the dumps and finding a dead rat that morning. I was surprised, because she was a doctor, with rights to a villa. Warning her that Housing would say, "*Bukra. Insha'allah*," I suggested she not budge until granted her wish.

Housing did exactly that. They didn't know what to do when she plopped her butt down for two hours, saying she was not leaving until they found a newer place for her. She was told that there were no villas available, and she said a flat would be fine. The flat she was assigned turned out to be huge, three times bigger than mine, and included comfy furniture. It faced an orchard of date trees, which was a blessing compared to every other view of the sandpit. She loved it and never bothered moving into her own villa.

Our up-and-down friendship began with a trip to the market, which was never a disappointment with its fruits, veggies, and spices. As I saw Mattie buying at first price, I laughed and asked her why she didn't barter. She got angry with me and said the prices were low enough; she didn't want to insult the vendors. I told her they expected bartering—it was their custom—but she wouldn't hear of it. She was clearly upset and moody, so I decided it was best to leave her and go barter to my heart's content. At the end of the day, Mattie paid approximately $80 to my $15 but refused to learn or accept that their custom meant yelling back and forth, and walking away saying, "*Ashand awanti*—too much!"

I was living in a way that was a near polar opposite of my first expat experience. I went from having too many friends to having none, from having so much to do with so many to feeling very much alone.

Apart from a few outings with Mattie and the occasional night with Christine, I stuck pretty much to myself. Christine and

I spent quiet evenings talking about work and drinking. Mattie and I would have latte's and grocery shop on the weekend, if she wasn't working.

To my surprise, there was an array of lesbians from all over the world, many from Lebanon and Egypt. I went to a few parties but for the most part, there wasn't an open inviting presence coming from anyone. I didn't get it—why was this whole environment so stark and bleak? Why didn't everyone want to blend together and support each other?

After being so devastated by my family, I think I was longing to feel cocooned. I wanted to nestle into a group of friends who played hard and loved hard together—like in Saudi. Tawam wasn't putting out, and the surrounding emptiness exacerbated my own internal barrenness.

The same old heightened intensity of emotions existed, however. People fell fast and furiously into love. Sexual relations were on active duty, but this time, the straights outnumbered the gays; I had no gay male friends. Hearts were broken quickly, and drama abounded, only now, I was on the fringe looking in.

I discovered Abraheem, who frequently took people on desert treks. He was famous for hiking at a brisk pace, and I was told I had to be in shape to go. I asked if he could bring it down a notch for those of us who couldn't jog through the desert. He laughed and said, *"Insha'allah."* His organization was hosting a desert barbeque on Christmas Eve, but we would be driving—no hiking yet.

An assortment of expats sat in a circle, drinking and partying around the huge fire pit. As the evening progressed, I sauntered into the darkness, just away from the fire, to get a peek at the constellations. At least a billion stars were sparkling. Two shooting stars fell side by side through the sky; seeing this was a first for me. What kismet our galaxy provided on this quiet Christmas Eve. I desperately missed Lorraine.

I drifted into the stillness of an Arabian night, lost in my thoughts about family and all that had so recently transpired. I was still stinging from my father's bite. I gazed into the glory of the heavens, wanting so much to be a part of the peacefulness. Such melancholy enveloped me, as I lay back in the middle of a hundred strangers. Thank Buddha, Lorraine would soon be coming. The sound of jingle bells snapped me out of my thoughts as I looked up to see Santa Claus—in shorts.

I spent Christmas day with Christine and an international assortment of women. After Christine attended mass "with all the saints and sinners alike," she prepared a great chicken feast, complete with wine and liqueurs.

It was also my coming out party. With so many lesbians on compound, I felt safe, and besides, I wanted to be who I was. It now seemed silly to be secretive. No straight person ever has to make an announcement. This announcement would therefore be my last. From that point on, I discussed Lorraine simply as my partner, just as anyone would discuss theirs. No more being on the outside, because of being gay. To me, it was the heterosexuals who chose an alternative lifestyle. Two of the ladies at dinner were also gay. We continued on without missing a beat.

The only hint of rejection was from a girl I worked closely with. Hearing her make derogatory remarks about all the lesbians on compound, I knew I needed to be honest. When I told her, she said she had guessed. "Just don't come on to me," she added.

"Don't flatter yourself," I murmured.

Ramadan followed on the heels of Christmas. There was a bonus in that both Muslims and westerners got to work half days. I was enjoying President Sheikh Zayed and his generosity. Water still had to be hidden behind doors, there was no gum chewing or eating except in the draped cafeteria, but getting off at 1:00 p.m. was a joy. Being so busy and having nothing to do on compound, I usually worked my normal hours during Ramadan and got paid overtime, which turned into almost a second cheque.

Mattie experienced her first Ramadan and commented on the hospital being full of patients with stomach problems from binging and lying down still full of food. Fasting Muslims walked around with sullen faces and said they were very weak, but, *"Insha'allah."* It's a dramatic time, and as in any society, there is a full share of martyrs wanting the world to see their enormous sacrifice. I could see Mattie's disgust and impatience; she was already having a hard time accepting what she witnessed on an everyday basis.

My relationship with Dr. Tirón continued to be difficult. His arrogance was burdensome. He would constantly make chauvinistic remarks about women: "She sure has a mind of her own!"

"Have you ever, in the history of mankind, heard that comment addressed to a *man*?" I sarcastically asked as I walked out of the office, not giving him a chance to react.

God, he was cruel, but this time, I didn't spend hours weeping, crying, and feeling like a wounded little girl, who had been severely beaten up by her Dad. Yes, I was angry and disgusted at his behaviour but it was *his* behaviour and had no reflection on me. He had already begun yelling at me in front of doctors and professors from the university, including the dean. Doctors would say they didn't understand how I put up with his behaviour.

The gossip in the corridors was that he tried to westernize Tawam, which was a sure ticket out of the Middle East. He refused to understand the Arab mentality and culture.

His last signature before vacation was a letter to His Excellency, asking for more money, more vacation days, less work hours, and more perks, including another car. I was embarrassed for him; any medical directors I had previously known worked longer hours than I did, but he managed to leave on time every day. His arrogant response when he saw me watching him leave was, "I worked twenty-four hours a day when I first started. You'll leave early when you finally get the hang of it as well. I'm just a fast learner." What a jerk!

One thing I was learning was to speak to my "enemy." If I had a problem with someone, or they had a problem with me, I was finally able to open up a dialogue with them—not aggressively or condescendingly, but as an honest talk. I was open to learning and growing, so much so that some didn't like my honesty. Others, however, grew to love it. If I were in the wrong, I would own up to it, learn, and move forward. This was very freeing for me, but I had to understand that not everyone wanted to be honest. This was *my* journey, and I couldn't thrust it on everybody.

Just before Dr. Tirón left, I spoke with him regarding his feelings and behaviour toward me. He pompously said he did not think I was worth a grain of salt.

I was taken aback by his boldness and didn't know how to react. His arrogance was like a slap in the face. I wasn't going to engage in conversation with that kind of an opening. My first reaction was a desire to tell him to sod off; my second reaction was to turn around and walk out. I was just learning to have a voice, and I cowered under his nastiness.

Within days of his vacation commencing, rumours started to fly that he was fired. Some of the doctors would fill me in on what was happening, and sympathize with me for having to work with such a difficult person. His previous secretary had lasted only a few months and the one before had walked out within two weeks.

When rumours begin, there is usually truth behind them. There was a sudden increase in the amount of closed-door meetings. Dr. B., who loved to gossip, hinted that he was asked to replace Dr. Tirón.

One morning, the office door swung open, and we heard a loud and sarcastic, "Ah. Look at your faces! You thought I was gone!" I was startled to see him and even more disturbed at his superiority.

Within a day, he began having his own closed-door sessions with each department head, and it quickly became clear what was happening. Doctors would leave his office smirking. Then it was my turn. I pretended not to know. I even went so far as to fake empathy for him—why did I feel the need to do that, considering how he treated me?

"I know there are rumours that I was fired but I'm here, aren't I? I was not fired, but I have decided to quit."

I felt sorry for him because his self-importance didn't allow him to see how embarrassing his behaviour was. He even went so far as to submit a three-week notice of resignation.

I was summoned immediately to His Excellency's office, given a letter, and told to hand it to Dr. Tirón, regardless of who was with him at that moment. I did, but not before reading it. In it, he was told he must vacate his office immediately and hand over his keys to Dr. B., who would be replacing him. Dr. Tirón stuck around the hospital for the next three weeks, sitting in a back office down by the ER. He would come in periodically, but Dr. B. would hardly ever speak with him.

I had to type a letter and have it delivered to him; it requested the keys to the pink Cadillac, a perk for medical directors. Dr. B. had been furious that Dr. Tirón had not handed over the keys to that car.

Custer's last stand was to try and bring me down with him. He told Dr. B. that I was incapable of doing my job and needed to be fired immediately.

This time, I walked into the office and said, "I hear you have some concerns with me." Dr. B. was very surprised but sat down, his eyes lowered, and repeated what he had been told. He realized that he had listened to Dr. Tirón without giving me a chance. He apologized.

I had found my voice and, finally, was able to speak and to defend myself. Our working relationship turned out to be very good.

New Year's was fast approaching. I think Mattie and I remained friends out of boredom. We had lots of laughs, but my ability to piss her off always kept me on my toes. One thing we shared was that we were both away from our partners. Hers was in Antarctica for the winter, and mine was in Canada. Lorraine was, however, planning to come over soon.

Anka was also in Mattie's orientation class. She was an eccentric, wild German fraulein, with dyed black hair and green eyes. She barely spoke English and was having a difficult time in Tawam. Anka was one of many who eventually would do a runner, but for now, she was trying to adapt. She invited Mattie and I to a New Year's Eve desert camp out. I had never slept out in the desert and I was thrilled.

Our trip turned out to be a near-disaster. Anka's friend with the car was an absolute control freak and a very nasty lady. We didn't know it then, but everybody hated her; she had the reputation of being a bulldog. There were a lot of gay women on compound, some butchier than others, but Sonja was the dykiest straight chick I ever saw. She looked and acted like a weight lifter on steroids—big, loud, abrasive, rude, and demanding. Sonja bought the alcohol and food supplies and charged each of us more money than the supplies were worth. When it came time for the trip, she decided Mattie and I would not be able to ride with her. Mattie was furious. We had no way of getting to the desert, and Sonja couldn't care less. We ended up taking a limo all the way to the edge of the desert where there is always a group of 4x4s, ready to help with the convoy.

Hopping in with a Kiwi couple, off we went. It was his first time manoeuvring through the sand, and he was shaking with adrenaline by the time we got there. His partner performed the familiar sexually explicit encouragement while, feeling like voyeurs, we laughed in the back. You cannot stop once you begin, or your 4x4 will sink into the sand. We bounced heavily over ridges caused by wind and drifting sand; the nose of the 4X4 would point upwards as we climbed, only to come barrelling down the other side headfirst. It constantly felt as though the vehicle could turn over at any second as it rocked back and forth, side-to-side, over on two wheels and back again. The driver had to keep moving, charging forward, pretending the V8 was a herd of camels; at all times, it was crucial to stay with the convoy. There was no second-guessing or thinking that one hill looked easier to manoeuvre than the one everybody else was taking.

There was only one driver who got stuck—Sonja. She was the example of what happens when one doesn't respect the desert rules. Sonja never listened, and we heard later that her passengers fought with her throughout the trip. She cursed and swore at the cars ahead of her and wanted to take charge. Although she had never been to this spot in the desert, she felt she could get there quicker than anyone else. Her 4x4 was neatly sunk into several feet of sand, right in the middle of the already set-up camp. Other expats had arrived earlier, a huge bonfire was going, and tents dotted the site. I could only imagine the campers' fright when they saw Sonja's 4x4 barrelling toward the centre of camp. Thank Allah, she sunk before hitting anything, or anyone. I didn't know how they planned to dig her out, and I didn't care.

Mattie and I went climbing while the group worked on getting Sonja's jeep out of the middle of the party. Dune climbing is one of the hardest aerobic exercises I've ever done. My heart was pounding, and it took me twice as long as Mattie to get to the top; she scrambled up the mountain like a gazelle.

Arriving at the top moments before sunset was dazzling. We walked along the taut ridge as if it were a tightrope; its edge, carved by the winds, was incredibly sharp. If our foot missed the tightrope, our legs would get buried up to our knees in sand. There were camels off in the horizon as the wind, soft and willowy, swirled the sand in gusts and circular movements, and sent it dancing through the air. Looking toward the horizon, we saw nothing but desert, sand drifts, valleys, and lastly, another stunning Arabian sunset. The stillness was like resting on Mars. Again, I felt higher than my body would physically allow me to go. Rhapsody on earth.

Back with the pack, we drank in the New Year repeatedly. With expats from all over the world, the clock rang midnight over and over again. As Sonja drank, she became even more belligerent, called me an "f-ing bitch," and cursed at me in German; she looked like she wanted to spit on me. I actually think she did hurl one at me as I passed by. Anka kept apologizing for her; she felt forced to be Sonja's friend, especially because she herself didn't speak much English. Luckily, there were lots of people there, and I just mingled, ignoring Sonja as best I could.

Although I was capable of having a mouth nearly as tough as Sonja's, I realized I didn't have to attack back. I finally understood that if I called my spirit back into me, and did not allow my energy to be consumed by her rage, I would remain intact. As she cursed me, I ignored her and looked quietly away. She didn't know what to do, because she was expecting a reaction from me. I physically saw her implode. From that moment, Sonja turned her rage into hysterical crying and Anka comforted her through her drunken stupor.

As the quiet before dawn approached, so did a heavy, ominous fog, bringing with it a sense of claustrophobia. Moisture droplets hung from our eyelashes and hair—so much for stargazing. It was a weird sensation to feel the fog entomb us in the middle of a desert.

Everyone slipped into their tents. Mattie and I put a tarp over us, crawled into our sleeping bags, and blissfully slept outside for the few hours before sunrise.

As the camp lay passed out, I had to get up. With the sun rising above the dunes, life felt so quiet and still. The intensity of the sun would soon stir everyone out of slumber. I sat in the quiet morning—what a wonderful way to bring in the New Year. Soon, Lorraine would be arriving. Oh, how I missed her during these moments.

Ahlen wa Sahlan, My Habibti

Long gone were the days of referring to one's partner as "lover" or "friend." How sad that we didn't feel worthy to belong to the world of acceptable relationships—and thank Buddha that finally ended, as we elevated ourselves into mainstream society. My darling, my life partner, my girlfriend—was about to be welcomed into my new desert home. Lorraine has dual Canadian and British citizenship. British passport holders are welcome to stay in the UAE for three months at a time, and so, we began to plot her arrival. The new female compound had an un*manned* security gate. We were willing to take the chance.

Seeing Lorraine for the first time in months was glorious. We stayed in Dubai over the weekend to get reacquainted before sneaking her home.

After the long ride back to Al Ain, we went to my favourite restaurant for dinner, prior to hopping the hospital bus back to the compound. The Ali Baba waiters had a habit of swarming around your table while you ate. If you put down a fork, they took it immediately. If you took a break in eating, your plate disappeared. I would be sipping a soft drink, put it down and go to have another gulp, and it would be gone. It was dizzying as these young men worked in overkill.

After ordering our favourite Arabian dishes—hummus, tzatziki, baba ganoush, all rich and dripping in oil—we talked about how Lorraine just needed to blend in, to act like everyone else and just walk past security.

She was suffering from jetlag and nerves, and became dizzy watching the twirling dervish waiters perform. Along with the rich food, it was too much for her. Her face turned ashen, and she said she needed air. Seeing her sense of urgency, I paid immediately and we walked outside. Standing at the hospital bus stop, she leaned over and threw up in the flowers. Thank Allah it was dark because I don't think a western woman throwing up would go over well with the natives.

The hospital bus came. I dared not tell her about the insanity of drivers. I didn't know how she would make it. We sat at the back, and Lorraine could barely keep from vomiting again. The drive was frenetic as usual, which certainly added to her nausea. Finally, we got off the bus, and as we were heading toward the security gate, Lorraine doubled over, again throwing up violently—fifteen feet from Security. My eyes darted back and forth, from her to them. *Oh, Allah. Please don't let them see this.* After she finished, we continued on past the guards and down the road to our flat. It was very, very hot, and the walk was about fifteen minutes through open desert, with nowhere to rest. Finally, we got to our apartment—we'd made it this far.

Everyone accepted Lorraine. Security ended up knowing her better than they knew me. They saw her every day! We would go swimming every night over on the old compound.

The only event the hospital put on was a pool party every other month. This was to welcome new staff members, and the occasion usually involved drinking and dancing; there were always prizes to be won. Everyone and every nationality, excluding the outdoor Afghani workers, would come. Lorraine and I would dance the night away. Mohammed, a 6' 3" security guard, started dancing with us, and from that point on, every time he saw Lorraine, he flirted.

Once, we both won door prizes; mine was a Dubai weekend getaway in a fancy hotel, and Lorraine's was dinner at an Indian restaurant in Dubai. Her "blending in" was working, and no one argued over her winning a prize. Soon, we were off for the weekend, including going to the Festival of Gold, a yearly event where all the gold souqs sell their goods for discounted prices. With tourism heavily promoted, Dubai had more security than Saudi; considering how much gold was openly available, a caper pulled off would have netted billions.

Our weekend was one of the nicest memories of our time together in the UAE. The restaurant experience was delightful, complete with a band playing Indian love songs. The sitar was mesmerizing; the musicians and singers all sat crossed-legged on a green, velvet couch, wearing their indigenous dress. Azam had teased us that we were going for real Indian food, "not like Red Indians."

After dinner, we went to Dubai's Global Village where there was a carnival, complete with Asian acrobats, music, popcorn, and goodies. This would be unheard of in Saudi; it was nice that the UAE had more normal living, especially during hot beautiful nights. The whole weekend took on a festive feel, ending with magnificent fireworks lighting up the night sky. How wonderful it was to get out of Tawam and back into life with my precious girlfriend.

Back home, we continued a friendship with Mattie, whose hatred of working in the Middle East was now off the charts. The abuse to women in such a male-dominated society proved to be almost impossible for her to accept. She could not find any means within her to respect the culture, the men, or even the women, because of what she saw as a physician.

She dealt with woman after woman who had diseases and infections from men. Women's vaginas were ripped open from forced sex and no lubrication. Infections and tears happened after childbirth because the women were circumcised, and then, when they gave birth, their wounds were torn open. Understandably, Mattie couldn't bear it and became more and more incensed.

Parents had brought a young girl to the hospital because she was getting so fat, and her feet were swelling so that she could no longer walk. We knew where this story was going. Mattie insisted the family leave the room, but the maid stayed as Mattie did the exam to confirm pregnancy. She had no choice but to inform the parents. We can only imagine what happened to this young girl. There were certainly honour killings, and it was a legal right for a man to kill any woman in his family who brought shame. Mattie was past the point of showing compassion, however, and no longer cared what happened to the girls. Besides, it was a steadfast rule that she had to divulge to the parents the truth— doctors could not hide or protect patients from consequences.

I also had a lot of contact with patients and their families. Every day patients would appear with their Viagra prescription, and an administrator would have to sign an approval to fill it. The male doctors laughed, but I was disgusted that they were giving Viagra to these men. Did no one consider the women? The idea of giving Viagra to these men was repulsive to all of us, and Mattie refused to fill out the prescriptions.

Sadly, Mattie's anger was also redirected toward the women for *allowing* the abuse to happen to them. "Let them bloody kill each other." With that kind of attitude in the world, it's not hard to wonder why wars happen. She wasn't the only one losing patience, though.

Like their Saudi counterparts, women of the UAE also had to fully cover themselves. It was incredibly strange to see them driving from behind their veils. As in any other Arab country, driving was surrendering your life to the gods. To make matters worse, the roads were designed British-style, complete with roundabouts. Imagine a six-armed-octopus of traffic lanes merging in and out of each other, zigzagging to and fro, but nobody knowing what they're doing. Just driving in a straight line is a mind-altering experience, never mind trying to manoeuvre a roundabout. The nurses and doctors I worked with talked of the horrific injuries they had seen, all from motor vehicle accidents due to a lack of driving skill.

If it wasn't a veiled woman who could not see properly as she nervously wound through the crazy male drivers, it was taxis that made so little money, they had to fly you to your destination so they could pick up their next trick. The Arab men were no better. Everyone seemed to have monster 4x4s, and some drivers were as young as thirteen.

I finally snapped. All my patience for riding in cars with lunatics at the wheel had been drained. I just couldn't stand the bus driver slamming his foot against the brake every few seconds, only to speed up, then brake again—over and over—as he honked at everything that moved.

Before I could think, I screamed from the back of the bus, "*Stop it! Please!* You drive insane! *Schwai. Schwai.* Please. I just need peace!" Staring in his rearview mirror, cursing at me, the driver almost got us killed. How dare a woman yell at him! The passengers on our bus became uncomfortable and sat quietly while he became more and more explosive.

He pulled into our compound and drove up to Security; he screamed and pointed his finger at me. Afraid, Lorraine and I jumped off the bus and ran into the gardens. She went one way and I the other. The bus driver drove around the compound and upon spotting me, yelled, "*Bukra. Bukra.* You go to Administration." I yelled back, "I *am* Administration," and walked off. I felt explosive and fed up with the men of Arabia and their insanity.

And then there was our little swimming pool in Tawam.

The older Arab girls had to swim in their clothes, pants, *abaya*, and scarves. The men, however, could bare all, including some massively hairy chests and backs. Children were allowed bathing suits, as were western women. In Saudi, the pool was restricted to women only. It was unthinkable on so many levels to have a male/female pool. Our two cultures didn't share the freedoms of bathing suits and men and women together.

My only source of exercise was swimming, and I requested that two lanes be roped off. There were already signs in Arabic and English saying that these two lanes were to be used for laps, but nobody adhered to this. Staff relented and put in a rope. The westerners respected the boundary, but the Arabs couldn't care less. They had their toys and rubber dinghies all over the ropes and continued to play in the swim lanes. We would beg them to let us swim, but they soon began to torment us and get a laugh out of disrupting our laps.

Some staff were giving up any attempts to swim laps, but I felt I needed to dig my heels in; if Tawam wasn't going to supply any other source of recreation, then I felt a need to make this one tiny demand. I tried asking the Recreation staff but, being Asian, they felt inferior to the Arabs and could not bring themselves to tell them what to do. I would go to the parents and plead my case, but they would only laugh, send their children to the lanes, and allow them to encourage others to join in the fun of kicking us as we swam by.

Even a father got in on the fun. I was the only westerner swimming laps. Using a snorkel, I noticed a large object floating at the end of my lane. The feeling in the air was that of a spaghetti western soundstage. I swear I heard *The Good, the Bad, and the Ugly* theme song playing in the background as the desert tumbleweeds danced in the wind. Showdown in Arabia had begun.

I swam toward the obstruction, thinking quickly about what to do. Everyone was now waiting for my hand to come around and bump into my intruder. There this father was, laughing to the people around the pool as he told his daughters to watch him. He was in a large dinghy that took up the entire width of the swimming lane. His legs were dangling out, and if I had been a shark, I would have attacked. Instead, I swam up to his dinghy, grabbed the side, and hoisted myself up.

"Are you proud? Is this what you teach your daughters? Is this how you teach your daughters respect? Do you respect yourself? Is this how a father shows his children how to interact? Do you teach them to disobey rules as you are doing?"

"Who makes this rule? Show me!" he exclaimed, thinking he had just won.

"Look at the signs. They are in English and Arabic. Look. Here. Here. *Here.* They all ask you to kindly allow people to swim in this tiny lane. You may have the whole pool. This is all I ask of you."

He was temporarily silenced and moved out of the way; he shouted at his children and pretended that he had proved to me who was the boss. My heart was pounding.

The next day, there he was again, sans dinghy. He had another plan. He and his two daughters were at the end of the pool waiting for me. I had had enough—again. I swam down and rather than talking calmly, I screamed, "What the hell are you doing? *You people have no respect!*"

"My *people!*" he shouted in fury.

"That's right. *Your people!*"

In a rage, he demanded to know my name, where I worked, and where I lived. I swam away and soon saw Security crouching at the end of the pool, waiting for my return lap. *Oh shit*, I screamed, as Lorraine quickly reminded me that she was here illegally, and that this was getting out of control.

I told Security that I would not say my name because I was afraid of him—this had nothing to do with my job. Security was afraid and did not know what to do. Promptly, all the Arabs began screaming and yelling at me. Security pleaded with me to apologize to a young mother because I had yelled at her child. I had previously lifted her brat out of the lane three times and asked the mother to please tell her child to stop.

Security said I insulted her. "Please. Please ma'am. She is a mother. Please apologize only to this mother." As I swallowed my anger and apologized, she spit toward me as she picked up her babies and left.

Being told this incident would be reported, I said, "Please. You must tell them to abide by the rules. Is it so wrong to want to swim?" The man reminded Security that I'd said *your people.* I apologized, admitting it was rude and that I had gone too far.

Not knowing what to do with my apology, he and the guard left.

I tried changing my swim times to late evening, but that turned out to be even worse. There weren't any bedtimes for kids and late at night the pool was packed, and not only with kids. Arab families sat around eating dinner and having social visits. It would appear my only option was swimming at midday, when the heat was too much for most to bear.

I stayed out of the pool for a few days, but on my return, all hell broke loose. Parents urged their children to line up along the rope and to kick and throw themselves into the lane, and on me, as I tried swimming. They did this with the momentum of a surging tidal wave. I had children diving on top of me. The mothers encouraged it and laughed; then, when I would look at them, their eyes would turn to hatred. They won. My last lap ended with me gagging at the sight of someone's bowel movement sitting at the bottom of my swim lane. I left the pool, sad, angry, and fed up at the complete disrespect and dishonouring of our one source of entertainment. I wished that I had my quiet Saudi women-only pool; they had the smarts to realize that East and West did not meet peacefully in a swimming pool!

I felt like we were all failing our divine potential. The swimming pool was like a cesspool of the nature of man. I was so disheartened that we couldn't even share a pool—never mind Israel and Palestine sharing a wall. Forget about the world living in harmony. *Oy vey*—all that from a swimming pool.

It was time to hit the desert again. Entrusting our lives to the leadership of crazy Abraheem, a group of us expats joined up for a desert trek; this outing included Mattie and a few doctors from Tawam.

It was summertime and very, very hot. Lorraine wisely froze water the night before, knowing it would become lukewarm within a few hours. We also had ice packs on our necks and head as we pressed forward into the desert. July wasn't the best month to be desert trekking. The temperature soared past 140F.

This desert trek was strenuous on many levels due to the heat and the slippery shale, but primarily, with Abraheem upholding his reputation of going very fast, everything felt heightened in difficulty. I was pulling up the rear, and he had no choice but to wait. This was a blessing for the group because, as they stopped and waited for me, they were able to rest. I sadly had no rest because it was always me they were waiting for.

Everyone was struggling, although no one was admitting it yet. I wondered if mirages came with sound effects, as I heard the sound of soft running water. Abraheem scrambled past a glorious wadi, as if it held no possible interest for his weary followers. He promised we would return on the way back, but I couldn't endure any more. You cannot walk by water at high noon in a desert, with heat waves visible in the thick air, and not expect a revolt. Abraheem's brother, Mohammed, waited for me and said he knew of another wadi just up the mountain slopes. "Just a few moments," he promised. It turned into a half hour at my speed, but Lord have mercy, when we saw the wadi, it was truly paradise. In the middle of absolute barrenness—no shade for miles, crevices, rocks, and shale everywhere in all four directions—this was more beautiful than anything I had seen up to that point in my entire life!

Abraheem wanted to complete his designated trek with another promise to return to this wadi as well.

I said, "Noooo!"—we were staying. As they continued up the mountain, heading closer to the sun, Lorraine and I waved *ma'arsalama*.

It was either pure faith or heat exhaustion that made us quite willing to let the entire team disappear and leave us in the middle of a desert, while we trusted them to retrieve us. I had complete confidence in their Bedouin blood. They, if anybody, knew exactly how to navigate this rugged terrain.

As they scampered up the mountain, Lorraine and I danced a dance of joy as we stripped down to natural causes and dove in. This water, coming from where, we didn't know, was very deep, very clear, and ice cold. There were rock formations and cliffs surrounding us, giving a sense of seclusion. Of all the times to see Bedouins, please Allah, not now. This was naked bliss.

My head was pounding from the heat, and we were starving. We lay in the wadi for a long time, then beached ourselves on the rocks, which happened to have a perfect overhanging cliff protecting us from the hot sun. Enjoying our picnic, we kept a watch out for Bedouins and/or wild camels before once again lying in the waters, with our heads resting on the ledge. It felt like forever before we considered getting dressed; we laughed at how neither of us cared if anyone saw us naked—except desert Bedouins.

They were gone a long time and, of course, small doubts started creeping in. *Are they coming back? Do they really know the desert?* We entertained the thought of having to make it out ourselves and scanned down the ravine to see if we could remember our tracks. Eventually we heard the pitter-patter of people scrambling down the mountain and crashing our peace. Half of the group bypassed us, taking another route with Abraheem back to the first promised waters.

The few that came to pick us up didn't have time to jump in but the looks on their worn faces said everything—they were dismayed, exhausted, and cranky. We had to hurry and head out to catch up with Abraheem and the others. By the time we got there, everyone else was in the water.

It was a small river flowing through a canyon of rocks. We jumped in again, and the current over the rocks took us down to a waterfall. This, too, was a beautiful site. We couldn't help but notice that lots of the folks were cranky. One of the ladies began throwing up from heat exhaustion.

Abraheem, we were told, had raced up the mountain and kept them going and going. By the time they stopped for lunch, they had left us forty-five minutes earlier and were starving and delirious. There was one small shadow of a tree, with all of them having to squeeze in together, desperate for shade.

We were the only ones that had cold water left and naturally, we shared it with everyone. They guzzled like they had never had a drink before. This was crazy. I asked Abraheem what fun it was to race through the desert, always looking down, rather than stopping and looking at the view and enjoying the beautiful wadis—without being nauseous from heat. He didn't understand.

After frolicking in the crashing waters, it was time to head back again. Lorraine and I soon had the company of a few of our comrades as we held up the rear, and nobody minded waiting this time; exhaustion had set in. I told the doctors about us getting naked and they roared with laughter. Everyone joked that the Bedouins no doubt were up in them-there hills, enjoying the sights. They are the eyes of the desert!

We all landed back at Abraheem's, had a beer, and headed back to a bath and bed. Abraheem had offered to take us out again in August but warned it would be even hotter. Naturally, only two athletes went. Lorraine and I declined.

Summer was highly amusing in Tawam. Free health care parlayed into free vacations for the locals. They came in hoards, demanding prescriptions to be written, stating their need to get medical help from the United States or Europe. It was Dr. B.'s responsibility to approve these, regardless of need. Dr. B. would laugh at the crazy requests for MRIs in America, or for surgeries that weren't needed. If patients received a written prescription authorizing their health care outside of the country, even if it was just an MRI, Sheikh Zayed would pay all expenses. It didn't matter that Tawam had its own MRI—this was a well-*oiled* machine.

With all the craziness of the nationals storming into the office demanding a prescription for a trip to America, London, or Paris, it was also time for Lorraine to renew her visa. Every few months she would have to fly out of country and return with a new visa. Usually, she would fly to Qatar, come back, and re-enter the UAE within an hour. I had only a few weeks left in my contract, and so, she planned to meet up with her parents for a visit. Afterward, she and I would fly to Asia.

1999

Dying to Forgive

I was alone again, returning to dreary compound life without Lorraine. Even Mattie and Christine missed her.

Arriving for work, my usual routine was to open up my personal e-mails, before diving into work stuff. Two caught my attention, as my eyes fell to the subject: *Urgent!* And then, with no time to react, I saw the next e-mail: *Urgent—Call home immediately.*

"I think my father died." I said to a co-worker sitting behind me. She didn't say a word as I got up and headed down the hall to use the international telephone line.

Everyone was at Mom's—he had just died a few hours earlier.

Mom said, "Your father has died. His body just shut down. His breathing was so laboured that he was unable to clean his lungs of carbon dioxide, and the poison killed him. He had a heart attack. But he held on until your sister Wendy got there. He hung on until his whole family was with him."

Feeling hurt, I responded, "But his whole family wasn't with him. I wasn't there."

Ignoring me, Mom continued, "I told him you were unable to come back to Canada. The funeral is on Friday. I understand you won't be able to make it. He donated his eyes."

My thoughts blurred into each other. *I had always wanted my dad to see me, to see my pain, and now, in his death, he physically gave his eyes away—how jarring. It would have taken Wendy twenty-four hours to get there—the same as for me. I was halfway around the world and the funeral was in two and a half days. I was not welcome. Mom didn't want me at the funeral. I would be the other woman. This is my mother's moment, and I am not to be in this scene.*

I tried to understand, but I hurt—it was so blatant.

The last time I saw my dad, I told him I would be alone when he died. Wow. I had no idea I would literally be completely alone. How symbolic to be in the middle of a barren desert.

I walked home, recalling that it had only been two weeks ago that I had shared a bit about my dad with Mattie. I even said that I felt he was going to die soon. I was trying to plan my feelings, my plan being to not mention his death, and just carry on working, not allowing it to have an impact on me.

It now felt odd trying to prepare for death and restrain my reaction—you can't control grief.

I had no friends, outside of Christine and Mattie, who had openly declared her disgust and couldn't understand why I would feel anything other than hatred toward him. I just wanted Lorraine.

Alone in my flat, I kept going over my words to my father that I would be alone when he died and would grieve privately. Not in my wildest dreams did I think I would be literally in the middle of the desert, more alone than I could ever have imagined. This would turn out to be ordained by the Divine.

This was the time to let the weight of sorrow be lifted from my heart. It had caused enough damage. I had tried to forgive, saw that he hadn't changed, and had to forgive all over again, only this time with no expectations. Realizing that I was actually now in the last stage of my grief over my dad, it hit me that there would be no more opportunity to change anything. I had to let go of any miniscule hope of having a "daddy" who loved his little girl. Even saying the words *daddy* and *little girl* made me feel grimy because I was unable to erase the "dirtiness." I cried.

Every time I had a question or a fear, I would open up the one book that finally made absolute sense to me: *Conversations With God*. The way God spoke within those pages was magnificent. His words came off the pages and into my heart, especially during this time. Thank you Neale Donald Walsch for having the courage to share God's voice.

Without speaking, I felt myself nodding in response to my soul, as if I were communicating telepathically. I lay there, saying in my head, *Uh-uh. Yes. I know. Mmhh-mmhh. Okay.* It was very much out of the flesh, as if I were answering to Spirit. Finally, I surrendered what is not to be and embraced what is.

I didn't know the man my family eulogized:

> Our dad was a strong, kind, and generous man. He taught us to be moral, ethical, hard-working people. Dad was a man who possessed a strong work ethic and an incredible sense of personal discipline. There were many times in his life that he struggled against various obstacles. Still, he raised his eight children, kept them fed and clothed. No matter what the obstacles were, he always said that God would see us

through. Dad hung on to his faith through his long illness. We take comfort in knowing that Dad is with the Lord, and that he finally has the peace that he sought throughout his life.

With love from all your children.

I wrote my own eulogy, which turned out to be very different than the one my family had written:

> Each life is worth a final tribute, even when we feel there is nothing to say. Value and sense have to come from life. Or what is the point in living? No man's decisions and personal choices are ever intended to hurt or be wrong. Choices come from a heart that is learning and desiring. Which one of us doesn't make errors in choice? And which one of us doesn't desire to be loved, valued, and cherished?
>
> I think of the young boy who had an alcoholic father, who turned to drink himself to shake off his reality. And the cycle continued, but he found a woman to love him. I am sure that at that point, he wished to make a new reality begin. The sadness is that no one can take away our sorrow from within—no one but ourselves with help from our angels and God.

Lying on the floor crying, I suddenly felt my father's presence in the room, but I wasn't afraid. Way down in that place where I know Spirit talks to me, I heard Dad's voice.

In quiet humility, his spirit spoke to me, saying he was undertaking a life review and had just now experienced how his choices hurt me. His angels put him in my shoes for the first time. My dad's spirit told me that he had walked through the life we'd had together. Thus he was able to see me, able to see into my soul, and feel the hurt and sorrow he had caused me. He was allowed to enter my heart space—to truly feel my innermost turmoil over our life together.

As I heard him, I began speaking telepathically again—all within. It was like stepping out of my body and seeing myself lying on the floor as my spirit hovered over me, breaking the earthly barriers and stepping into infinity.

I thought of my sister Lorita and knew she would understand. She and I had shared a similar experience a few years earlier, while at *Writing-On-Stone*, a native provincial park, full of spirit guides—if you listened. There were ancient native petroglyphs on the sheer sandstone cliffs, images carved from the wind, depicting whales, Indian chiefs, and an array of folklore. It was a desert with a mystical landscape of mushroom-shaped rocks, known as "hoodoos," that stood within steep-walled ravines. It was a spiritual, native sacred ground, right in my own backyard.

There, we had stood watching the night sky when, suddenly, a white owl appeared—literally out of the sky. As we both gasped, the owl returned back into the sky—a flap of sky opened up and enfolded her back in. Lorita and I just looked at each other and embraced in awe at what we had just witnessed. We laughed that nobody was going to believe us. I was already described as "trippy" and this would just be another "out there" experience. This time, I had a witness, though.

And now, here I was with my father, infinity holding us in her palm.

I sensed that Dad was finally getting it and began asking him, "Do you see how what you did and said has affected me? Do you understand the grief of being blamed and hated by you? Do you see how my heart has been broken? Do you see how you lied and wouldn't deal with your truth?"

For the first time ever in my life, I felt my dad knew and understood. It was brilliant and poignant and cleansing and forgiving.

The Divine took us even deeper. Together with Dad's spirit, I went through each one of my chakras with him. I had crystals in the colours of the eight chakras hanging in the sunlight on my window.

Holding my chakra, I said, "Dad. This is the first chakra—red; it reflects "fight or flight" and also symbolizes having roots and support. It is located at the base of the spine. Dad, I felt so unsupported throughout life. I've had years of chronic low back problems, which, to me, represent this chakra being blocked. With incredible synchronicity, my low back problems began at the same time you started displaying inappropriate "love" to me.

"Dad, this chakra represents being supported and strong and able to stand in the face of diversity. I have had none of this with you. I had given all my power away. I was not there for me, and you, my father, most definitely was not there to support me. I have had two traumas to my lower back, and I am still learning how these injuries presented an opportunity to heal the emotional blockage.

"Dad, I take back my power to the depth of understanding I have in this moment and forgive you for not supporting me." I kissed the chakra and moved to the next.

"This is the second chakra—amber; it reflects personal power, creativity, and sexual energies. It is located at the hips and sexual organs. I have been so violated by you. I had years of distorted sexuality, and I still battle with anger toward men. I transferred emotional pain into physical pain and injury. It shouldn't be a surprise that I had surgery to remove cervical pre-cancer cells. I even went as far as to stop my period—to stop the flow of blood, allowing no more creation of life. My womb was a tomb for me.

"Dad, I am just realizing how my spirit has dealt with my pain. I have hidden the emotional pain—or so I thought—but I have developed physical illness in almost all of my chakra energy centres.

"Dad, I take back my power to the depth of understanding I have in this moment and forgive you for your abuse." I kissed the chakra and moved to the next.

"The third chakra—yellow—reflects emotions and is located right in our gut. My emotions have been so confused. I wanted you to be my dad and you were not able to be. This area, the solar plexus, carries all of my life's worries and fears and emotions. Again, I had surgery in this part of my body as well. Dad, can you imagine the emotions of a young girl just off the streets and drugs, already full of life's problems? And then, within a heartbeat, her father begins acting incestuously toward her. You attacked an already wounded animal. My journey with you has been an emotional roller coaster.

"Dad, I take back my power to the depth of understanding I have in this moment and forgive you for your abuse." I kissed the chakra and moved to the next.

"The fourth is the heart chakra—green. I had such a broken heart. So broken was my heart that I needed open-heart surgery to have an entire valve cut out and replaced with someone else's valve. Dad, I desperately wanted you as my father. My broken heart needs healing.

"Dad, I take back my power to the depth of understanding I have in this moment and forgive you for your abuse." I kissed the chakra and moved to the next.

"The fifth chakra is blue, located at the throat. I had no voice. I could not speak. Remember I told you that I knew I was going to be alone when you died, and I would talk to you then. This is my moment but I feel that I don't need to say much for I know that you are going through every moment with me, that you are experiencing "us" through my being. You now know what it was like to be your daughter. How sad that I had to wait for your death before I could take back my voice.

"Dad, I take back my power to the depth of understanding I have in this moment and forgive you for your abuse." I kissed the chakra and moved to the next.

"The sixth chakra is known as the spiritual eye, and is indigo. It is located on the forehead. Dad, I am learning to see from a spiritual plane. I am learning to step aside from my emotions and to look through the eye of spirit. This is new for both of us, as you also are now seeing through spirit.

"Dad, I take back my power to the depth of understanding I have in this moment and forgive you for your abuse."

Breathing deeply, I held the chakra and said softly, "I breathe in spirit and truth. I step out of my own way and allow spirit to flow through me." I kissed the chakra and moved to the next.

"Purple is my favourite colour and that of the crowning seventh chakra. This is the constant flow of energy through each of us, to the heavens, and back again. It is like blood circling through the entire body, continuously allowing life to ebb and flow. Dad, you are now in the spirit world and can now make choices and decisions about what to become next. Please learn from your choices in this lifetime and choose differently in your next life.

"Dad, I take back my power to the depth of understanding I have in this moment and forgive you for your abuse." I kissed the chakra and moved to the eighth.

"Dad. I have one more chakra hanging in the window. It is white and, to me, symbolizes everything coming together in purity and light. It is true spirit. As I hold this chakra, I must send you on your journey now—our time is over in this life.

"I thank you because all of your actions toward me are what caused me to find my higher self. Although it took almost my entire life, I am finally seeing gratitude come from darkness. I release you and send you on your way. Go into the light."

I kissed the chakra and blew a kiss to the heavens, symbolically sending my dad off on his journey.

Late in the night, I suddenly awoke from a sound sleep. Everything was very dark and very still. For the first time, I had an enormous fear creep over me. I felt like I was seeing spirits in the room, and nothing felt safe. I immediately called back my spirit to a safer place—something I had learned through reading Caroline Myss, a spiritual guru to me for the last few years. This sense of a darker spirit trying to capture my energy was far too scary for me, and I needed all my power not to succumb to it. I had to stand within myself and my own light. I spoke out loud:

> Lord, I feel fear coming over me. Suddenly, I feel the spirit world is even stronger than the physical world. I choose not to let the darkness enter my consciousness. I know this time spent with my dad has been protected by the Divine and has been spiritually intimate in a beautiful way, but now, I sense strongly that I must let him go.
>
> I thank you for being with me, and I trust I am safe. No harm will come to me.
>
> Dad, I ask you to continue on your path, but I

need to release you from me. I acknowledge that I do not want you to be with me spiritually. I know people find peace in knowing their loved ones are with them, but Dad, our journeys must now be separate.

It is time to say good-bye.

A quiet peace came over me.

You Can't Run without Your Big Toe

Who would think that a toe injury would hold a deep spiritual significance? Though I knew that health had always played a part in teaching me, I didn't immediately grasp what I could learn from my big toe.

Every few months, gregarious Jill would throw a huge party. I wasn't in her daily social group but was always invited to her parties.

I had been through a few days of feeling shut down from emotions. I was feeling nothing—finally. It felt like my body just needed a break. I needed to get out. This night, it was an Austin Powers party. Yeah, baby!

Everyone dressed in sixties clothes; I went as a hippie. One of the partyers was very drunk, and her dancing became increasingly like black-belt karate kicks—one of which hammered my big toe back into my foot. It was funny to everyone except me. I kept asking if it was possible to break a toe.

I told Dr. B. that my toe felt separated from my foot, and he ordered me an MRI. It was serious; an uncommon injury usually seen in sports. Trying to explain the sport of dancing–karate proved difficult and got lost in translation. Dr. B. said he knew I wouldn't be back to work.

Fortunately, Mattie was going on a six-week vacation and offered me her spacious, comfortable flat, with a telephone and computer. If I'd had to stay in my little space, I would have gone crazy.

Having this injury and being barely able to walk rendered me dependent on help—but no one helped.

Just like when my dad died, no one cared, offered to help, or to buy food; it was sad to feel so unimportant. I felt very sorry for myself, and very alone again.

Lorraine was able to fly back from England on a cheap ticket, thank Buddha, because I wouldn't have been able to care for myself. Holing up at Mattie's was a miracle, and we were enormously grateful, especially considering that our friendship was slightly strained. It was Lorraine's and my first time together since Dad died. Lorraine had a hard time because she was so angry at how I had been treated by my family, especially my father. Her compassion lay in her knowledge of how deeply I wanted to have a dad.

After his death, I'd had extremely limited communication with family. I called twice—once immediately upon his dying, and once, after his funeral. The only other communications were e-mails between Rona and me.

Lorraine was more than a little annoyed because of money. My parents had none, which meant that the kids had to pay for the funeral. Lorraine thought it was crazy for me to give money, but I had to. I couldn't *not* give money, and eventually, she understood. The weird thing was that half my siblings professed not to have money and didn't contribute. I also had to pay an additional few hundred dollars for the phone calls I had made.

At the end of the day, my brother Jimmy sent an e-mail. There was no *Hey, how are you?* There was no friendly message whatsoever. It simply said:

> Dear Edna,
> This letter is simply to inform you of our father's funeral expenses and how they were paid.

He proceeded to list the costs, including a wake and booze, but excluding the phone bills. He also noted how much each of us paid; my name was at the bottom, as I'd paid quite a bit less than my three older siblings—the four youngest all got to pay nothing, stating they had no money. By this point, I just felt *aaaahhh* and had to let it go.

It was good to share with Lorraine what I did after my dad died. She had always known that I needed to forgive and to stop hoping for the impossible. "It is what it is," she would always say. Lorraine was way ahead of me in her state of peacefulness; she loved my searching, because she knew I needed to find peace. She was already there, comfortable within herself. I loved to watch how she would deal with her emotions and quickly reach a place of understanding, as she chose who, and how, she wanted to be. My precious Lorraine was, and remains, truly an angel in disguise.

I wasn't a mess by the time she returned. I was tired and drained but there was a layer of sorrow lifted from me. It truly felt like I had finally been able to let it all go. Oh, Goddess, it was great to be with my girlfriend again. I loved—and love—her so much.

An Aussie angel, by the name of Jaybird, had just moved in next door. Jaybird was like me: spiritual with an edge. Our passions flowed; we had joie de vivre, loving our spiritual journeys while maintaining our wild side.

The three of us had so many great nights, laughing and talking; she and Lorraine would dance around the living room and have a gay old time—except Jay was straighter than straight. We were like sisters. It was wonderful to have a friend.

Jaybird not only loved native spirituality but was also into energy, chakras, psychic readings, spirit guides, and past lives; she also believed that in a past life, she had been the daughter of Black Elk, a Shaman of the Sioux Indians. There was a time I would have thought she was the devil's spawn talking like that, but now, I was open to all mysticism and did not want to put Spirit into a boxed religion. I smiled internally at how serendipity placed an Aussie in my life, one that just happened to be rooted in North American native spirituality.

I had originally been offered Jaybird's job but had turned it down, taking my current job instead. It made us ponder where our paths would have turned if I had accepted; Jaybird would not have been in the Middle East—everything would have been different—but I felt that we still would have ended up in the exact same spiritual place. Our destinies *had* to be fulfilled.

Jaybird joined me in my nightly ritual of watching the sunset, waiting for the first star, and quietly making a wish.

After I'd witnessed both darkness and light when my dad died, Jay brought comfort, because she saw light in everything. Her strength reminded me that I was protected and helped me to stay away from dark thoughts and fears.

It all ended quite unexpectedly. Jaybird had a love affair, a quick, intense eruption of feeling. Within a matter of days, she was smitten, but it was not to be. He wasn't ready. The earthly part of Jay's heart took over, and she had to get away.

On top of her heart being broken, she was very unhappy in her job. People from her department were known to do runners, and she joined the sprint—but not before she left an indelible mark on my soul.

It was just Lorraine and me again.

I had been told to stay off my foot for ten days, but the pain was unbearable. I knew something was wrong and called Dr. B. who ordered another MRI. It was decided I needed a cast up to my knee for a week—which turned into a month. My contract was coming to an end and, although able to leave, I was stuck.

I revisited the symbolism of the first chakra, which includes the feet. I had always stopped at my low back problems, not realizing the importance of feet and balance. As I read, clarity jumped off the pages and into my consciousness. The energy of the first chakra included taking steps to heal, standing up for myself, sustaining a sense of identity and of belonging to a group, as well as family bonding. Significantly, the first chakra also carried the energy of both a tribal code *and* a personal honour code. This was an amazing awareness for me, and also a sad one. I felt I'd come so far but saw how I still carried an intense need to belong.

This need blocked my evolution into the person I truly wanted to be. I realized I needed to develop a personal honour code. I needed to stand within *my* power and learn to balance *my* energy. I finally had an answer for Lorita about why illness and injury were a part of my life. Everything that happened in the physical realm held a cellular *and* a spiritual symbolic meaning. Whether my physical injuries or illnesses were ever "healed" was not the point—it was the understanding that each held the potential for spiritual health to shine through the pain. In my world, this was a colossal newfound understanding. I could begin to let go of my guilt and self-abuse.

My big toe was about to step into yet another desert storm.

Mothers and Daughters and Mothers and Daughters

I opened what I thought was an innocent e-mail from Rona and almost fell off my chair. In my grief, I had mistakenly shared my soul and told Rona about my chakra cleansing with Dad. Besides telling me my beliefs were a million miles from Jesus, she said:

> Mom has been sorting through Dad's stuff and came across his letters. Apparently Dad kept every letter and Mom had never read them before. She sat and read every last one of them. She's very angry—the demons are out of the closet.
> There's more. Jimmy was handling the paperwork and noted errors in the marriage licence and birth dates. He asked Mom, and he found out that she had given birth to Paula before ever meeting Dad. Apparently, Mom had an affair with a married man, got pregnant, had Paula, and married Dad when Paula was two years old.
> Mom is sending you pictures of Dad in his casket and is writing to you.

Mom had an affair and a baby before marrying Dad? Paula is my half sister? I was stunned. After all the abuse she hurled at me about my pregnancy and never, ever showed compassion or understanding. I was a whore, slut, and good-for-nothing. I just couldn't believe this secret! After having a period of being shut down in my emotions after Dad's death, I felt a surge of unimaginable sorrow. This was beyond my soul's grasp.

And then her letters arrived. The first one was very brief, saying, "I don't know what killed your father more—the illness or the persecution." Enclosed were all those pictures, first from a distance then slowly creeping up to nearly being in the casket. I looked out of guilt for not having been at the funeral, for not having to go through all the motions that other family members did. I felt I had to look, but I wished I hadn't. I could tell my dad had no eyes, and it was very disturbing.

What did she mean by persecution? Was she blaming me for his death because she found those letters? If she read all his letters, did she not feel any compassion for her kids? For *me?* I guess not. I knew that there were many letters I hadn't even seen. There had been times when my siblings would tell me they received a letter from Dad, about me, but it was so vile and disgusting, they refused to share it with me. Now, my mother was privy to all of it.

Unaware of her ambush, I opened the next letter. Photos of strangers dropped around me like snowflakes falling in slow motion. A cuddly little girl with strawberry blonde hair and big blue eyes looked into the camera and now, into my heart. I was suddenly flooded with a wrenching anguish. Somewhere inside, I knew her.

Disoriented, I read my mother's words: *I found your daughter.* The next photo was of two girls, now in their twenties, but there was no mention of who was who. I was left to guess which one was my "daughter." Her identity, name, and address were all withheld—kept in the diabolically controlling hands of my mother. She did not have the decency to say *your daughter is the one on the left or right.* It was more than malicious.

Ensuring I was left dangling with the noose around my neck, my mother concluded by stating she would let me know how their *meeting* went! I could not contain my horror. I heard a moaning from the depths of my soul. A sour acid came up from the pit of my stomach as I vomited my mother's poison.

My shock was overwhelming. It was a crushing blow that my mother could speak so casually of someone I had never openly shared. My baby had been mine alone; her memory was all I had of my precious little girl. How was I going to crawl through this grief? How was I to bring life back from the grave? Oh, my God.

Lorraine was speechless, as she held me and just sat with me, allowing me space to absorb this. Thank God, we were alone; I could not have borne sharing this with Jaybird or anyone—not now. Lorraine and I both felt it was the last thing my mother could do to hurt me, maybe because of Dad. A part of me wondered if my mother thought my baby was my father's.

I had a nightmare that I was lying in an open grave, while my mother was shovelling dirt over me—burying me alive. I woke up trembling, aware that I was surrounded by desert. The sand around me felt like a grave about to swallow me whole.

I had come to the end. No more. This was beyond cruel. I made my decision in that moment. I would never see my mother again. It was time for me to leave this family.

I don't know any of my sibling's reactions to what my mother had done, because none of us communicated, except for some initial information I received from my sister Rona. I had asked for details, and Rona sadly seemed to defend Mom, saying it appeared to be something that she needed to do before dying. The only other information I received was that my little brother, Danny, had helped in the search. I was so disappointed. Danny had always tried loving me, at least when we lived in the same city. Why wouldn't he share this with me, or ask my permission? Especially because he was adopted, and must have had some understanding of the emotional anquish. I knew he was in the clutches of my mother's control, just as Rona and my other siblings were, and I knew he needed her approval and love, but it seemed beyond comprehension that he'd do something so blatantly behind my back.

I was still trying to digest the news of my mother's own teen pregnancy—not to mention the accusatory tone in her note about Dad. And now this. There was nowhere to go.

I had felt a little guilty for going to that Austin Powers party, but now, thank Krishna, I was given an evening of laughter. It felt like I was never going to smile again. I ached.

Way back, when my mother and I toured Europe, and visited my dad's relatives in England, they had shared a story that resonated within my very core. My granddad had left England at the age of sixteen, hopping a ship to Canada. He set sail, never to turn back, and never to communicate with his family ever again. It wasn't until over a half-century later, when we visited, that his family heard about his life, marriage, children, and grandchildren. By that time, granddad had been dead for many years.

I understood his actions and had always felt like my grandfather. I, too, needed to set sail, never to turn around again. I needed to walk away.

New Endings, New Beginnings, New Millennium

As I sat gripped by colossal grief and heartache, I realized my toe injury had kept me at Tawam much longer than I should have been. If I had left at the end of my contract, my mother would never have had an address to reach me. I also understood that my body and soul were asking me to *stop running*, to stand still and just be. I wasn't running *away* from my past—I was run *by* my past. My bruises were quite visible from constantly running into it.

Having just gone through a healing journey with my dad, I knew I would now need to do the same with my mom. I went through an array of emotions—this was not going to be easy. I felt completely shattered, exhausted, and in too much pain to carry my anger for long. I felt so betrayed. I needed to get into my heart space, to hold on to all that I had learned, and to believe that I would survive this. What was I going to do with life now? Who did I want to be within all of this? The heavens certainly didn't waste any time. I had to find safety and trust in all that was happening. Through my shock and sorrow, I remembered the message given to me the last time I saw my father—*Forgive them and let them go. Let the weight of sorrow be lifted from your heart.* I had put all of my energy into my father, and now, I heard that still, quiet voice once again—*Now is the time; you are not alone—be not afraid.* I had not yet forgiven my mother, or myself.

Thank the Divine for Terri and e-mail. With a bout of intense spiritual counselling, I began clinging more and more into a trust in Father and Mother God, in Goddess, in Divine Wisdom. No matter what name I used, they all wrapped into Light and Love. I knew I didn't want to act out of fear; somewhere, I had an understanding that I was returning to the Beginning. Mother Earth. Father God. Mother God—my beginning. My baby girl was alive and this would now be another sacred journey.

It was happenstance that I noticed a small room in back of the shop. The sign above the door said, "Tarot Readings." I felt drawn to that back room but was scared. Should I see what the cards say? I wandered around the store, observing from a distance, feeling like I was being urged to go in. This had always been black magic to me, but upon meeting her, I felt connected to Tema Dawn; her spirit was so gentle. As I sat down, the ambiance of that little room resonated comfort. The universe was about to give confirmation of my journey and its symbolism, and reveal how I would be able to move forward.

As I turned over my cards, it was as if an angel were present. The cards were a gift, telling me to trust, to heal, to let go. I cried as Tema Dawn spoke to me:

SHAMAN, BIG MEDICINE WHEEL, VISION QUEST, SPIRIT GUIDE

These are your four biggest cards in this reading. They are Major Arcana that represent the important changes and significant cycles in a lifetime. I will read the cards in the order you drew them.

1st:
Heart/Essence/You in the Now/4 of Air/Contemplation

This is the time for deep contemplation on important questions at hand. You know within that some deepening is needed to be still, silent, and thoughtful. It is a time of watching, waiting, and creating a safe space in which to detach yourself from normal activity.

2nd:
Atmosphere/Where Your Questions Come From/5 of Air/Fear

There are fears of letting go, of change, or loss. These fears are conditions of the mind that keep you from seeing clearly. Fears of failure and self-doubt remind you at this time to take a deeper look at your fear, and that this is a time of looking within before rushing ahead in confusion. Watch the conditions/illusions arise, and let them go before making any decisions.

3rd:
Your Challenge/or What Needs To Be Integrated/2 of Fire/ Will

What you need to integrate into your life at this time is Fire energy of Instinctive Determination and Confidence. It's like pointing an arrow and letting it go—after it is released, there is no need for control. Just stay centred now, and everything will unfold. If you trust yourself, your higher consciousness will flow with volition of its own, and events will effortlessly happen. Then you will see you are on the right track!

4th:
Unconscious/The Root/Foundation/5 of Water/Loss

Coming up through your deepest unconscious is the instability of leaving the old and the emotions based on attachment to the familiar. At the same time, the *veils* of ignorance *are being lifted!* Be brave—this is the beginning of a kind of liberation and it's quite useless to fight against the tide. You will get clearer about your feelings now, which come from deep patterns from childhood. Profound, yet painful, this will free you as you come into awareness. When this card comes up in this position, it indicates that some real soul-searching is in place.

5th:
Immediate Past/*SHAMAN*

In the recent past, you have come into a real wisdom, gotten in touch with your intuition and your instinct for the deep underlying forces that are guiding you. The Shaman inside you is capable of merging with the wisdom of the elders. You are getting in touch with what truly motivates you, what continues to motivate you, and what is essential to you at this time. You know that you have been fulfilling superficial desires. This is why you are now taking the time to explore your innermost being. You have tuned into what you don't need anymore, letting it fall away. Be thankful that the power of this wisdom has come and encouraged you to contemplate how to spend your time!

6th:
The Mind/Consciousness/Your Thoughts Now/7 of Air/Futility

Your mind is full of negative expectations, rigid thought patterns, survival fears, and fears of the unknown. You need to become aware of your childhood conditions, so they won't dominate your life. The fear of being inadequate, unable to accomplish anything really worthwhile, usually comes from our past and really doesn't have anything to do with you now. Develop new mental tools and forgive yourself. Before you take action, let go of this sense of futility by calming your mind—notice this theme of contemplation!

7th:
Immediate Future/*BIG MEDICINE WHEEL*/The World

This is a big card.

Very soon now, in your immediate future, you will feel the wheels of change turning, and a creative opening—an entirely new paradigm—transforming you, as you recognize your rightful place in life. This card is about all stages of learning as you move through a physical and spiritual rebirth. You are completing one stage of your life and preparing to move into another that will take you out into the world in an exciting new way. You will have much to celebrate as you let go of your past. This is a great opportunity to wake up and begin a different life! See yourself on the wheel of change and above, flying like an eagle, looking at the whole big picture. This is about realizing your maximum potential!

8th:
Self-Concept/How You See Yourself/5 of Earth/Insecurity

This is a very big opportunity for you to let go of a lot of limiting self-concepts.

Again, fears of inadequacy, loss, and worries will keep you in self-condemnation. This is an old negative mind loop. The cards are urging you to let this go! Find out what's going on! You allow yourself to be hypnotized by your negative thoughts. Let that dark cloud of worry pass out of your mind by becoming still; relax and you will soon see that everything looks a lot brighter.

9th: *VISION QUEST*
Hopes/Fears/Initiation/New Outlook/Sincere Search for Meaning

Your greatest hope and greatest fear is this letting go of the familiar and all the values attached to it. You want to totally, wholeheartedly, surrender to this Vision Quest, but at the same time, there is the fear of the initiation, and the plunge into the inner emptiness of the unknown. To be willing to let go is Grace in itself and will bring spiritual assistance at this time; this is a very important part of the spiritual path for you now. You will have to see things from a completely different perspective, and your world will turn upside down. Focus on letting old structures drop away, and don't interfere with your inner growth process. The unknown will open the doors to your perception and you will not run from this major shift in your life now!

10th:
Psychic Space/The Home—Mother of Cups/Compassion

Around your home and in your personal space there is a sense of great warmth and compassion where you can open up to your intuitive powers and healing. The Mother of Water represents your natural powerful feminine aspect, and she is the one who wants you to value them as well as the masculine qualities within. There is a balancing of your male/female aspects that will contribute to your emotional security and overall peace of mind. But now, more than anything, you must trust your feminine qualities to understand yourself and your situation. This viewpoint will give you what is needed to take you through these big changes.

11th:
General Outcome/*SPIRIT GUIDE*/Awakening

Without a shadow of a doubt, you will very soon be receiving powerful spiritual assistance and profound guidance. There may be messages from the other dimensions and/or psychic experiences. This is the time to ask for help and watch for the signs and answers to your prayers. Let yourself be guided now. By being receptive (the natural feminine intuition), you will feel the presence of helpful influences in your life and be inspired by the wisdom and compassion of your guides.

This is a powerful final outcome to the reading in relation to the combination of your cards and connection to the Shaman and the Vision Quest. This indicates clearly that you are on a spiritual journey that will transform your life and take you into your infinite potential. You have the most wonderful guidance at this time that will help you let go of all your fears and deepest insecurities. There will be much creative energy released with this unfolding.

I was in awe. Everything I had been going through—all my struggles, all my searching—Tema Dawn had summed up without ever having met me before, without knowing anything about my journey. I *was* on a vision quest. I did have spirit guides; they were like the stars—I didn't always see them, but I always knew they were there. How did she know that I was using this language? Her message parralled Terri's reading of my astrological natal chart from a few years ago—both readings were tools that I had once believed to be of the devil, but now, I saw my life's journey through their words—I felt their Divine interconnected wisdom.

Tema Dawn said the cards she used were inspired by native teachings, as well as based on traditional tarot originating in Europe, making it a blend of pathways, cultures, and spiritual teachings. I would never have thought a tarot reading would align to my personal beliefs, and be so in synch with my journey—another tool used by celestial alchemy. She was gracious enough to write out my reading, allowing me to review, absorb, and delve into the words given to me. There could have been no deeper way for the Divine to sit down and talk with me than through Tema Dawn and her cards. As she spoke, I said nothing. I never confirmed or denied. I just listened—and cried..

Oh Lord, I was going to get through this. Finally, I knew I wasn't alone. I knew I was saying good-bye on so many levels to my past, and I was so scared of my future. Only now, there was such a confirmation of what I already knew in my heart of hearts—that I had my angels and guides to help me walk through my fears and let go.

A vision was given to me, of an old Shaman sitting before me. The Shaman was both male and female. I was an Indian princess. He/She was speaking, but her face looked sorrowful; his words were not being heard. As I sat there, watching her, I understood that, within my whole life, I had never felt heard, and now, before me, was a spirit guide requesting the same favour—to be heard, to be listened to.

Sitting up on the rooftop, I did my own life review; I thought of all the times I had felt desolate in my own wilderness. Images raced through my mind's eye of moments in time, both the painful and the joyful.

Stepping outside of my skin, I could see how I had never been alone. I saw blessings in each step of my journey. If I had not gotten pregnant, I would have continued my destructive and deadly behaviour—already using needles, getting deeper and deeper into drugs. Because of Ferzat and becoming a born-againer, my promiscuity stopped at a time when AIDS hit the world with a deadly surge. My heart surgery *opened* me to forgiveness; my toe… and on and on. Nothing seemed to work against me if I only chose to look at life not as desolate and hostile, but as a tangible, awesome piece of art.

Even my father played his part—in seeing such darkness, I was able to know immense light.

I would get through this as well.

God, Goddess, and the Divine never missed one heartbeat of my life—from sunsets to desert roses, from Pinnacle Point to the Dead Sea. They were with me every moment, including when I was scared, abused, and afraid. It is an impossibility for my spirit to be separated from Divine Spirit—where could I hide? All those times I wanted to dance while on top of a mountain were my spirit calling out, telling me I could. Peace was mine, no matter what. I needed to cling to this; especially now, I needed to remember I was not alone.

It was through Tema Dawn's reading that I realized I had been spinning in circles, repeating old patterns over and over. I continually reinforced the circumstances of dysfunction.

Crises equalled running, and I always ended up in the desert. I just got it. I just figured out why I would get off the plane and immediately feel angry and be surprised that I wasn't thrilled to be on the other side of the world. I had just brought my portion of the world with me—I wasn't on the other side of anything.

God, it felt good to look inward—finally—to really look inward. The symbolism of Tawam was magnificent: there weren't any more women who needed me to rescue them. I felt so alone in the desert. I had no one to save but me.

My co-workers had stepped into the role of my family. None of them supported me but, instead, criticized and judged me. There had been lots of buzzing and gossiping about my not going home for my father's funeral; people couldn't understand why I was grieving if I didn't even go home. My grief was judged to be inappropriate.

Mattie had come to see me the day Dad died, and I could see her thinking that I was crazy to be feeling anything. She only stayed a few minutes. After that, I never saw her for weeks. Even sweet Christine had a hard time dealing with my situation because it brought up unresolved issues from her own "pappy's" death. She handled it by disappearing. I stood alone in the middle of everyone—in an empty, barren desert—just as I stood alone in the middle of my family.

Bravo to the Divine—I don't think she could have made it any more clearer to me that none of this was a coincidence. My cocoon in Saudi would have been full of love and support. Tawam did not give me the cocoon I had hoped for.

It was time for me to become a butterfly, time to shed my cocoon and spread my beautiful wings. Could I even become as majestic and powerful as an eagle—and soar?

And now, in the situation involving my mother and my baby girl, I *needed* to stand alone, within myself, and to honour my spirit guides. I struggled with the fear and apprehension of what was ahead; I *needed* to remember that I had only two choices—fear or love. Although I didn't know it at the time, my angels were already preparing me for an introduction to my first Shaman and medicine woman, Dr. Karen Quinn—just as my tarot cards said. I would soon discover that she held a spiritual understanding of life that far surpassed anyone I'd met on this earth. She would eventually take me, step by step, teardrop by teardrop, through the labyrinth—the circle—of mothers and daughters. *Yeha-Noha*—Sacred Spirit.

No one had discovered our rooftop hideaway. Lorraine and I had often slept up there, under a million stars. This night, as I sat high above the buildings and gates of the compound, able to see unobtrusively to the west, the evening was still. A gentle, warm breeze blew through the cluster of palm trees just outside our walls; their leaves danced and shimmied in its wake. A lone mountain to my left stood in a silhouette of solitude as the sun slowly lowered herself directly in front of me. I secretly had often looked to the stars and moon, wondering if my baby girl was looking at the same sky... she was alive.

The circle of life: from Mother God, to Mother Earth, to mother, to daughter, to mother, to daughter... I was being asked to let go of my fear, which I knew held me back and was my worst enemy.

I embraced Mother God—her womb, her love. All those years of wanting a mother to love me, and there she was. She'd always been there, with outstretched arms. This time, I let her wrap those precious arms around me as I nestled into her bosom.

As beauty surrounded me, I could see and feel the trees, sky, sun, stars, moon, mountains, wind, and air; and for the first time, I felt I was an actual part of life. I was not separate from creation—I was part of it. I felt safe.

Facing the east, the north, the south, and the west—greeting the new day and all that it brings—has become a way I start each day. As I face each of the four quadrants of our world, I softly say, "I step into the energy of life. I am one with all that is. I bless this day and all it brings with her."

I still intentionally say "all it brings," not excluding anything "bad." Life is full of good and bad, dark and evil. I believe it is all part of one spirit, and I choose to learn to embrace all of life. It's who and what I'm going to be in the middle of good and bad, dark and evil—that's my focus now. The elusive peace I had been searching for was inside my spirit all this time—I now need only to make the choice to step into that peace, no matter how difficult my external life becomes.

On my last day, waking up to the sunrise, as we snuggled on our rooftop, I consciously understood that the circle had been completed. The east represented the Middle East; the north, native Indians; the west, our western culture; and the south, the aborigines and their desert quest. Each direction held such spiritual diversity—Islam, Judaism, Hinduism, Buddhism, Christianity, and so much more.

I remembered previously flying east to Hong Kong and then on to North America. East soon became west, as time blended them together. As I daydreamed, gazing outside the window of the plane, I witnessed the sunset become the sunrise; the dusk of night became the dawn of morning—a circle that had no beginning and no end.

Seeing symbolic meaning in all that existed felt neverending—a circle of life. The four winds, the four seasons, the four directions, each blending into each other. All was one within the Divine—we were *all* one.

Evening came. The prayer call echoed through the dark evening air. Saying goodnight to the sun, the clouds illuminated the skies in soft greens, pinks, and aqua, swirling and wrapping around the stars, as they scintillated into view.

Just as the white owl had been enfolded back into the night's sky, I felt infinity once again open up—this time, she took me in. I wasn't watching the glories of the universe—I was part of them. It was like being mesmerized by the waves of the sea, watching them one by one, until, finally, you become the wave...

I felt myself entering an oasis within my soul, to be cradled in infinity. Thank you Lord, Allah, Yahweh, Buddha, Krishna, God, Goddess, Father God, Mother God, the Divine. Thank *You*.

Without one *ma'arsalama* party, I bid farewell to the Middle East. Sitting quietly on my rooftop, I listened to the last call for prayer, as the sun set on Arabia.

As our plane came in for a landing, I listened to the soft voice of the stewardess, "I wish to take this time on behalf of your crew and the pilot, to thank you for taking this journey with us. The forecast is for a beautiful sunrise, sunshine throughout the day, and a gentle breeze blowing. I hope you have enjoyed your trip. Whether staying here or continuing on, I trust your journey will be a pleasant and safe one."

ABOUT THE AUTHOR

Edna Whitehouse now goes by her nickname, Samadhi—which means "Being one with the Divine and being in the moment." Each time she hears Samadhi, it reminds her that she is part of love—a continuous affirmation.

Samadhi began her writing career by winning two contests; the first was for Focus On Women, a Victoria-based magazine. Her essay, *"Two Hearts In One,"* spoke of her healing journey through her first heart surgery, and the correlation of illness and forgiveness. Her second essay, *"A Gut Reaction,"* for the on-line magazine, Outback, showed the risks as well as the fun of exotic travel abroad.

At the age of forty-eight, Samadhi decided it was time to dive into her passion and give full-time writing a chance. The outcome is *Circles in the Sand*. She is currently working on her second book, *"Separated at Birth."*

A writer who has never forgotten what it feels like to be young and to be silenced, Samadhi's messages are: Break the cycle of dysfunction. Be heard. Take back your own power. Go girls!

After years of travel, including visiting, living, and/or working in Europe, Lebanon, Syria, Israel, Saudi Arabia, Jordan, India, Egypt, Oman, the United Arab Emirates, and Thailand, Samadhi now lives in Victoria, British Columbia, on Vancouver Island—surrounded by the ocean and its life force.

ISBN 1-41204190-2